Praise for

A Hostel on the Nolichucky

This unique Appalachian Trail story reveals a slice of trail history in an entertaining narrative. John Shores, known by everyone on the trail as "Uncle Johnny", tells us of how his search for purpose on the trail led him to a life on the trail providing lodging, supplies and assistance to fellow hikers. **David "Awol" Miller, author, *AWOL on the Appalachian Trail*, and *The A.T. Guide: A Handbook for Hiking the Appalachian Trail***

An Appalachian Trail book like no other. For almost two decades, John Shores has been practicing the rare craft of hosting Appalachian Trail hikers. In this fascinating memoir, the legendary keeper of Uncle Johnny's Nolichucky Hostel shares his myriad experiences hosting the A.T. traveling community that passes close by his hostel every day. A captivating read, Shores tells the remarkable story of the building of his hostel on the Nolichucky River. Funny, moving, and informative, **Elmer Hall, Keeper of Sunnybank Inn at Hot Springs**

To know John Shores is to know a love for the Appalachian Trail—and those who hike it—that runs as deep as the Nolichucky Gorge near where he established his hostel. In this one-of-a-kind memoir told in a creative non-fiction style, Uncle Johnny, as he is fondly called, and author Stephen Tyler join forces to tell the story of how Uncle Johnny's Nolichucky Hostel became a can't-miss stop just 68 feet from the A.T. Set during 1997 and 1998, this is a tale that weaves together local history, legends, and some unique true-life characters that you just have to meet. The respect and affection both Shores and Tyler have for the A.T., its community and the trail towns through which it runs is obvious throughout the text. It will make you want to put on a pair of hiking boots, grab your gear and head out for a hike through Unicoi County and beyond. **Keeli Parkey, Managing Editor of *The Erwin Record*, Erwin, Tennessee**

John Shores
1998

John was coming off the trail to resupply in Erwin, the only trail town Jan Curran had disliked. An entire chapter of Curran's first book was devoted to a detailed description of his bad experience. The men he met were crude and rough. A motel refused to rent him a room. His shuttle driver was rude. When leaving Erwin, a mystery truck had followed, had quietly circled the Beauty Spot parking area, and Curran was forced to hide from shadowy men flitting along the edge of the forest. For a few moments, Curran had feared for his life.

"I wonder," John thought as he merged onto the hard surface road just above the Chestoa Bridge and walked down the hill.

What the heck am I going to run into here?

Coming along the west side of the Nolichucky River, John noticed a rugged little house just beyond four county roads that intersect at the foot of the bridge. An old man was standing on the front porch.

Is he waving at me?

John slowed.

Must be. There's no one else about.

No ... John stopped and squinted.

He's not waving. He's motioning ... a very insistent hooking of his left hand and arm as if to say, "Come over here, will you?" He's waving me over forcefully as if I were trespassing or he had a beef to discuss.

A Hostel on the Nolichucky

How John Shores became Uncle Johnny

(More or less)

A story by John Shores
as told to Stephen Tyler

Trailside Books

Trailside Books. LLC
151 River Road
Erwin, Tennessee 37650

First edition paperback printing September 2016

ISBN: 978-0-9979139-2-7

Printed in the United States of America

The interior typeface of this book is set in Sabon Lt Std 11/15 pt. Sabon is a traditional serif font, which was developed in the 1960s by Jan Tschichold, a Leipzig-based designer. The heading font throughout is of Century Gothic, a sans-serif typeface in the geometric style. Century Gothic is a digital typeface that has never been made into actual foundry type.

A Hostel on the Nolichucky is a work of non-fiction. However, some names and identifying details have been changed. Most of the characters you will meet here are real people. A few are fictional introduced to advance the story. While the author has made every effort to portray the scenes and events of the story that took place in 1997 and 1998 as accurately as possible, the dialogue is, of course, imagined. As for those readers who discover themselves in this story and who may remember things differently, the teller of this story, being limited by his own knowledge, offers his apologies.

This is for Charlotte, the love of my life,
and for her beautiful daughter Claire

John Shores

For Patricia Kathleen Veronica Reese,
without whom this book would not
have been written

Stephen Tyler

Acknowledgments

To Mr. DeHaven, who waved me across the road and changed my life; Roger, Bobby, Richard, Mike, Cindy, J. M. Harris, Al "No-Drip" Higgins and the dozens of volunteers who built our hostel, cabins and bathhouse; Dan "Wingfoot" Bruce, who believed that I would open on time and put me in his book; Laurie Potteiger, the store staff and all of my friends at the Appalachian Trail Conservancy who also trusted me and put me in their guide; Don Newton, whose photographs of our hostel have been used many times, including this book's front cover; A special thanks to photographer, Charles Edwards whose newsprint photograph of me taken in 1998 is opposite the title page in the book; The talented reporters and photographers with *The Erwin Record*, *Johnson City Press* and *The Knoxville News-Sentinel*, whose articles about our hostel lifted my spirits; Bubba Evely, who trusted me and didn't care if my business plan was hastily scribbled on a yellow legal pad; Mickey Townsend and Clarke Stallworth, trusted advisers and close friends; The bartenders at The Birmingham Press Club; Bob Manual, another trusted adviser, an effective attorney, and a member of MENSA; Debbie Tittle, David Sullivan, Bill Gaines, and Wendie Blair, all extremely competent and helpful public servants; Mrs. Erma Freeman, the world's greatest mother-in-law, who found the time to proofread our book; Mikey Pettijohn, a wonderful volunteer with a pure soul and superb proofreading skills; Gary and Frank, who worked extra hard allowing Mikey time to work with me on the book; Anjanette Harris, whose enthusiasm is contagious and represented the Unicoi County Chamber of Commerce well; Zack "Chief" Cross and all the scout leaders who taught me outdoor skills and helped me develop a set of personal values; Skinny "K" Hallmark who certified me as a SCUBA diver; Danny, Leslie and Daniel Honrath, awesome hostel neighbors and all great cooks; Elmer Hall, Innkeeper, who has a much-deserved 5-star rating, a wonderful mentor, and Bob

Peoples, operator of the Kincora Hostel, another of my mentors; Daniel and Wayne with Bluff Mountain Outfitters who shared their knowledge on how to create a successful outfitters store; Nolan Davis, his wife and staff at Sports Outdoor Marketing who supplied us with some of the finest hiking gear made; Brady and Lisa Sleeper, good friends who fed my hikers tasty burritos as large as footballs; Sarge and his friend, Paul Sherman, my buddies with exceptional graphic and computer skills; my mother and father, who prepared me for life; and last but certainly not least, to the thousands of wonderful guests who, over the last 18 years, have made Charlotte's life and mine a never-ending adventure.

American Whitewater gave us permission to use their description of the Wilson Creek Gorge rapids. We urge all of our readers to visit their amazing website. Thanks guys.

Stephen and I would like to extend a special thank-you to our small army of beta readers, those kind and patient folks who read early manuscripts and offered advice and encouragement. Thank you Patricia Reese, Kenny and Phyllis Reese, Harry and Sheri Reese, Walter and Kimberly Reese, Phillip and Heather Reese, Kenny Dunckley, Glen Tyler, Ann and Sid Hayes, Beatrice "Memama" Tyler, Mikey Pettijohn, Erma Freeman, and Pete and Patricia Rutter.

Finally, we extend our utmost gratitude to Thomas L. Coffman, Ph.D. (Social Psychology, Princeton University), our principal editor. Tom grew up within a few miles of the AT, in Virginia, was an Eagle Scout, and so came to us with a natural interest in this book. His editorial skills stem from an academic research career of writing and reviewing scholarly articles for professional journals in psychology and gerontology. Tom willingly and with great enthusiasm spent a good chunk of his time over the last five months spreading red ink over nearly every sentence we wrote. One memorable phone conversation lasted six hours. Tom, your patience with us was simply amazing. Thank you.

The longest journey begins
with a single step

---Lao Tzu

Prologue

John Shores

The Appalachian Trail runs right down the main street of the little town of Hot Springs, North Carolina, and over the French Broad River. After a little jag along the far bank, the trail turns sharply and climbs through several switchbacks up Mill Ridge, an elevation change of about 500 feet. The principal overlook at the top goes by the name, "Lover's Leap," and provides a panoramic view of Hot Springs, the French Broad Valley, and the mountains along the border with Tennessee.

John Shores crossed the French Broad with the intention of reaching Lover's Leap by noon. Like most people, John Shores was hiking the AT for a reason. He had just passed through a hard stage in his life. His struggle began a few years back with an unexpected divorce. Then his seventeen-year career with the *Birmingham News* ended. John had seen the writing on the wall. Big-city newspapers were experiencing financial problems, especially afternoon papers. Each day brought more employee reductions, hiring freezes, and budget cuts. It just wasn't fun anymore. He left the *News* opting for a deferred retirement and collected his severance pay. He was fifty-one.

All this new-found freedom had prompted a cascade of confusing opportunities. That was the problem. He needed to collect himself. He needed time to sort through a dizzying array of possibilities. The 190-mile hike from Hot Springs to Damascus, Virginia would give him that; and healing. He planned to self-medicate with the aerial diffusions of fir, balsam, bay, rhododendron, beechnut, and lily washed down with daily doses of high-mountain spring water.

Aroma-therapists are the artisans who specialize in the practice of utilizing blends of therapeutic oils applied by massage or inhalation to stimulate a desired human response. Aroma-therapists can make a fortune with the right client list, but nature along the Appalachian Trail provides the service free. The provocative odor of wet leaves and decaying deadwood, mixed with the aromatic compounds issuing from the conifers produced a sweet-smelling bouquet that filled the air during John's ascent. He needed something. He needed stimulation, and the atmosphere of the Appalachian Trail was his drug of choice. Conscious of all this, his enjoyment, sense of well-being, and overall perception of the trail grew as he hiked.

There are people who process smells differently, hearing them as sounds. The forest smells become whispers. The wind, influenced by the musty and rooty forest floor, becomes bits and pieces of song. A bird's call wrapped in the moldering, piney brume of an early dawn becomes a name spoken clearly.

Just after noon, John reached the narrow pathway that circumnavigates the wall of stone climbing over 250 feet to Lover's Leap; a rocky bluff overlooking a bend in the French Broad, the town of Hot Springs, and to the far west, a range of mountains known as The Devil's Backbone.

First it was her scent. Then her face shimmered before him in a bloom of light auburn hair. And clear as can be heard she whispered, "*John ... hey John.*" It was Charlotte's voice in the wind through the trees. "Wish you were here, baby," he said softly. And he stood on the narrow path skirting the high outcropping of stone looking out over the valley. "Wish you were here with me now."

John and Charlotte were canoeing and hiking enthusiasts, and had first met canoeing the scenic Hiwassee River with fifteen avid boaters. At the campground that afternoon, dark clouds rolled in, followed by a torrential downpour, and John had spent the afternoon with another couple in Charlotte's big tent playing Rook. From that point, they were aware of each other, and often found themselves in the same group canoeing here or there, or in the same raft of shrieking, whooping boaters shooting a Class V rapid on the Upper Gauley. As time went by, they grew closer. Eventually the inevitable happened. They became a well-known couple among the outdoor adventurers with whom they played.

But their time together was made difficult by John's commitments. Back then, he headed human resources at the *Birmingham News*, a responsibility that filled his long workday to the brim. With a couple of partners, he owned a dive shop. John and the others taught scuba diving at a local quarry. Every other weekend, it was his turn to man the store. Moreover, many vacations were spent guiding trips to the Florida Keys and the Caribbean. John Shores was a very busy man. For John and Charlotte, time alone together was a precious commodity.

From Lover's Leap, he struck out along the spine of Mill Ridge heading for the Spring Mountain Shelter, one of the few remaining shelters along the trail constructed by President Roosevelt's Civilian Conservation Corps. Some portions of the hike from Hot Springs to Damascus are considered rather boring. This was why John chose this section of the trail. He wasn't only in it for spectacular views or remarkable trailside features. He was also there to think.

The Spring Mountain Shelter would be an early stop for the typical hiker, but John knew better than to push on the first day. Trail legs, they call it. John didn't have them. By the third day you become stronger, and you can aim for the further destination. Fully supplied, his pack was heavier now than it would be in a few days. The climb up Lover's Leap, though not especially long, was steep and tiring. The next shelter, Little Laurel, would add another eight-plus miles. Better rest today and push hard tomorrow. Otherwise, it would become a pain-filled five days of hiking to reach his stop in Erwin, Tennessee.

John awoke with the light of dawn, rested and thankful the shelter was still empty; thankful that a group of exuberant, youthful hikers had not shown up after dark, as is often the case when one hikes the Trail in search of solitude. There are many places in the wild where isolation and serenity is assured and certain. The Appalachian Trail is not one of those. It has to do with the popularity of the Trail and the fact that there are people who hike fast, and those who are slow. Naturally the faster hiker catches the slower and the two of them might gain on a third. If these three people are well-matched and like-minded, they all begin to accommodate each other's pace. Then these three might gain on and blend with another three hiking together. Now there are six affable people hiking along together, grumbling and sharing complaints, laughing about the dumb things they did yesterday, and sharing life's experiences.

John was not interested in hiking with others. He wanted to sort through and appraise the things in his life that were changing. "What has happened has happened," and "It is what it is," were the thoughts running through his mind, as water for his breakfast came to a boil. He was ready to accept the facts and move on; to simply make the best of it.

Two packets of instant oatmeal and a handful of raisins went into the water. A few minutes later, breakfast was over. He rinsed his cup, slipped the little stove into its place, hoisted the heavy pack onto his back, and turned his thoughts into a question, "What has happened?" he said aloud, with emphasis on the *what*. A question put that way is an inquiry, not a plea.

It comes as just a tinge, something that plumbs the depths of memory producing unconscious feeling; a burst of vividness that fades in an instant. During that moment, he was at Camp Arrowhead. He could feel it, smell it, hear it. The pounding of tent stakes. The smell of wood smoke. The distinctive rattle of a Boy Scout mess kit. A protesting teen voice. The face of Chief came to him. A scurry of leaves became his voice. "OK, Scouts --- Listen up." Zack Chief Cross had been a force in his life.

Chief. Everybody, the president of the United States included, called him "Chief." He was a key figure in Alabama scouting. He had been the camp director every summer, and when John became a camp counselor himself, they became friends. It was a mentor, mentee relationship he came to value and cherish.

The face of his father had come to him several times during his trek toward Spring Mountain Shelter the day before. "He was a good father," John thought. "Wish I'd told him that more often."

John was not yet six the first time they went fishing on the Warrior River in his dad's big, flat-bottomed johnboat. The boat looked huge to John's eyes then, and it was. His dad had built it and painted it a very dark green, like the shutters on their white house. His dad and his partners built these boats with cypress wood. They were very heavy, had three wide bench seats, and the transom was designed for mounting a small outboard motor. Capable of operating in extremely shallow water, they were especially suitable for float-fishing and duck hunting. The hull, being nearly flat, limited the use of the boat to calmer waters, but the advantage of that design was stability. You could fish standing up. Two men could pass each other trading ends.

John loved those trips on the river with his dad, and he loved the river too. Just being on the water made him happy.

These outings and his father's encouragement had put him in the Scouts. By age seventeen, he was an Eagle Scout and soon after, a member of the Order of the Arrow. As a Scout, he had become an experienced hiker of the AT. It could be said that because of his father and scouting, he was hiking the Trail today. They had given him a deep sensitivity, a keenness of mental perception and understanding for what lay before him —the white-blazed trail becoming endless vista; the great, blue sky becoming night; the mesmeric roar of whitewater; the beguiling danger of the deep dive. It was an abiding love for the wild that equaled any he ever held for a human soul.

In many ways, the direction of John's adult life sprang from that of his father. His dad was an enigma. None of his friends had him figured. The most common thing you would hear regarding John M. Shores Sr. was, "You mean he's *that* John Shores?" He led four distinctly different lives, and in each of these, he could shift his personality to match what those roles required. First, he was an electrician with U.S. Steel, the largest employer in Birmingham. On the side, he was a general contractor with a reputation for building excellent houses. He owned a boat works with two partners and they repaired boats of every description. And, of all things, he owned a bar. Not your ordinary everyday bar, this bar was in the boondocks down a narrow gravel road on the banks of the Warrior River. Imagine that. Imagine the clash of experiences that led to John's becoming an Eagle Scout on the one hand, overlaying the experiences of spending many summer days in a rowdy fish camp bar popping cans of beer. And the smell came with the memory. And the sound. The spew of hoppy beer and the popping crunch of the long-handled can opener that cut two holes at once---the one you drank from and the little one on the far side. The cans were steel in those days, and crushing one in your bare hand was a true test of fish-camp manhood.

John's father had purchased a WWII hand-cranked telephone and had laid over a mile of connecting wires through the woods from the fish camp to the top of the hill where the gravel road branched off. Twelve-year-old John was the look-out. Very strict Blue Laws were in effect in Alabama, and you could not buy beer anywhere on Sunday; that is, except at the Warrior River Fish Camp. On Sunday the beer went into a twelve-ounce Dixie Cup. When the old WWII phone rang, meaning a strange or suspicious car had turned down the lane, a tarp was thrown over four half barrels of iced-down beer and the cups disappeared from sight until the "all-clear" was given.

The Warrior River Fish Camp was where John, as a teenager, had first experienced diving. He had purchased a used air-line diving rig in good condition from a friend of his father. The reason for this purchase was the fact that mounting an outboard motor on the back of a sixteen-foot johnboat became more difficult if the fisherman doing the mounting had spent the previous two hours re-filling his Dixie Cup. The motor could easily end up ten feet down in the water drifting who-knows-where; maybe tangled in the limbs of a submerged fallen tree. The $5 fee John charged for retrieving the motor was a lot of money back in the '50s, but insignificant when weighed against the cost of a new motor.

Funny how the mind can cruise so easily from one memory to another; from the stinging smoke and crackle of a Scout fire circle, to lying on your back in the leaves by a WWII telephone listening to distant laughter and music, to the sound of an air hose blowing muddy water from the cylinder of an outboard motor, to the faces of friends, and dive buddies—all flash by in an instant. And when the forest broke into fields of wildflowers, his thoughts returned to Charlotte.

Hiking through Bearwallow Gap toward Big Firescald Knob, John caught up with two hikers. He had passed several section-hikers with lighter packs earlier in the day. They, all of them, would certainly reach Jerry's Cabin Shelter, John's destination tonight. The strategy forming in John's mind was to stop at the shelter, tolerate the folks who would assemble there, rise just at dawn, and push hard hoping he would leave them behind. With luck, he would not run up on another such group ahead. John needed space to think.

The next day John was up and packed and hiking while the others still slept. As the rising sun began peeking through the trees east of the trail, he looked for a place to take breakfast. He considered not eating at all, but he knew that was unwise. Every hiker has experienced a loss of appetite on the trail. Three causes might be in play here. First, it's a pain in the butt to drop your pack, dig out the food and equipment, and then clean up using precious water you might have hiked a half-mile down the side of a ridge to acquire. Secondly, trail food is not appealing --- oatmeal every morning, for instance. Dry soup mix boiled in water with a can of tuna. A freeze-dried beef stew that tastes like it was created by DuPont. And finally, wild cravings replace hunger; you just stop feeling hungry for trail food and begin craving cheeseburgers, pizza, big salads, and chocolate milk. Typically, the hiker discovers he's starving when his legs give out. Or when he awakes in the morning as tired as the night before. Or when the pack he had slung effortlessly on his back yesterday is too heavy now to pick up. That's when forced feeding begins.

Something about the hiss of the WhisperLite backpacking stove generates the face of Clarke Stallworth fifty feet down the anchor rope of the Sea Hunt II, Lanny Rinehart's dive boat. The Sea Hunt is anchored above the Empire Mica, a huge British tanker sunk in 110 feet of water by a German sub off the coast near Apalachicola, Florida. John is moving down the rope with Clark, and their glassed-in faces are inches apart. Stallworth is giving the thumb and index finger OK sign. John is nodding and returning the sign, but he could count on one hand the number of times Stallworth had dived. Not enough experience to be diving this wreck.

John, now hunched over his steaming oatmeal, again feels the anxiety that gripped his heart that day as Stallworth continued to pull himself down the anchor rope. "God, I'm responsible for this," John feels himself thinking. Not certified to dive this deep. I must be nuts to have let him do it.

Finishing his oatmeal, John smiled. The remembered anxiety of this event dissolved. His friend was a natural. They had a great dive that day, and as a PADI/SSI instructor qualified to certify deep diving, John had given Stallworth his diving certification with complete confidence in his friend's ability.

Stallworth was a good bit older than John, but they became close friends. He was youthful and energetic by nature, a bearish man, an old-style fire-eating journalist, smart as a whip and full of stories. When John joined the *Birmingham News*, Stallworth was Managing Editor. Years later, John had seen a TV interview with General Norman Schwarzkopf.

That's Clarke. Just like Clarke.

For John, it was an honor to know Clarke Stallworth. He was a master storyteller who could awaken all five senses. You didn't just see and hear his stories, you could feel, smell, and taste the worlds he described. His specialties were Birmingham and the history of Alabama. So it was a surprise to John when management assigned Stallworth to his department as a writing trainer. It was confirmation, too, that the paper was in serious trouble. He and Stallworth had talked it out over mojitos in a Cuban bar several years ago. They both concluded the paper would not last until their retirement. It's the kind of discovery that a man his age does not want to recognize right in the middle of his career.

The best job I ever had. Right in the middle of my most productive years.

"What's next?" John heard himself saying aloud. After leaving the *BN*, he had done some consulting, but didn't enjoy it. The consulting gigs were okay, but he missed people-management. He missed the hands-on impact he could make in people's lives. He liked being around the staff, especially the reporters, who were a singular sort. They couldn't get enough of each other. They had lunch together, they met for breakfast, they gathered at the Birmingham Press Club every evening. But, most of all, from John's point of view, they were smart people. John operated most efficiently when surrounded by smart people.

The climbs out of Sugarloaf Gap and Devil's Fork Gap were stupidly steep. "Who built this damn thing." John said out loud, slipping and catching himself sideways. "Look, for god's sake! The trail could go through there, up that way, a switchback right up there. Why the hell didn't they think of that!"

Pushing on, grabbing at roots, the weight of his pack nearly tumbling him over backwards when he missed his grip, John spoke to himself again. "The agony and the ecstasy, that's what I'd call it! If I wrote a book about the AT, the agony and the ecstasy!"

Those are the kind of thoughts that dominate the mind when hiking the trail shades on misery. You could predict it. Tough climbs produce frustration; even anger. Pleasant thoughts, conversations with Mom, remembrances of lost loves would serenade the trail over grassy, sunlit balds; along burbling streams; through fields banked in goldenrod. And when these visual delights recede and the trail passes along an easy grade through the viewless forest canopy, the mind turns toward review and serious inquiry.

So, during the easy stretches through the forest, John's mind would turn toward weighing his options. He had been a trumpet player. A musician. A good one. He had made the Alabama All-State High School Band. He spent his stretch in the military playing in the 282th Army Band out of Fort Jackson, South Carolina.

With a little practice, might get back into that. Go back to school. Get a Master's and become a high school band director. Two years, Maybe?

Things like that would drift in and out of John's mind as he followed the line of white blazes curving slightly upward through rhododendron and pine.

Become a contractor.

He had worked with his dad's construction crews; spent one whole summer framing houses.

Always wanted to own a bar.

He was counting options on his fingers.

A fish-camp.

A few more steps.

I love canoeing and kayaking, how about canoes? I could build canoes.

He had liked hanging around his father's boat works. The men working there were true craftsman. During one school holiday, he had helped construct a fiberglass hull and liked the process.

Or wooden boats. Cedar-strip canoes.

All these scattered thoughts were slowly coming together, picked up and examined, surveyed for truth, tested for fit, like pieces of a puzzle.

John's breakfast at the Hogback Ridge Shelter had taken longer than expected. A young hiker, her confidence shaken by the presence of a bear during the night, was ready to quit and go home. Before hiking out that morning, John had spent an hour or so calming her down, describing some of his experiences, and dispelling the bad information she had picked up about the nature of bears.

Then the trail had taken him over Big Bald, one of the most spectacular vistas in the Southern Appalachians. From its broad, treeless summit at 5,516 feet, one has an unobstructed panoramic view of the Smokies, Mount Mitchell, and the Unaka Mountains. John had lingered there enjoying this magnificent place before getting back on the trail. By the late afternoon, John realized that he would be hiking in the dark before reaching the next shelter.

His last night before reaching Erwin would be spent at the No Business Knob Shelter. The water source near the shelter had been used by moonshiners for a century. The mountain men would remind each other, "Haint nobody got no business over there."

In the gathering dusk, the ridge crests stretch forever in bas-relief against an iridescent deep-blue sky. The wild is forever restless with its birds and insects, its wind-trembled leaves; its ticking and dry-cracking fallen limbs. But, as day dissolves into night, the forest becomes quiet. The scuffling winds, alive with sight and sound, die down. A regime change occurs as daytime animals, birds, and insects stand down and nocturnals cautiously emerge. The ecosystem pauses, anticipating the night. An uncommon stillness prevails in respect for this change.

John became conscious, first of the eerie light, and then of the stillness, as his own sounds, uncommonly loud, uncommonly near, wrecked the silence. The straps and accoutrements of his backpack whispered and groaned aloud. The tips of his hiking poles clanked against rock like pistol shots. The unaccustomed sound of his own lungs rasping, pulling for air, intrusively breached the quiet. The eeriness, John realized, comes from the fact that he is still moving while all others have stopped. He felt the eyes. They were watching. They were watching him.

Coming out of Spivey Gap, the sky growing black into a moonless night, John pulled on his headlamp for the last two miles. The grade was nearly flat coming toward the famous water source, and hiking through the night was not difficult. But, with his fresh batteries stowed away in the package waiting for him at the post office in Erwin, the steep climb up to the shelter was a concern. “Hope these batteries hold out,” he muttered to himself.

Five hikers were at the shelter when John arrived. “It’s okay,” John thought. “All of them are older, thank god.” Four of them were huddled around the fire pit, and by the light of it John noticed right off, they were exhausted. During the routine exchange of hellos and the announcement of miles hiked and points of origin, the men explained they were two weeks into a three-week section hike, and that all of them worked for Georgia-Pacific.

John rolled out his sleeping bag to claim space in the shelter should other hikers show up, and fixed his supper. By then, the others had crawled into their sleeping bags and two were snoring.

John quietly slipped into his bag and thought, “I could get back in the dive business.” Thoughts and images of boats and scuba gear and sunken ships flicked through his mind as he slipped into that acroamatic asylum, that dark hall of mirrors and somber landscapes one enters just before sleep. Then he heard a passage from Annie Dillard. Not exactly. Not her precise words. But, the sense of it, as if she were speaking to him.

Things come if you wait. They come. They do come and it pours over you like a waterfall; like a tidal wave. You're walking this trail without expectation, and that which comes rocks and topples you; shreds you; grinds you; spins you dry.

The words "clarity will come," echoed through the hall like a prayer, and, without his knowing, small scattered pieces of his life's experiences awakened. Forgotten shards of his true self buried in the busy-ness of his life, now began to emerge and gather like bits of a picture puzzle. When completed, that picture would portray an image no more imaginable for John at this moment than if it were of him crowned the King of Spain.

The next day, climbing up from Temple Hill Gap, a steep gap ravine, John topped Cliff Ridge. Around mile 340, the trail begins its descent toward the trailhead at Chestoa. That trailhead is about four miles from downtown Erwin, and marks one of the most fascinating features of the Southern Appalachians; the Nolichucky River Gorge. The Nolichucky is an ancient river pre-existing the mountains themselves. As the mountains pushed up over eons of geological time, the river reversed course and cut through metamorphic rock dividing the Appalachian range into the Bald Mountains to the south and the Unakas to the north; a chasm too wide, too steep, and too deep for the trail to cross. Hikers, both northbound and southbound, must come down out of the mountains in order to cross the Chestoa Bridge spanning the Nolichucky River. The gorge levels out at Chestoa, but the river is wider. The bridge, high up over rushing water, is nearly 100 yards long.

At the foot of the bridge, north-bounders like John turn right, cross the bridge, and re-enter the forest on the other side. From here, the trail follows the river for a bit, and then turns sharply up into the mountains, climbs to an elevation of 4,440 feet, and continues its northward trek. Along the way, coming down and going up, there are many breathtaking views of the river, the gorge it runs through, and the valley around and beyond Erwin, Tennessee.

For the northbound hiker, the climb down is the hardest. There are eighteen switch-backs; a forty-minute, stiff-legged, pack-swaying march that's hard on your knees. Once down, you still have a long walk into Erwin.

John reached the high point of Cliff Ridge overlooking the Nolichucky, a river he had canoed and fished. Three switchbacks further along and he was overlooking the little town of Erwin. From there, he could hit the bridge with a rock, it seemed.

Erwin, Tennessee.

John stood somberly taking in the view with arms crossed.

Erwin, Tennessee.

Since that day back in Birmingham, with maps spread out on the kitchen table, since that moment when having put his pencil on the trail crossing the bridge and from the point of his pencil noticing the word *Erwin* on the map next to it, John could not avoid connecting the sound of that name with the barefoot man in the woods. The barefoot man had said just a few words and the enormity of the devastation and heartbreak of the Vietnam War had dropped on John and nearly crushed him.

After high school, John had joined the Army. The war in Vietnam was heating up and he was exactly the right age to have been drafted. John could not stand the thought of being coerced, or of being compelled to do anything. He never could. So, he volunteered. After basic training in Fort Benning, Georgia, they sent him to Fort Jackson, South Carolina where soldiers receive advanced combat training. Not John, though. He was assigned to Fort Jackson's band, the 282nd, one of the

Army's most historic active duty bands. His military occupational specialty was to play trumpet.

Part of his duty was funeral detail. A military funeral requires two officers or sergeants, depending on the man's rank, seven riflemen to fire the 21-gun salute, six pall bearers, and a trumpeter to play Taps. One of these assignments took him from his base near Columbia, South Carolina, through Erwin, Tennessee, and over the Unakas to a little church in the rugged mountains of western North Carolina.

The Fort Jackson bus carrying the detail traveled up old US 176 to Hendersonville, North Carolina and turned north on US 23 just at dawn. With the rest of the detail asleep, John was alone for over an hour, alone to witness and marvel at the quaint little villages, the bare-hilled, beggarly mountain farms, and the scenic beauty of the highway's winding route through mountains like none he had ever seen. It had been a number of years since he had hiked the Appalachians, and spotting the sign marking the highway's crossing of the Appalachian Trail had been a thrill. For an instant, the serenity of hiking through this remote region possessed his senses. He could smell it, hear the sound of it, feel it on his skin. So, coming over the mountain at Sams Gap, just those few minutes, became a pivotal moment in his life. The name of the little town of Erwin became for him a memory peg. He determined he would return. He would hike the beautiful mountains of Tennessee as soon as his commitment with the Army was over.

The driver had stopped to refuel in Erwin, and the men took their breakfast at a lovely, home-style restaurant nearby. From there, the detail traveled over the mountain to a church in North Carolina. The trip was steep with switchbacks. Pavement ended at the top. Heading down on the rutted gravel road, the howling, lurching, bounding bus in its lowest gear, John was on the edge of his seat, thrilled but awestruck. The experience was beyond description for the young trumpet player who had grown up in the Alabama flatlands and was now stationed in South Carolina, mean elevation 350 feet.

John played Taps. That was his job. He and the other trumpet players in the band did it over and over by turns. He played Taps and the mother would collapse, either to the ground or into somebody's arms. It happened every single time.

To get through his performance under these circumstances, John would put himself mentally in another place. If the funeral happened to be non-formal, as was the case on this occasion, he distanced himself physically from the devastated family. Taps can be played anywhere nearby.

On that day, the graveside portion of the funeral took place in the churchyard cemetery. John had walked behind the church and up into the woods. After the final volley of the 21-gun salute settled, he played taps. As the last, long note ended and its echo disappeared into the steep, surrounding mountains, John was startled by the sudden appearance of a very tall, thin man in bibbed overalls. No shirt. No shoes. Mud squeezed up between his toes. He was slowly approaching. John wanted to back away because the man was staring directly at him. He kept coming, his blank, lifeless eyes revealing nothing. When he reached the little clearing where John had played, he stopped. He stood looking for a moment, his lips moving wordlessly, and then he spoke in that high, East Tennessee accent that in the north would be taken as somewhat feminine.

"Y'all jes bureed muh bess fren. All we deed was huntn feesh. Now'ees gone 'n I got no idee when nor where nor why. I wouda seed him off, but I ain't got no shoes." Then the barefoot young man turned and walked off into the woods.

* * *

Coming down from Cliff Ridge through seemingly endless switch-backs, his mind darkened by these memories, John reflected on a book he had read for inspiration prior to his trip. Jan D. Curran, an Army lifer, had retired as a full-bird Colonel complete with Bronze Star. Curran had thru-hiked the trail in two seasons and had written a different book about each of those efforts. John read the first one, *A Journey of Discovery*. Like John's, Curran's hike had a purpose; a reconciliation of his life. Curran was 57, and his observations and memories were that of an older, experienced, world-traveler. Like John himself, Curran had just retired, and the hike up the Appalachian Trail was an undertaking designed to prompt an inquiry as to what he intended to do with the rest of his life.

Now John was coming into Erwin, the only trail town Curran had disliked. An entire chapter of his first book was devoted to a detailed description of his bad experience. The men he met were crude and rough. A motel refused to rent him a room. His shuttle driver was rude. When leaving Erwin, a mystery truck had followed, had quietly circled the Beauty Spot parking area, and Curran was forced to hide from shadowy men flitting along the edge of the forest. For a few moments, Curran had feared for his life.

"I wonder," John said as he merged onto the hard surface road just above the Chestoa Bridge and walked down the hill.

What the heck am I going to run into here?

Coming along the west side of the Nolichucky, John noticed a rugged little house just beyond four county roads that intersect at the foot of the bridge. An old man was standing on the front porch.

Is he waving at me?

John slowed.

Must be. There's no one else about.

No, ... John stopped and squinted.

He's not waving. He's motioning ... a very insistent hooking of his left hand and arm as if to say, "Come over here, will you?"

The Main Story

The Nolichucky Hostel

Uh-oh. That's not a howdy-neighbor wave.

..............?

He's waving me over forcefully as if I were trespassing or he had a beef to discuss.

As I crossed the street, I thought about James Dickey's famous book *Deliverance*. And not twenty minutes ago, coming down the mountain, I had recalled Jan Curran's description of the sullen, ignorant men he had met in Erwin, the frightening experience of this highly-decorated officer hiding from gnarly mountaineers he believed to be tracking him down. Curran carried a snub-nosed 48 Police Special. I carried...well, these trekking poles.

I could see the old man's serious demeanor. Hands on hips watching me. Approaching the porch, I called out with as much child-like innocence as I could muster, "Yes-sir, what can I do for you?"

"You got that backwards, hiker. Where you goin?"

"Northbound."

"Well, son, I can see you're northbound. How far?"

"Damascus."

"You're runnin a little late. You missed Trail Days."

"Well, I wasn't particularly interested in..."

"Name's Don DeHaven, he said, chuckling. What's your name, son? ... your trail name."

"Uncle Johnny."

"Well, Uncle Johnny, why don't you take a break, have some coffee and chocolate cake?" he said motioning me up. "I make a pretty decent chocolate cake."

His manner had taken on a very pleasant fatherliness. He was a wiry, handsome man, average height, lean, and youthful. He had shoe-polish black hair, which may have been an excellent dye job. He looked to be in his late seventies. Much relieved, I took the three steps up to the cracked, concrete porch.

"Drop your pack over there." He pointed to the porch glider. "Is that a Gregory?"

"Yes-sir, a Gregory Evolution."

"That's one big-assed sucker. Got that external frame." He opened the screen door and waved me inside.

"I just made fresh coffee," he said, pointing toward a worn, dark brown leather couch as he disappeared into the kitchen. In a moment he reappeared with cake on a china plate. The plate had an underglaze pattern of hand-painted bright flowers, green stems, and leaves. Coffee was in a matching cup and saucer. The fork was heavy, old-fashioned silverware. I'm not the most graceful person in these circumstances and it required a delicate balancing act on my part. There was no end table or coffee table near the couch. I set the coffee on the arm of the couch and reminded myself not to clip it with my elbow. He took his seat on the other end holding his cup in both hands. No saucer.

"It surprises me you recognized my pack."

"I been sittin in that porch rocker watching you hikers coming down that hill for over forty years. All of you like talking about equipment and what you're gonna buy next time. So I know a lot about equipment and the trail. You'd be surprised what you learn just listenin to folks."

An awkward moment passed and we both sipped coffee. I took a bite of cake, and with my mouth full heard him ask:

"You're section-hiking...where'd you start?"

"Hot Springs," I mumbled through rich chocolate icing.

"How much weight you carryin?"

"About forty-five when I started. Probably thirty-eight or so now."

"What's your real name?"

"John Shores"

"Well, John, you've got one hell of an accent. Where you from?"

"Birmingham, Alabama."

"What you do there.?" he asked with obvious interest.

"I just took early retirement from the newspaper business…the *Birmingham News*. I was their Human Resources Director."

"Me, I'm retired too. The railroad."

We chatted on like that. He had a calm, easy style, and his interest in me seemed sincere. He explained that when the Army released him, he had come to Erwin with some buddies to apply for work on the Clinchfield Railroad. The Clinchfield line had its corporate offices in Erwin, and a large yard where Clinchfield repaired damaged cars. The ending of the war had produced a huge demand for every kind of product, and cheap coal was at the heart of the boom. The Clinchfield, running straight south out of the Kentucky coalfields, connected with a dozen or more lines running east and west. Being at the center of coal delivery, the railroad was expanding rapidly. They were recruiting new hires as fast as they could find them. DeHaven's Army buddies caught wind of this, so they came.

"You got a wife, John?"

"No, sir. Not right now. Been married though. No children."

"I've got three kids all grown up. Lost my wife eight years ago, but I'm newly engaged," he announced with a big satisfied grin.

DeHaven got up, went in the kitchen, and returned with one of those tall, blue-porcelain, cowboy-style coffeepots and poured more coffee. The chit-chat went on for almost an hour.

When the conversation turned to politics, DeHaven's manner took on a twinkling, mild cynicism. Like many southern men of his station, he had a low tolerance for gov'ment tomfoolery, as he put it. He said that last night the breaking news on television was the lawyer for Paula Jones, the woman suing President Clinton for sexual harassment. The lawyer explained in the interview that he had taken sworn testimony from a woman working in the White House indicating there was a full-blown affair going on. From talk of Clinton's recurrent sexual scandals, the conversation turned to Iraq and Clinton's campaign to oust Saddam Hussein. Regime change, he said Clinton called it, and I almost laughed aloud at the way he drew those words out while dropping his head and looking at me from the corner of his eye. DeHaven was charming and funny, and he was surprisingly knowledgeable of current events. He talked on about the Middle East, and of things I didn't know.

"I guess you'll want to resupply here in Erwin?" he asked

He understood hikers. That was becoming clear to me. After all, he had lived here, he was especially eager to point out, since 1955. I would imagine he had met and talked to hundreds.

"I have a package to pick up at the post office, I need some groceries, and I'd like to take a shower at the YMCA."

"Look here, son, you must've liked my cake. You want another piece?"

"No, sir, I've got to get back on the trail. I'm trying to make Hampton in five days, and it's some distance into Erwin, isn't it?"

"Son...Uncle Johnny...I'll tell you what. I've got to go to town myself. I'll carry you in. But first, I've got to gather some things and put on my boots. Ain't going in these slippers. While I do that, you eat another piece of my cake. Just go in the kitchen there and get you some."

* * *

We got into his old, white Ford Econoline van. Barely out the driveway DeHaven turned to me and said, "Johnny, you like beer?"

"I love beer," I said. It was 10:30 in the morning.

* * *

We pulled into an alley and passed along what looked like abandoned warehouses. On the left, in the center of a large paved lot, sat an unattractive one-story building. By the sign hanging near the corner, the place was the Rendezvous.

Seven patrons turned to see who was coming in the door. After a second of silence, they all shouted at once. The clamor coming from the men was punctuated with cheerful Don's and DeHaven. It was the typical old man's bar, smelling of stale beer, dirty and dark. The room was deep with a long bar down the left-hand side. Booths lined the right wall. In the back were two, well-used pool tables.

"Here's another one of those crazy hikers," DeHaven announced. "Meet Uncle Johnny." More clamor carried the words Uncle Johnny while I gave them a little wave with my gray Tilley hat.

The bar was L shaped. It took a turn on the front end toward the left-hand wall, closing off the back-bar area. From the bar stools here, one could look down the line at the other patrons. DeHaven sat first. I sat to the left of him.

"Where you going?" one of the men asked. They, every one of them, were DeHaven's age and all seemed to be friends. I noticed too, all of them were drinking long necks, Pabst Blue Ribbon in a bottle. All of them. Odd.

"He's a section-hiker," DeHaven interrupted with a smirk. "He ain't goin the whole 2,100 miles," he sang out, pointing in the general direction of Maine. "Least, not this year."

"Ri-i-ight," dragged out one man faking a critical tone."

"You sure ain't getting there from down here in this bar," said another, laughing."

"Hang in there, Johnny. Don't pay attention to these nuts," the man next to DeHaven said.

All this commotion came out at once as DeHaven gave me a fatherly pat on the back.

"Two PBRs over here, John." And when they were delivered, DeHaven introduced me to the bartender, a tall, slim man about my age who had been smiling at me and laughing at the ribbing these old guys were dishing out.

"John, meet another John...John Shores, ex-newspaperman from Birmingham, Alabama. He's celebrating his recent retirement by hiking the trail. Damned noble of him, don't you think?" Before the bartender could answer, DeHaven said to me, "We're like a club here." And he tipped his head sideways to indicate the other guys along the bar. "Most of us come here every day. John here gives us a special discount...PBRs one dollar!" He announced proudly. "So drink up. The beer's on me."

"Uncle Johnny," a man about midway down was leaning forward looking in my direction. "What do you think of our town?"

"Well, sir, from what I've seen......"

"The name's Paul," he said with a little dip of his head toward me.

"Nice to meet you, Paul. Yes, from what I've seen so far, this is a real nice town. A beautiful spot too. From up on the trail you can see most of it and the valley is beautiful."

He smiled broadly and saluted me thumbs up.

Right then, a wiry man of medium height and with thick, snow-white hair got off his stool and walked our way saying,

"I'll tell you about Erwin. I'll tell you what kind of town this is." He came over to my side where he wiggled his empty bottle at the bartender.

"Back in '36, we had a big snow. A blizzard. The Blizzard of Thirty-Six." He looked at DeHaven and back at me. "I was fifteen." His beer came and he took a swig. Then he leaned casually against the bar facing me, his left forearm on the bar top, his right hand holding the beer.

"Over three foot of snow and drifts ten-foot deep. It was a surprise. Middle of March. Nobody had no idea it was a-coming. Some of the trees were leafin already and my mother's jonkills were blooming in the front yard. No weather report that I heard of. There weren't no warnings from the radio talking about a big snow comin. It just hit us…wham! It was Thursday. The kids in school. It come a-snowing bout eleven thirty. Just a little whiff of fine snow. No wind. The wind didn't come 'til the next mornin. By noon though, it was a-pouring down; couldn't see twenty-foot through it. Well, don't you know, the kids did a full day. There wern't no early release back in those days. No-sir. Kids come home at three and that's the way it was. No kids stragglin home at one or two in the afternoon. Where would they go? Who would know? Those kids got a full day of school, snow and all.

"Well, the buses come and there was more'n a foot of snow on the ground. The buses sure weren't going back in them side streets and twisty roads up the holler. So, the mothers, they all walk down to the intersections. Here the bus is a-comin and the parents waitin in the pourin snow to walk the kids home in it. One of them bus drivers tried take his bus up Unaka Springs Road, and it got stuck on the steep part. Slid right into the ditch. Wasn't long, here come the mothers walkin down the hill. They probably spected it would happen. Kids got home all fine, but it was a week before they got that stuck bus out the ditch and back to the lot.

"Next mornin, we had three foot of snow on the ground and big drifts everywhere, but you know what? The milk got delivered. The groceries got delivered. Mr. Swain got himself a team and a high-wheeled wagon, and he delivered them groceries. Mr. T.J Love out at Loves Dairy? He couldn't get his truck going, but he had a team and wagon, and that's how the milk got delivered. And all those folks living south of town, that's how they got to work. Mr. Love's wagon plowed the way to town with a whole bunch of folks walking behind the wagon.

"The sheriff was on duty. The policeman was on duty. All the doctors and lawyers were in their offices. All those highflutin executives at Clinchfield, they were in their offices. Nobody missed work back in those days. There was responsibilities to tend to. That's the way people are in Erwin. When there's work to do, we're working. The girls painting them flowers in the pottery, all of them got to work, God knows how, you know, comin down out the mountains and all. But the story got around all the pottery people were in. Them kill'ns baking and smoking all night, somebody had to get them plates out when time was up.

"And you know what? They sent a special train to Johnson City. They sure did, and the JC people who come to work in Erwin, they got to the station on their own. The buses weren't running. Their cars weren't going nowhere. They knew the train would come and they went to the station to catch it. Nobody gonna miss a day's work back in those days, not for a little snow on the ground.

"The Mayor…Ol' Uncle Jake, bless his heart, the Mayor lived nine miles out Asheville Highway. He walked those nine miles to his office. He sure did. Got there about noon, just in time to go to Coley's Drugstore for his lunch like always. Walked in and there were all the town big-wigs worrying about the calamity the town was facing. Ol' Doc Monroe was there too. Always ate his lunch sitting on a stool at the lunch counter. A call come in to Mr. Coley that one of Doc's patients was in trouble. Doc walked three mile through deep snow and delivered a baby girl over in Rock Creek. He sure did.

"That's Erwin, Uncle Johnny. That's the people of Erwin, and we're still at it like that. We work hard and take care of each other. Oh...yeah. Here's a good'n.

"Miss Annie. Miss Annie Cross, she must have been ninety. Lived way back in a deep cove. Can't remember which one, but it was way back. Well, people got to worryin about her and was she alright. This was about three days later...we were snowed in for a week, more up in the hollows, but the Red Cross they come and they were helping people. When they heard about Miss Annie, well three of um got horses...there was lots of horses around back in those days...they rode horseback up the holler to Miss Annie's place way down a little dirt road through the woods by the creek. When they got there, they went up on the porch and knocked on the door. Well, when Miss Annie opened the door, they announced they're from the Red Cross. Miss Annie shook her head, and in her sweet little voice said, I'm real sorry fellas, but I can't help you none at all this year. It's been a hard, bitter winter."

All the men at the bar laughed. But I think the laughter was for my benefit. They, I suspected, had heard that story many times.

DeHaven started telling me a story about a big snow he had experienced and the white-haired man strolled back to his bar stool at the other end. The conversation at the bar murmured on with Waylon Jennings' comic song *Wrong* playing in the background. Suddenly the men burst out laughing.

"Did you hear that, Don?"

DeHaven responded, "Hear what?"

"Paul here said if a chimpanzee walked in the Oval Office wearing a skirt, Clinton would try to screw it." And the men burst out laughing again.

DeHaven looked at me apologetically, and shook his head. "Yeah, I heard on the radio something about the Clinton investigation. Looks like Clinton's reckless skirt-chasin's catching up with him. That Paula Jones has accusin women coming out the woodwork."

"I don't git-it," another man said. "He's got the whole world by the balls. Why would he risk all that for nothing? She ain't no good-looking woman to me. Got a nose like an ax handle."

"Well, she looks better'n a chimpanzee, don't she?" Paul called out. And they laughed again.

We were half-way through our third beer, and I was about to nudge DeHaven and suggest we move on, but I liked these men.

What I couldn't help noticing was the absence of anything like Jan Curran's descriptions of the people of Erwin, Tennessee. These men were salt of the earth. A friend once told me he figured there were only about forty different kinds of people. The types even look alike, he said. We were in a bar and he pointed and said, look at that woman, see, talking to those three guys. Looks just like Julia Roberts. And she did. Had the same facial expressions, same speech pattern. That crossed my mind here as I looked over these friends of DeHaven. I knew them. They looked familiar. I had met men just like these guys over and over throughout my life. I could look at one of them and almost tell you what he's thinking; they were that ordinary and typical. These were not some James Dickey stereotype mountaineers genetically predisposed to go out hunting hikers. These were ordinary Americans, retired from long lives of hard work and responsible living; fathers, husbands, retired now and living the good life.

I found the same thing true of the clerks at the post office. Wendy, a very attractive young woman with long blond hair cheerfully announced, "Honey, we've been looking for you to come in. How you been doing," she said with a great big smile as she handed me my package. And that's what it was like with every single person I met. I couldn't help thinking; this is a good town. These are good old-fashion southern people. In fact, I thought, I would not mind at all living in a town like this.

* * *

The package was a typical resupply box sent by my good friend Roger Perrin, a paddling buddy from Birmingham. My intention was to pick up the package at the Erwin Post Office and get right back on the trail. Based on Curran's characterization of Erwin, I hadn't expected to spend any time here. I had planned to take a zero day in either Elk Park about fifty miles further down the trail or in the town of Hampton which was seventy-two miles from Erwin. The package contained supplies that would get me to either of those two towns. Meeting DeHaven changed all that. Like war plans, your plan to hike the Appalachian Trail changes the minute you engage the enemy. In this case, the plan changed when I met a certain trail angel named Don DeHaven.

So, I bounced the package, sent it on, unopened, to the Hampton Post Office, and bought my groceries at the local IGA.

The next stop was the YMCA. While walking towards the small, attractive building, I suddenly realized I had forgotten to bring my pack-towel and soap. I really needed a shower. When asked, the young man on duty didn't bat an eye. "No problem at all," he said handing me a large, soft towel and a bar of soap. "You hiking?" he asked. "We get hikers in here all the time. Most of them want a clean towel. Like to get up there myself someday."

Later, as we drove to the IGA grocery for resupply, DeHaven mentioned he was building a new house up in the mountains, outside of Ernestville near Spivey Gap. This led into a discussion of contracting problems, new construction, and how I had spent summers working for my father who had been a home building contractor.

"You're a carpenter?"

"Well, yes, I guess you could say that. I've banged a few nails."

"You a framer?"

"Worked with my father's framing crew a couple of summers during college. I got pretty good at it. I guess you could call me a framer."

We reached the IGA and he waited in the truck while I went in to buy food for the trail. When I came out and hopped back in the old van, DeHaven was quiet. He drove for a little bit, and then he asked, "Would you do me a big favor?"

"Of course. You've certainly done me a big favor."

"Would you ride with me to Spivey Gap? ...it's just down the road apiece. I'm worried about those guys building my house. They look a little loopy to me. I think they smoke dope, you know, marijuana. I'm worried about the job they're doing. Would you take a look? Inspect the framing? See if it's up to snuff?"

It was getting late, I needed to get back on the trail, but I went with him. I liked him. I couldn't turn him down. He was bright and intelligent, and like many older men in the south, he possessed a folksy, philosophical understanding of life that he delivered with rascally charm. So, I went with him.

The house was fine. Maybe the guys did smoke dope. They were young. But, they were good carpenters. Everything appeared square, plumb, and true to line. They drove clean nails without splintering and dinging up the wood. That's one sure way of judging the skill of a carpenter. The site looked well-managed. Scrap pile out back. New wood stacked neatly. No lunch-bag litter that I could see. This told me they had some pride.

We rode back to Chestoa, shook hands warmly, and I got back on the trail a little after three. Getting to the campsite on the other side of Beauty Spot would take me at least five hours.

Some could do it in less, but I knew I'd be hiking by headlamp that night.

* * *

When the trail leveled out along the ridge, I began thinking about my visit with DeHaven. Somewhere back there in Erwin an idea had come to me. Now, as I hiked alone in the late afternoon, the idea began to turn around in my mind. If DeHaven was getting married, what did he intend to do with his old house? He had mentioned that the place disgusted his fiancée. She told him straight out, he said, that she wanted a new house. He could afford it, she said, and she expected him to provide it. I got the impression she was a good bit younger, and that he was profoundly smitten. Would he be selling the old property? This property something like sixty feet from the Appalachian Trail? A property that every single hiker northbound and southbound must pass? I had just resupplied in Erwin fully aware of the difficulty the long distance between Hot Springs and either Elk Park or Hampton presented to every person who hiked that section. I began thinking about a hiker hostel practically sitting on the Appalachian Trail. Was this another door opening for me? I had puzzled over what to do with my life with no current obligations. Was this it?

Those thoughts just went round and around in my mind with no resolution, no firmness. But, I couldn't stop thinking and wondering. I had some money, not a lot, from my severance package with the *Birmingham News*. There was substantial equity in the house I owned. The economy was booming. Property values were skyrocketing. My house, in the prestigious neighborhood of Mountain Brook, would sell at a good price.

I arrived at Beauty Spot and the panoramic night-time view of Erwin. There was no moon at this point. I shut off my headlamp to enjoy the billions of stars overhead and the soft lights of Erwin. Sitting there in the dark, my mind eased back into hiker mode. So, I hiked on toward the campsite. I had a tent to pitch and supper to cook. And before that, a need to organize my food bag. I had hastily stuffed my IGA purchases in any nook or cranny my pack would accommodate.

Just about that time, I saw what I knew instantly were the headlamps of two hikers. All I could see, though, were light beams jerking and stabbing here and there in the pitch black forest. Suddenly both beams whipped around and stood steady, silently stabbing at me. "Hello hikers," I called out cheerfully. It turned out they were hiking the section between Hot Springs and Damascus also. I wasn't unhappy with the company. Much of my hike so far had been solo. These guys looked okay.

We exchanged the normal. From where? Going where? Trail names? Seen any bears? Have you heard anything about the water situation up ahead? And we set about pitching tents by headlamp in the dark, and heating water for supper. Like most hikers just off the trail, I had over-purchased junk food. I dug out some Nabs and Twinkies and passed them around.

They were Friar Tuck and Speechless. The one looked just like his name. He was stout and had a perfectly round face rimmed with a band of black beard he kept trimmed short. His bowl-cut raven-black hair parted at the crown and lay splayed in all directions. He could easily have played the part of Friar Tuck against Kevin Costner's Robin Hood.

With a good fire beating back the chilly night air, we turned off our headlamps. I could see that Speechless was tall and thin. He had graying hair pulled back into a short ponytail. His pale blue eyes peered through round, steel-rimmed glasses. The quintessential aging hippie. You could tell in a single look, he felt he knew everything important to know. From his point of view, there was no reason to speak to me. And he didn't.

They were Mutt and Jeff. Total opposites. Speechless was well named. He said hardly a word. The friar never stopped.

He spoke rapidly in a soft conspiratorial tone. Even while pitching his tent he talked and asked questions constantly of no one in particular.

When the tents were up and the camp in some order, we sat around the fire, each with his own camp stove boiling water for our suppers. It was then I noticed Friar Tuck's glass eye. His left eye stared disconcertingly straight ahead, while the other eye darted here and there nervously as he spoke. He was rattling on and on, quietly and somewhat privately, about a strange, unidentified bug he had seen back on the trail. Now and then he whispered a question in my direction. I picked up the word "bug," amidst the hissing sounds of the fire, our respective camp stoves, and the friar's odd lisping style of speech.

"Did you stop in Erwin?" I asked.

They did, Friar Tuck said. Like me, each had a resupply box waiting for him at the Erwin Post Office. They had hitched a ride from a bright little high school girl who had waited at the post office and then brought them back to the trailhead. I told them my story. I busted them with how, had I not been there, they would surely have enjoyed an excellent chocolate cake and strong black coffee followed by cold beer and good conversation at the Rendezvous.

Without a word from me, the friar began talking about the good people they met in Erwin. The girl that brought them back to the trail was so nice. The blond chick, as the friar put it, the clerk in the post office, knew they were coming, knew from how the packages were addressed that they were for hikers. "They were interested to see that I got it," the friar said, quietly astonished. We were eating our suppers, and this is how the conversation went, with Friar Tuck doing all the talking for their side.

Maybe it was conscious on my part, but we were just talking and somehow the subject changed to the need for better services in Erwin. We all agreed, it's just too far between Hot Springs and Hamilton. Erwin would be the ideal resupply spot.

But four miles into town on a rainy day? Not so good, we all agreed.

This conversation was reinforcing the thoughts that had been running through my mind, and I blurted out, "What would you guys think of a hiker hostel at the foot of the bridge over the Nolichucky River?" Speechless looked at the friar and the friar looked at me. "Wow! Yes! Great! It would be great!" Friar Tuck nearly shouted, then, with a quick glance over his shoulder, he turned back to me and muttered under his breath, "...wow...yes...great...would be great." Speechless said nothing. The friar squinted the good eye and looked around carefully, then turning, the glass eye sought me out like a darkened searchlight. "What are we talking about here?"

So, I began to fill in the details of what I had in mind.

"What do you think, guys? If he's willing to sell at a price I can afford, and if I can get all the permits and stuff, would a hiker hostel work in that spot?"

"Righteous," Speechless said, as he lit the joint he had rolled.

"Killer," Friar Tuck said. "No-brainer," he added. "So? What? You seriously thinking about this?" he asked, his good eye dancing. "You got the bread? You gonna walk back there and propose, dude?" He began to talk rapidly now. "I wouldn't wait until you get to Damascus, dude he's already building another house, he's gonna do something with this one, I'd have that house on the market already, it might *be* on the market already, it's a hot market dude my brother he ..." The joint was passed to Friar Tuck. He took a hit and inhaled sharply, then held the smoking joint out to me. I held up my hand palm out to decline, and the joint went back to Speechless. Friar Tuck's dead eye staring straight into the woods, the good eye flashing back and forth between me and Speechless, he snorted a couple of times and exhaled the smoke. "... was transferred to Chicago and sold his house in ten days...dude think about that think about that...you might walk back there tomorrow and he'll say oh no I sold the house last month you know he might I would've. Did you talk about the house at all? Did you ask if the house was up for sale? Man...what you gonna do?"

* * *

What I did was hike the eleven-plus miles back to Erwin. I crossed the bridge, walked across the road, stepped up on the porch, knocked on the door, and DeHaven appeared.

"Hell, Uncle Johnny," he exclaimed. "I thought you'd be in Maine by now...haw, haw, haw," he erupted in fake laughter. "Come on in. Did you come back for more cake? ...haw, haw, haw."

"Well, no, but I'll take a piece, and coffee if you have some. I came back to talk to you about something." DeHaven disappeared into the kitchen and came out with his prized chocolate cake on a china plate with matching cup and saucer.

"What do you want to talk about, John?" he said taking on a serious tone.

"I came back to ask you what you planned to do with this property ... you're building a ..."

"Hell, I'm gonna sell it. You want to buy it?"

I hesitated, shocked by the sudden appearance of the very thing I had hoped to hear.

"I don't know if I can afford it."

"Hell, yes you can afford it. If you need, I'll finance it for you."

We talked another fifteen minutes. All the time I was thinking about zoning laws, the neighbors, utilities, gas, water, sewer. DeHaven added that he was just getting ready to advertise the property at thirty-six five, said he would not take a penny less.

"If I give you five hundred earnest money, would you keep it off the market for two weeks while I check some things out?"

"I ain't gonna do that!" he said standing up. Then he turned and looked at me for a moment.

My heart sank.

"You seem like a fine young man to me. Here's what I'm gonna to do. You got the right of first refusal and it won't cost a penny. Take two weeks. No earnest money needed."

I stood and we shook hands. The deal was done. Just like that in forty-five minutes, maybe less. Lost for words, I turned a full circle looking for my pack. The room was spinning. Spotting my hat on the couch, I picked that up. Moving towards the front door, I stood for what seemed a long moment inching my fingers around the brim, DeHaven quietly watching. I was thinking about what I had to do in just two weeks; a list forming in my mind. It struck me that my hike was over. That brought clarity.

"Mr. DeHaven, I need a place to stay. Can you recommend ... somewhere downtown ... would be ... I'll need to..."

"We only have one motel," DeHaven quietly interrupted. "The Best Southern, out on Jackson-Love Highway. Ain't real close to downtown, but it's the only one." Then DeHaven paused, and pointed his finger at me. "Well ... there are a couple big old houses on South Main that rent rooms. Not so nice, though. I'm betting they wouldn't let you drink in there, and no air-conditioning. The Best Southern's probably it, Johnny."

"I don't know, Mr. DeHaven. An older thru-hiker named Curran wrote about his adventure. I read his book. He describes his stop in Erwin, and he said the Best Southern refused to rent him a room."

"Hog-wash," DeHaven shot back with an angry look. "That's just bullshit. You treat them nice, they'll treat you nice. I know the manager...and his wife." DeHaven studied me for a moment, and then said quietly. "They're good people, Johnny. He's a retired Air Force officer. A real nice guy." DeHaven paused. "Montgomery, that's his name. Can't remember his given name. Don't let him charge you more'n fifty bucks, though," he suddenly added. "And if you need, I can give you a ride. I'm heading to the Rendezvous, over in the same direction. Wanna grab a cold one?"

"I'd love to Mr. DeHaven, but I've got a lot to do in just two weeks. I'll take a rain check. On me, next time, how's that?"

* * *

When he dropped me off in front of the motel office, DeHaven pointed in the direction of downtown Erwin and said, "bout two-mile that way, John. Just walk the road behind the motel and keep going. Take a right on Carolina. You can't miss downtown."

Starting to pull away, the old work van stopped abruptly, then slowly backed up until DeHaven was looking at me through the open passenger window. "John," he said. "One more thing I forgot to mention."

"Sure, Mr. DeHaven," I said, walking up to the window.

"I'm not selling 'til January," he said emphatically. "That okay?" his eyes dead on mine. "I'm not selling until I move into my new house. That'd be about first of January. Can we agree?"

"That's okay with me, Mr. DeHaven," I said. He confirmed with a single, slow nod, looking me right in the eye, turned, and drove off.

I watched as the old, Ford van pulled back on the highway. Turning toward the motel, I spotted a man with a bucket entering a door marked "Office."

Frank Montgomery was a tall, thin man in his late 50s. His military background was evident in the way he moved and spoke. He greeted me with a friendly smile, and before I could ask, he told me he did have a single vacancy, fifty dollars a night. I noticed his eyes drift toward my pack.

"I suppose you'll need to do some laundry."

"Yes, sir."

"That'll be an extra four dollars," he smiled, nodding. "I'll use my machine. Includes the detergent."

"Do you have weekly rates?" I asked.

"Certainly. How long?"

I explained that I had business in Erwin and I'd be here at least two weeks. He asked if my business was with the railroad, and I told him I was looking at some property. I needed to examine the deed, take a look at all applicable laws, restrictions, that sort of thing. His price was $300 per week. While I signed the registration book he remarked that he had the only motel in Erwin. Salesmen calling on the Clinchfield Railroad's corporate offices and other businesses in town usually stayed with him. He allowed that he was almost always full, but he would be charging me the same weekly rate as he charged them. He said this with a proud, professional smile.

"You hiked here to do a business deal?" he asked, suddenly.

He had stopped cold and was looking at me with uncomfortable seriousness. "No car?" I could see his mind connecting dots. I had heard that small towns in eastern Tennessee were facing a crisis of illegal drug distribution, the result of a revolution in methamphetamine production that user's call "shake-and-bake" or the "one-pot" method, a simplified way meth is synthesized from cold and allergy medicines like Claritin D and Sudafed.

"Well, sir, that's about it. I met somebody along the trail. Picked up an interesting tip. I'm just following that up. Suspended my hike because, well…you know, best laid plans of mice and……"

"Strike while the iron is hot, right? Yes-sir. I understand that." His serious face dissolved into a smile, and his inquiry went no further; thankfully. It had occurred to me during this exchange that a hiker hostel could be seen as direct competition. Hikers staying over in Erwin had no option but the Southern.

Paying for the first week, I grabbed my pack and headed toward the door.

"I'm going to need some regular clothes," I said, turning back. "Can you suggest something nearby?"

"Well, John, there are no clothing stores in Erwin. We do have four thrift stores. That's where I get my clothes," he said laughing. "But, if you're looking for new stuff, the Dollar General is just a couple hundred yards down the road on the right."

"Okay, that sounds good. How about a place to eat? Anything good close by? I'm starving."

"Three places, John. All pretty good. You've got the Dairy Ace for burgers and milkshakes." He had come out from behind the counter signaling directions with his hands. "That's just up the street. Out the door here and to the left. It's an easy walk up there. Then, We've got JD's Market right next door the other way. I go there myself pretty often. Down home cooking. Different menu each day, you know, southern cooking; greens and cornbread. That kind of place. You're from Alabama? You're going to like JD's. Then there's Pizza Plus further down on your right. They have an unlimited pizza buffet and salad bar at lunch every day. Your basic salad bar, but great pizza. They'll deliver to your room if you want."

* * *

The room showed its age. I could tell by the look of things the place had been built in the '50s. The room was neat and clean but the carpet was old and hopelessly matted. The bathroom was tiled pink and black. There was an old-style bathtub shower. The yellowed shower curtain was decorated with pink flamingos. The tub itself was brilliant white, recently re-glazed using a paint brush. You could see the brush-marks. The main room had two queen-sized beds flanked with nightstands complete with cigarette burns. There was the standard TV. The ancient card by the TV showed your basic cable listing. All of this was unimportant. What the room had that I needed even more than the bed, was a telephone.

My first call was to Roger Perrin, the Birmingham friend who had mailed the resupply box for me.

"Hey Roger, I need some help. No, I'm in Erwin, Tennessee. Something's come up, buddy. No. Not in trouble. An opportunity popped up out of nowhere and I'm pursuing ... that's right. No, don't need money. I need my car. I need for you to drive my car up here. Yes, I know it's a six-hour drive. Can you get away? Two weeks? Alright. Yes. That's okay, Roger. Then I'll ... sure, Roger. What happened ... I'm coming off the AT heading for Erwin. I see this old guy standing ... he invited ... well, long story short, Roger, there's a piece of property for sale something like fifty, sixty feet from the Chestoa trailhead, right at the foot of a bridge over the Nolichucky. Here's the thing, Roger. Every single hiker that hikes the AT now and forever, must come down out the mountains and cross that bridge whether coming or going. What I'm seeing on that property is a hostel. Well, Roger, you know what a hostel is. That's right, and this one catering to the needs of the trail community. Hikers coming off the trail need ... sure there's money in the hostel business. There's a dozen of um up the trail. That's right, like a bunkhouse...twenty bucks for the bunk, then ... yeah, got camping, there's a nice grassy back yard, they can pitch a tent out there for ten bucks. Three shuttles into town every day. No, that's a service we ... that's right, meal shuttles into town are free. Hikers, our guests need resupply, they've been dreaming of restaurant food. Well, I know, Roger, but we'll offer other shuttles, like a taxi service, pick um up from the bus station, airport, carry section hikers up ... yes, and other income streams. Hikers will gladly pay five bucks for a hot shower. Yes, we provide the towels, yes. And soap...of course. No, we'll launder the towels here ourselves. Yes, we'll have a laundry. Hikers need to wash their clothes. Five bucks for that. Yes, we'll provide the detergent. I know, I know … listen … Roger … I don't think I'm getting the full picture across. When you get here, we'll talk. Well, I bet you do, Roger, you've never had a problem expressing your opinion, but let's just wait until you get here. I can show you the place and … yes, all wrapped up. The house is mine if I want it. We've settled on thirty-six, five. Well, that's what I thought too, pretty damn cheap for a house and an acre … yes, it has a roof! Doesn't have shingles, Roger, it's a 110-year-old tin roof. I'm not worried about the roof, Roger, no. Yep, I'm working on all that now … zoning, sewage system, codes, licenses, all that stuff, Roger, but I'm going to need my car. Okay buddy. Can't tell you how much I appreciate … okay, see you when I do."

After hanging up the phone, I sat on the bed thinking. I would be talking to bankers and lawyers, and I needed to get my story straight. Roger's questions had raised my own doubt, and I needed to be clear and positive in my presentations in the future.

I needed a decent shirt, too. I was wearing old hiking boots that had been worn on many hikes, so I needed shoes. After pulling my pack apart and gathering up dirty clothes, and dropping dirty laundry in a pile by the door, I headed out for Dollar General. There, I found a nice, collared, short sleeved shirt, blue and white; a Carolina blue I liked. I might have to see the same people more than once, so I picked out a similar shirt in white with red trim. I had a decent tee-shirt in my hiking gear that could serve for a third visit. Next, I walked over to a small display of work clothes, hats, and gloves and picked out a pair of khaki pants. The only pair that fit my waist had cuffs lapping onto the floor.

With new sneakers, underwear and socks, a couple of notebooks, a three-pack of ballpoint pens, and a yellow legal pad, I returned to the motel prepared to meet the real world of Erwin, Tennessee. I stuffed all my dirty trail clothes into a pillow case from the unused extra bed, handed that over to an attractive motel employee who said she would take care of it for me, and headed next door to JD's Market. It was way past noon and I was famished.

Not much of a market, this was an odd combination of gas station and drugstore-style lunch counter. A few shelves of canned goods, hardware, and some household items like light bulbs and brooms stood in the middle of the room. Locally-grown produce was heaped in boxes and baskets along one wall. Across from the produce was a huge assortment of cigarettes packed on shelves nearly to the ceiling. A long, glass case displaying snuff, chewing tobacco, and corncob pipes stood in front of the shelves. A dozen or so hand-lettered signs announced discount prices for this or that brand of cigarettes. The cheapest seemed to be a brand called Golden Gate priced at 99¢. I remember back in my dad's bar, Camels from a machine cost a quarter. Fishermen would grumble that they could get a carton of ten packs for only $2.21. Some of the cigarettes from these machines would come with three pennies in the package.

The daily special was meatloaf, but I chose a bowl of bean soup, a bowl of turnip greens, and a plate of country ham topped with cornbread. With tax, this came to all of $4.72. There were six or seven small tables, but I sat at the counter on a rickety stool with a red-vinyl seat that squeaked loudly with the slightest movement.

* * *

"Frank, I've got another question," I said, holding the pants at my waist and looking down at the extra flowing onto the floor. "I don't suppose there's a tailor around here, know anybody could fix these for me?"

Just then, the office door opened and the same attractive motel employee who had taken charge of my laundry stepped in.

"Well, speaking of the Devil, this is your tailor, Mr. Shores. Darling, meet John Shores. He'll be staying with us for a while. John, this is my wife, Debbie."

"Nice to meet you Mrs. Montgomery."

"John, show Debbie your pants. Darling, can you hem these? John's got business tomorrow serious enough to require new pants."

* * *

Dressed in my new clothes, I rounded the end of the motel heading for the route into town DeHaven had described. The street behind the motel intersected with Spring Street, not Carolina Avenue. Turning left, guessing it would intersect with Carolina, I struck out at a decent trail pace toward downtown Erwin. I had asked Frank Montgomery about transportation. Seems Erwin was missing a lot of ordinary businesses. No clothing store. No taxi cabs. No buses. No office supply store. Amazing opportunities here, I'd say. I briefly considered buying a cheap bicycle. I looked in the phone book's yellow pages. No bicycle shop.

Montgomery suggested calling USA Raft, a river adventure company on the Nolichucky. Many hikers staying over at his motel had used shuttle drivers from USA to carry them back to the trail. I called, and USA's office put a river guide named Ben on the phone. We talked for a few minutes, I asked the key questions a person of my experience would ask, was satisfied with his answers, and Ben agreed to be my driver. His fee would be twenty dollars per trip, he said. We made arrangements to meet at eight sharp in the morning.

But, for today, it's a two-mile walk into town. I needed to visit the court house. I figured on hitting the Chamber of

Commerce next. They keep up with everything. They're in the business of helping businesses, especially new businesses. Last night before turning out the light, I'd sketched out my plan. I had searched the yellow pages of the phone book. From a dozen legal-pad pages spread out around me on the bed, I'd written out a long list of questions in my little pocket-sized, spiral-bound notebook.

Somewhere along the way into town, it dawned on me that the resupply box I'd bounced to Hampton would be stranded. I needed that box. It contained a couple of really nice tee-shirts, a new pair of shorts, two books, a razor, nail clippers, and some quality snacks. The post office would be my first stop. Maybe there was a way to get the thing returned.

Carolina Avenue ended at Union Street. I could see downtown was to the left. Approaching Main Street, I met a man in a wheelchair coming my way. He listened to my question and motioned for me to follow him back to the corner of Main and Union. Pointing to a sign over a door at the next corner down the block, he said, "That's the Chamber. You'll want to ask for Anjanette Harris. She's the director."

"And the post office is on down this street?"

"Yes, on your left. You can't miss it."

My first view of the post office was from across the street. Having always been interested in architecture, especially the architecture of historic buildings, this particular building grabbed my attention. The front façade presents a traditional, sort-of federalist-style architecture but without the federalist roof. That style will sometimes showcase geometrical concepts, and here the effect is seen in the tall, Palladian-style windows flanking a similarly-designed entry. They were simple glass arches with muntins dividing each window into many small panes. But, this particular building had a flat roof. I couldn't help imagining the more typical hip roof featuring a simple center gable over a pediment incorporating the arched windows and entryway, and for a moment I was working with my dad framing up what I imagined should be there.

Six white marble steps led to the front door. Entering the lobby, I took note that the old mahogany table where patrons would pause to address and stamp envelopes must be as old as the building, which I learned had been built in 1927.

The clerk watching me survey the place was Wendy, the same nice-looking young woman who had helped me the last time. What luck, I thought. Lot less explaining.

"Hi, Wendy"

"Well, hello Uncle Johnny. I thought you'd be long gone up the trail by now. What brings you back to us?"

"You remember me?"

"Who could forget an Appalachian Trail hiker named Uncle Johnny?"

"Well, thanks, Wendy. I'm impressed." I said this and paused, collecting my thoughts. "I'm back because I've got a problem. I bounced a package to Hampton, remember? Well, I've suspended my hike. You remember the older gentleman that introduced us? Well, I … he and I … Wendy, is there any way we can get the post office in Hampton …?"

"Oh, that's not a problem, Uncle Johnny. Sit tight. I'll be right back."

She left and I began looking around. This was an old-style post office. It was attractive but simple. The paneled walls and woodwork looked to be fir, stained to a dark walnut. The right side of the lobby housed the letterboxes, a stunning array of polished brass letterboxes in several sizes. The customer area was too narrow to be pretentious or overly dressy, and whoever designed this space opted for simplicity. The floor and the wainscot were of Georgian marble. The steps out front were also Georgian marble. I remembered laying a marble floor in the foyer of a house one summer.

Beautiful white sanctuary marble just like this floor. From Georgia. The Clinchfield. Probably shipped here by rail.

Clinchfield runs to Spartanburg, South Carolina. Horse and wagon lugged the stuff to the railhead from Pickens County, Georgia. The vein of marble seven miles long, half-mile wide, 2,000 feet deep. Ancestors of the Cherokee discovered it. Quarried there three thousand years. Famous Marble Valley of Pickens County. God! Dad had these sudden impulses to travel! Drove to Jasper once to the Marble Festival. A full-blown parade down the main street. Tours of the marble industry and ......

"No problem, John. I just talked to Hampton and they'll send your box back here. You can come pick it up in a couple of days."

* * *

"My name's John Shores. I'm from Birmingham, Alabama. I'm thinking of opening a business in Erwin." I was speaking to yet another very nice-looking young woman, who had greeted me as I entered the Chamber's offices.

"Well, welcome to Erwin, Mr. Shores. I'm Anjanette. What can we do for you?" she sang out cheerfully.

"Please call me John," I said, and we shook hands over the counter. "With apologies in advance, I've got lots of questions. Do you have time to talk for a little bit?"

"Certainly."

I gave a brief description of my plans, and her response was very encouraging. She seemed to clearly understand what I had in mind.

"John, that's great. We need something like that in Erwin," she said, smiling with bubbly enthusiasm. "We see hikers almost every day and wonder how they get into town. I've spent a lot of time thinking about what we could do for them. A hostel like that on the trail will encourage more hikers to layover in Erwin. Maybe spend the night. Patronize our restaurants. You can count on the Chamber's help. I'm here if you need anything at all."

She was petite. Not even five-foot two. One of those exuberant personalities that all men find irresistible. I had my little notebook and went down the list scribbling notes as we talked. Health Department, County Clerk, Property Tax Assessor, Building Inspector. Deeds and Records —I had listed every question that had come to mind as I mentally walked through the process of turning the DeHaven property into a successful Appalachian Trail hostel. Anjanette provided names and looked up phone numbers. She said that Deeds and Records could be found on the first floor of the court house next door.

"I'm interested in membership, Anjanette. Can you tell me about that?"

This question ramped up her energy again and I got the full pitch. The annual fee for me, as a one-man operation, would be just forty dollars. This included four breakfast meetings. I'd get my money back right there. I would receive periodic newsletters with important information about Erwin's business goin's on. And they were building a website, she proudly announced. I would get a free listing there and in the Chamber's printed directory as well. She shook my hand and beamed again when I wrote out the check and placed it on the counter.

"I'm going to need a lawyer. Can you suggest somebody?"

"Bob Manuel. Right next door, John. Just to the left as you go out. He's our lawyer and he's also the City Attorney. Very nice man. I'm sure you'll like him. He's a good one."

* * *

Bob Manuel was a casually dressed portly man wearing a white dress shirt, loosened tie, and slip-on dress loafers with wingtip-inspired accents. The shoes looked expensive. He wore a thick wedding band and I noticed photos on the credenza behind his desk. His wife and teenage children, a boy and a girl.

"This is going to be easier than you might think, John," Bob Manuel said after listening to my plans. He smiled and spoke in that lawyer-like tone we've all come to expect, and gave me a special look telling me I'd be getting insider information. "Your property is in Unicoi County. No building codes," he said, fishing through his wallet for a business card.

"So, I just start building whatever I want?" I said, looking at the card.

"Well, not exactly." Then, Manuel smiled, leaned back in his swivel chair, and put one foot up on a banker's box that happened to be sitting next to his desk. He continued in his instructional, lawyerly way. "If you improve the property, the county's gonna want to raise your property tax. They'll want you to give them a heads-up. You'll need to contact Bill Gaines. He's the county's Assessor of Property, an elected official in the State of Tennessee, John. This means he's interested in your vote and even more interested in your word-of-mouth campaign on his behalf. What I'm saying, John, he's going to be real friendly and helpful. His job is to list, classify, and value all property within the jurisdiction of Unicoi county for tax purposes. Your classification will change from residential to commercial. And you'll be improving the property. Just like most places, taxable property in Unicoi County is divided into two classes, real property and personal property. Real property includes land and all buildings, structures, and improvements to the land. Personal property is machinery and equipment, fixtures, furniture, and other items that are movable in nature. Part of Bill's job is discovery. Finding taxable property and keeping up with all the changes. So you go over to Town Hall and tell Bill what you have in mind. He'll appreciate that. Then you call him when you're done. Bill will come out and get the process started. Property tax is what interests them. What you build on your own property is your business around these parts. Now, John, be prepared for your property tax to take a jump. As residential property, DeHaven's house is assessed at 24%. When you change that to commercial property, the assessment jumps to 40%."

Manuel took a welcomed pause as I scribbled notes, and waved the sole of his raised expensive loafer back and forth a few times, and then:

"Couple of things. I'm pretty sure you'll need a new septic system to handle the bathhouse you've described to me. You'll need a permit for that. David Sullivan handles that part. His main office is in Johnson City. He spends just two days a week here in Erwin. So you should call his office first, see if he's in before you go over there. David's a real nice guy. You can get most information you need from him. He knows everybody. That kind of guy, you know. And you'll need an electrical inspection. Your electrician will take care of buying the permit and scheduling the inspector's visit. That's about it. If you have questions call me anytime."

Lawyer Bob Manuel was also the town's only travel agent. His office was a mix of legal and travel. Shelves of law books were cheek by jowl with large, colorful travel posters. The Rialto Bridge spanning the Grand Canal in Venice complete with gondola loomed over his credenza. The Eiffel Tower, the architectural wonder that attracts more visitors than any other paid tourist attraction in the world, stuck up between bookcases to the left of his desk. And a particularly large photo of the Parthenon hung on the opposite wall. Tables adjacent to two comfortable leather chairs were strewn with travel brochures and magazines. The faded gray bindings on the legal shelves looked washed out sitting beside a colossal cruise ship sailing under a brilliant Caribbean sky. I wondered briefly, if, after a successful case, Bob would propose a lengthy cruise as a reward for the newly-rich divorcée.

* * *

Following Bob's directions, I quickly found the County Courthouse and the office of Debbie Tittle, Register of Deeds. Shaking the hand of this stunning blond, I couldn't help thinking, every woman I've met so far has been attractive.

"What the heck's in the water around here?"

"The water? I'm not the person you need to talk to about the water, that would be ..."

"Dag, it must be the water. Every woman I've met so far has been gorgeous."

"Now, Mr. Shores, that kind of flattery will......" she looked down. Then, "What can I do for you, Mr. Shores," she said smiling with the unruffled confidence of a woman who must hear these things daily.

"I'm looking to buy a piece of property out on River Road. It's where River Road intersects with Unaka Springs Road and Chestoa Pike."

"Right there at the bridge?"

"The DeHaven place. Are you familiar with ..."

"Yes, I've actually fished the river there under that bridge. I've hiked up to Beauty Spot a number of times, too. How can I help you?"

"I'm wondering when DeHaven bought the place and how much he paid."

"You'll have to talk to the tax assessor about that. I can tell you whether the deed is encumbered, though," she said, turning toward a file cabinet.

From working with my father, I understood the importance of doing a title search. Title searches tell you if there are any debts or liens on the property that you could end up paying as the new owner. Some people hire a lawyer to run a title search, but the information is always available to the public from a county officer like Ms. Tittle. The possible problems a title search may dredge up include unpaid property taxes, various restrictions imposed on the property, and liens representing unpaid debts of the former owner.

"Well, Mr. Shores, there are no liens or restrictions on this deed. Mr. Gaines, the Tax Assessor, can tell you if there are unpaid taxes. His office is just up the hall. Out the door here and to your right. His office is on the right. Is there anything else I can do for you today?"

Leaving Ms. Tittle's office, I quickly found the tax assessor's office. In every practical sense, counties serve as an administrative arm of the state. Maintaining records, assessing property and collecting taxes, along with a growing list of other functions, all take place under the supervision of various elected and appointed officials. Quiet of manner and of voice, Bill Gaines was the quintessential super-serious county official. He looked to be in his late fifties. He had been elected to serve the people of Unicoi County, and what's so different, when comparing an elected county official with those who are appointed, is the degree to which explaining your need is necessary. Gaines looked at me with an expression of hopefulness that you would never, ever see in an appointed clerk. I could tell, just by that expression, he intended to help me any way he could.

"Of course, Mr. Shores. Come with me. Let's take a look at the plat book of your part of the county."

A number of record keeping and administrative activities are necessary to appraise property, determine property values, and calculate tax levies. Having worked with my father and later having bought and sold several properties on my own, I was familiar with those processes. The county assessor generally maintains maps and legal descriptions of taxed parcels as well as other records relating to evaluating property. Those maps and legal descriptions are kept in large bound volumes larger in size than a daily newspaper. Gaines called them "plat books." A plat in the State of Tennessee is a map, drawn to scale, showing the divisions of a piece of land. A county's plat books contain the public record of maps of subdivided land showing the divisions of the land into blocks, lots, and parcels. These large books were racked on shelves on the far wall of his office. Running his finger across the numbered titles of several volumes, he pulled one off the shelf and lugged it over to one of several long, heavy tables meant for the use of examining these books.

"Here we are, Mr. Shores. That's your property right here," he said, pointing with the eraser of his pencil. "Nice little community. I've knocked on all those doors. Got a cousin lives up the hill from that bridge," he said, tapping the bridge with his eraser.

He wrote the number of the DeHaven property on a scrap of paper, and I trailed him over to another shelf of books. These were deed books. These were similar to Ms. Tittle's Registry of Deeds. In fact, the process of deeding a piece of property would begin with Ms. Tittle and then pass along to Mr. Gaines. Showing me these records, Gaines noted that the DeHaven house appraised at a very low value. The current property tax was $150 per year. I explained my plans. Big bathhouse. Addition to the house for the hostel, large deck out front. And some alterations to the house itself. Because I would live in the house, Mr. Gaines said, the overall assessment, reflecting the residential part, would lower the commercial tax rate somewhat. Still, I would be paying triple what DeHaven had been paying.

"Does it say what DeHaven originally paid for the place?"

"Yes. Donald DeHaven paid $6,400 for the house and just over seven acres of land back in 1955. He sold most of the land piece-by-piece over the years. Your plot is just under one acre."

Sly ol' fox...he really made out on that deal. He'll get nearly six times his original investment back from the last piece he's selling to me.

* * *

The portico of the Unicoi County Court House was massive. It ran across the full width of the building. Facing northwest, it was warm and breezy on this clear, blue-sky day in June. A single chair sat to the left of the entryway.

I sat, leaning my head back against the cool masonry. Just a week ago, I hiked out of Hot Springs. I could hardly remember how I felt. I could see myself standing below Lover's Leap, totally uncertain about my future. I remembered looking at the trail winding through rhododendron and pine. I had wondered then where that trail would take me. Now, here I am, just days later, looking out at the main street of my new hometown. Erwin, Tennessee.

Then, with the balmy breeze, the murmur of the traffic, the fact that I was really tired, I relaxed. I could feel myself sinking into the chair. It had been a long day starting with the pre-dawn hike back to DeHaven's place. The shock of getting the deal with so little effort, the sudden realization that my hike was over, the stress of checking into the Best Southern, needing new clothes, needing all kinds of stuff, and not knowing where to go, my mind buzzing with the things I needed to know in order to make a commitment, all of this had worn me down. Sitting there, head back against the wall thinking about what had just transpired, I fell asleep and had a weird dream. As in every dream I'd ever had, I was lost, searching, not sure I would survive, and things I knew very well were coming from somebody else's mouth.

I remember shutting my eyes and wishing I'd taken the time to hike up the side trail to the top of Lover's Leap. Even as I hiked away along Mill Ridge, I wondered how the world would have looked to me from up there, standing on the spot where the Indian girl had jumped. Wondered what it would have been like to stand right close to the edge and imagine myself as her, ready to jump, and I couldn't think of her name. I started going through the alphabet trying to think of her name. I believe that's when I fell asleep, counting through the alphabet. ... what's her name? ... what's her name? I kept asking myself. Then I heard Clarke Stallworth's voice.

"Lovers have leapt ..."

He was there in my dream, wearing hiking boots, had a backpack and a walking stick. I've never known Clarke to be interested in hiking, so why he showed up in my dream, I just don't know. I heard his voice and turned to look and there he was, sitting, leaning back against his backpack about 18 inches from the edge of the cliff. And he was telling me the legend of Lover's Leap.

"Lovers have leapt from countless rock outcroppings, John. There are lover's leaps all over the world. And the girl's name was Mist-on-the-Mountains, a young Cherokee maiden barely in her teens. Now, here's the story John. She had fallen in love with Magwa and at the same time was spurning the unwanted attention of another warrior, Lone Wolf. As you might guess, the two rivals each decided the other must die, and Magwa lost the contest. Misty was so distraught, she opted straight away to join him in the land of happy hunting. She jumped. Probably took a running start from the very spot where you're standing now. Wanna try it?"

Clarke Stallworth always had an attitude, and he was telling me this story as if I didn't know it. But I'm a reader. Love to read. I've read dozens of books and articles about the history of the American Indians, the 16th Century Spanish exploration, the French and English colonies, the early pioneer settlement of the Southern Appalachians, and the Appalachians themselves, how they were formed geologically. Those subjects have fascinated me all my life, and here was all of this coming back at me but from Stallworth in this dream.

"Man, you've got a mouth on ya, Clarke. I had no idea you were interested that kind of stuff." Where'd you get that story?

"I read, John. You should try it sometime."

"I read, Clarke."

"I read and I talk to people. It's my job. I came across a guy a year or two ago. A Bama graduate. Name's Hunter Lightfoot. Was part Cherokee and spent most of his life researching and lecturing about them. I thought the Cherokee had been here thousands of years, but he explained that the Creek and Cherokee nations had occupied the Appalachian Mountains, well, the southern part, that is, for only about 500 years. They were Iroquois. Split off from the Iroquois and migrated south. They and the Iroquois were descendants of the Ancient Adena; mound-builders who had migrated north from Mesoamerica bringing with them maize, beans, squash, domesticated turkeys, and dogs. They played a ball game involving hundreds of players at a time. Something like lacrosse. The Adena had a tradition of ball-playing, and by the time they became Cherokee, they would often substitute a vicious game for settling inter-tribal disputes. You know, instead of going to war, they settle it with a game. Cool, huh? Well, anyway, they came to the Southern Appalachians and they hunted the big animals: buffalo, elk, and each other, with devastating consequences. By the time of Magwa's death, they had organized themselves into peaceful, settled agricultural villages. They were simple farmers, John. Bet not many people think of the Cherokee as farmers, Planting fields of corn and raising domesticated turkeys. Then, the white people came. The invasion of these territories by white settlers set off a decades-long struggle that ended with the infamous Trail of Tears; the expulsion of these native peoples to the Oklahoma territories far to the west."

Then the scene changed. Suddenly we were up on Clingman's Dome Lookout. Nobody there but us and a strange-looking man I had never seen before. He was tall and thin with long grey hair. He had a long face and two braids hanging down by his ears. Neither Clarke nor I had seen him at first, and when he spoke, I jumped out of my skin.

"But that was not the end of the Cherokee and Creek Indians, nor their influence in the Southern Appalachians."

"Who's that guy Clarke? Where the heck did he come from?

"That's the guy, John. That's the guy I was talking about. Hunter Lightfoot. Hey Professor. Good to see you, man. Meet my best friend John Shores. Where the hell did you come from?"

"I've been here all along, Clarke. Standing on this very spot when you and John walked up the ramp. You're the ones doing the coming-from."

"Look, Clarke. We're on Clingman's Dome Lookout. That long, curving ramp, see? I know this place. Been here. Slammed with lots of people every time I've been here, but look, we're all alone now. How weird is that."

"I've been here, John. Know exactly where I am. Calm down, buddy."

The professor was leaning back against the central, round-part that held the structural steel of the lookout tower. I motioned for Clarke to come over by me, and we sat leaning against the outer wall. All of it was very strange. We were alone and it was very quiet, a gentle wind brought the sound of the trees below and bird song.

"Clarke, dammit, I'm here to put your story straight. The majority of the Cherokee had already, both easily and willingly, assimilated into the towns and villages of the peoples that had conquered them. Just the way it has always been. The human experience throughout the world. Every human society that ever existed prior to our time was conquered by somebody. Those Cherokee the government moved west were a small, belligerent remnant of the nation that originally occupied these mountains. Most of them had been living side-by-side with the white man, and their influence was profound. There are Cherokee and Creek names for thousands of landmarks, place names, and events throughout the Southern Appalachians."

The scene changed and we were walking single file through the spruce and fir forest, warm as toast in the normally cool, wet conditions that had produced the coniferous rainforest that covered these mountain tops. Professor Lightfoot was still talking; had not stopped talking, in fact. His voice muffled by the vast forest and the thin air at this height.

"But John, as a former Boy Scout and long-time hiker of the trail, you might find this interesting. The word Appalachian was never part of the Cherokee. How those mountains came by that name is the work of early mapmakers. Scribbly maps drawn by early explorers carried the notions and place names they invented. Early Spanish explorers sent these sketches home. Early maps became what the cartographers back in Spain could make of these sketches. In this case the Spanish explorer was Hernando de Soto, who in 1539 came across the Apalachee Indians, in a village near present-day Tallahassee. The Muscogee word apala means The Great Sea. Given the Muscogee personal participle chi, the name of the tribe was Those by the Sea. Apalachee then, has nothing what-so-ever to do with mountains."

Now Professor Lightfoot was standing on a stage behind a lectern. Clarke and I were sitting in movie theater seats eating popcorn. The lectern stood in front of a huge, backlit map of Florida and Georgia, and the professor was pointing out various locations with a lightsaber, the signature weapon of the Jedi Order and their Sith counterparts.

"Map makers Diego Gutierrez, Gerard Mercator, and all who followed for the next 150 years, transcribed the name as Apalachen. But Tallahassee is a long way from the Appalachian range. Here is what I think happened."

Professor Lightfoot was touching the map here and there with his lightsaber, and I couldn't tell if it was actually me up there or not, and I started looking around for my lightsaber. Clarke had disappeared. I discovered I was outside again, in the forest, and it was pitch black, no light at all, and I felt alone and strange. But, the professor's voice was quite loud and very present as I made my way along, feeling with my hands, looking for Clarke and my lightsaber.

"The Apalachee Indian leaders, probably carrying off a trick to get the nasty Spanish Conquistadores to leave them alone, said that in the mountains to the north they would find gold, silver, and copper in good quantity mingled in the sandy creek bottoms of every mountain stream. The Spanish departed in haste and marched, God knows how, through the swamps of the Georgia delta all the way to a spot somewhere in what today we call Cabarrus County, North Carolina. Lightfoot pointed to the exact spot. There, Hernando found a young Cherokee who explained how gold was separated from the sand, melted, and refined by his people. In gratitude, or for some other reason, they named the craggy, mist-shrouded range after the Apalachee whom they erroneously assumed had been there before them."

"John! Lookout! Here they come, the Apalachee! Can you believe it?

"Aaaahh."

I sat bolt upright in the chair. Three women had come out the door laughing and one of them had shouted,

"Can you believe it?"

"Oh, Maggie, I'm sure you misunderstood." another said. "Now look Maggie, all y'all, it's five o'clock somewhere and somewhere is right now, right here. Y'all follow me over to my place. I've got the makings for an awesome apple martini; apple schnapps, vodka and apple juice. Unbelievable."

Five o'clock?

......................?

Five o'clock!

* * *

Retracing my steps to the motel, feeling awkward after the unexpected nap, I had decided to think through where I stood so far. I had worried needlessly that there might be property restrictions for environmental purposes, given that the property lay next to the Nolichucky River. Surely the river had flooded many times in the past. Had the Nolichucky ever risen to the point of flooding that property? That's a concern I hadn't thought about. How would a floodplain problem affect my insurance? Yet another important question to ask somebody. I had called David Sullivan's office from Bob Manuel's telephone, and luckily, he was in town. The Health Department receptionist said he would be in the office until noon the next day. I decided that calling on Sullivan would be my first stop in the morning. I would grab a quick breakfast at JD's, and meet Ben, as we had arranged, at eight sharp. I planned to meet with Sullivan, ride back out to DeHaven's place for a closer look, take measurements, and draw a sketch of the place.

Walking back to the motel in the late afternoon, warm and thirsty, I remembered the Rendezvous was in the vicinity of the Best Southern. Just then, I spotted an elderly man sitting on his front porch who might know exactly where.

"Sir, can you tell me if I'm anywhere near the Rendezvous."

"Sure can, mister. You're right close. You jess keep walking on, and up yonder a bit you see a big warehouse on your right side. Along there is a street what angles off to the left." The old man stood and made vigorous curving motions with his left hand and arm. "Can't recollect the name right off, but you won't miss it. The street don't turn straight left, jess sorta angles off," he said, demonstrating the angle with his hands. "Well, down that street some little ways, you'll see the Rendezvous on your left side. Now, when you gets there, mister, drink one for me. Doctors won't let me drink no more. Spent a good part of my life in that place, I did."

The other John was tending bar and remembered me. I got my six-pack of beer for six dollars; a buck each.

Later, stopping at Pizza Plus, I ordered and paid for a deep-dish vegetarian pizza with an added topping of pepperoni. On my walk back to the motel, I could smell the wonderful aroma. I'd been craving this pizza for a month, it seemed.

The pizza was great and three beers later I fell asleep and slept like a log.

* * *

Ben arrived at 8:15. The first thing he said was did I want to get some breakfast. He seemed disappointed when I told him I had grabbed an egg sandwich and coffee at JD's. He was driving a beat-up old Ford Pinto. It was mostly pale green, with one steel gray door and an orange fender. The right-side headlight was smashed. The back bumper was dented as would be if one had backed hard into a telephone pole. Sitting in the passenger seat, I noticed a football-sized hole in the floorboard. Through the hole, I could see the asphalt roadway zipping by. There must have been other holes because the interior was rapidly filling with tailpipe exhaust seeping up through the heap of McDonald's bags, pizza boxes, beer cans, and soda bottles mixed into what looked like his wardrobe in the back seat.

"Great little car you got here Ben."

"Duct tape and bailing wire, John. River adventure isn't the highest paying job in the world, but I got nothing else; at least, nothing else interests me. What do you do?"

"I retired early, Ben. Human resources. Looking at some property here and my car's in Birmingham, Alabama."

"'How'd you get here…bus?"

"No, Ben. I was hiking a section of the trail. Some paddling buddies carried me up to Hot Springs, and I hiked from there to Erwin. Got a tip on a piece of property. Sweet deal. Now I'm following that up. I'm going to need your services pretty regularly over the next week or so. Think you'll be available?"

"Oh yeah. Pretty much. USA Raft chooses guides by seniority, so I don't work except when a big crowd shows up. River's kinda low now, so business is off a little. I'm thankful, John. In fact, let me thank you proper for calling me. Anything I can do, you just ask, okay?"

"You bet, Ben. I have lots to do over the next ten days or so."

Ben was an intense driver. He sat forward and held the wheel with both hands. He was constantly looking from side mirror to rear-view mirror and back to the road. I wondered how such a cautious man had managed to bash up his car so. He was smallish, and had a five-day beard ranging down into a stringy goatee. Wild, untrimmed auburn hair stuck out from around his ball cap.

Unicoi County Health Department on Okolona Drive was a low, brick nondescript building just off Love Street. Ben pulled into the parking lot, shut off the Pinto's engine, and swung his door wide letting in much-needed fresh air.

"Take your time, John. I brought this book along to read." He picked up the book as he said this. "I'm as happy reading here as I'd be if I were somewhere else. I'd rather be reading than almost anything I can think of, so I'll be sitting right here when you come out. Take your time." The book was Jon Krakauer's *Into the Wild*, a book I had packed in my resupply box, one of the reasons I was so anxious to get my box back from the Hampton Post Office.

* * *

A man I assumed to be Sullivan stood outside his office door shuffling through several orange call slips.

"Mr. Sullivan?" I asked, and the man looked up. "I'm glad I caught you on your day in Erwin. I understand you have an office in Johnson City?"

"I do, yes. I'm here in Erwin just two days a week."

"I'm from Birmingham, Alabama, Mr. Sullivan, and I've never known a county official to ..."

"Please call me David. And your name is?" As he said this, he fanned the call slips like playing cards in his hand.

"Shores. John Shores," I replied, watching him select a slip and return the others to his shirt pocket.

"Sorry to interrupt you, John. You were saying..."

"I was just curious. Nothing important. I just ... I don't think I've ever heard of a county official working for two different counties."

"Well, John, I don't work for either county. I work for the state of Tennessee. We are assigned to regions and I cover this part of the state, out here in East Tennessee, these two counties. We're not so much concerned with county health matters even though my office is here in the Unicoi County Health Department. My job has to do with environmental health relating to both residential and commercial properties, private homes, of course, but also restaurants, motels, campgrounds, that sort of thing." He paused a moment to let that sink in. "When you called yesterday, you told our receptionist you needed a septic system permit. Septic systems are handled by my office because they affect the environment even more than do the people using them." Sullivan removed the be-back-in-one-hour sign from his office door and, turning to me, he said. "So, what you got going there, John? Step into my office here and show me on the map."

I pointed out my property on the large map decorating one wall of his office and explained the project; that I would be building a big bathhouse to accommodate twenty or thirty hikers per day. Then Sullivan explained the difference between residential and commercial septic systems; an attempt to justify the much higher fee, it struck me.

"Okay. So, this is going to cost me $250? Should I write the check now, or do you need to run a perk test on the property?"

"John, you're not going to have any problem with the land out there. It will perk. All of that area along the river is very rocky. Your problem...well, you're going to have problems with the guy who puts the system in the ground. First thing he'll say is you have to pay more because of the rocks. They might even have to dynamite...and get permits for that. So, be prepared for higher bids."

"Can you help me with that? You work with these guys. Can you give me the name of somebody you think is reasonable and reliable?"

"Well, John. In my position, I can't discriminate. But I do have a list of all the system guys in your area." And with this, Sullivan opened the file drawer in his desk, pulled out a manila folder, and withdrew a piece of blue paper printed on one side. "If I were you, John, I'd call all of them," he said, handing me the page. "Everybody on this list is reliable. I can go that far with you. But call all of them. You never know whose son just wrecked the family car. When a contractor has all the work he can handle, he tends to clear the air with high bids. But guys who need the work will come in at a level they think will land the job. Some guy who needs work all of a sudden? ... Sorta desperate? ... He'll come in low. But John, you can't guess who's who looking at that list. Just call all of them."

As Manuel had said, Dave Sullivan was a nice guy who wants to help people. He was perfectly comfortable, and answered all my questions, relaxed and smiling the whole time we talked. Bob Manuel had described Sullivan as "very strict, but fair." I didn't see the tough side. I could sense no toughness at all. I guessed that the strict but fair part of Dave Sullivan applied to his interaction with contractors making the installation. Sullivan handed me his business card. On the back he had written Thur 9:00 AM.

"I'm going back to Johnson City tomorrow morning, John, but I'll swing out by your place and take a look. Can you be there no later than nine? I won't be able to wait if you're late."

* * *

When Ben dropped me off at the motel, I remembered his disappointment, and invited him to have breakfast on me at JD's, providing he arrived promptly at eight o'clock sharp.

He was on time. I suggested fried egg sandwiches on toast with heavy mayo. We had two each, and large coffees. The Pinto, all four windows rolled down, chugged along Chestoa Pike. He was driving slowly. I looked over at his side of the dashboard. "This route was frequently policed," Ben said. He had noticed me squinting at the speedometer. "Thirty-mile-per-hour speed limit, on this road, John."

We arrived at DeHaven's property twenty minutes early, but David Sullivan was already there on the porch. Sullivan was holding a mug of coffee, and DeHaven had the blue-porcelain cowboy coffeepot in his hand.

Ben parked the Pinto next to the old Ford van, and we ambled up to the porch and joined them. Without speaking, DeHaven motioned with the coffeepot, and in unison we pitched our cold coffee and received a steaming refill.

Holding a clipboard, Sullivan drew the layout for the septic field and drove a stake in the ground where the contractor would place the tank. I was surprised by the size of the leach field and how much of the yard this would require.

During the next week, I kept Ben busy driving me out to the property and to various offices to set up services for electricity, city water, natural gas, and so forth. Fortunately, the gas company had installed feeder lines down River Road years ago. I would need the largest gas water heater available for the bathhouse. I wanted to use the phrase *endless hot water,* when hikers asked about the availability of showers. As we had arranged, Ben charged twenty dollars per trip. Even if there were two or three consecutive stops, his response was always, "that'll be twenty bucks, John." Whenever I thought him overly generous, I tipped him an extra five dollars.

Of the five excavation contractors I called, only two were even interested enough to submit bids on the septic system. "Rocks" came up in every conversation. They were all familiar with the area.

I chose James M. Harris, an impressive businessman in his sixties. He owned something like twenty-four rental houses, he told me. His wife had two Corvettes. He did the backhoe work himself and he would not need to blast away any large rock, he said, shaking his head. "No, sir, he said." His price was not cheap.

At night in the motel room, I wrote out my plans, drew up various iterations of the bathhouse, and worked on lists of materials. I knew I was just guessing. I had no idea what the bathhouse plumbing would require, but I needed a figure. Bankers were going to want hard numbers. The numbers just needed to be logical and reasonable. Once I had the loan, I could create an overall budget. Any unanticipated costs in one area would be provided by compensating in another area.

I wasn't flying by the seat of my pants. I could feel my dad's presence. I could hear him talking to a couple who had come to him about a new house. They were sitting around our dining room table and they had a fat manila folder with photos and magazine clippings of all the things and products and features they wanted in their new home. They had sketched out ideas for the kitchen. They had arrows pointing toward labeled circles showing how the rooms would interact. They had spread all this out before my dad. He stopped them just short of disappointment.

"Here's a better way," he said. "First, you need to know that the average cost of a house in Jefferson County is thirty-six dollars per square foot. So determine how much you can spend, and we'll convert that to square footage. Next, you need to put together a budget that divides what you have available to spend into the fixtures and features you want. All this stuff," he said to the couple, waving his hand over their portfolio. "Once we have all that on paper, we can adjust square footage, the extras, the upgrades, and your can't-do-withouts down to an amount you can afford."

My own fat manila folder was in my head. I had been thinking through all the things I wanted for my Appalachian Trail hostel since my conversation with Friar Tuck and Speechless. Remembering them, I was struck by how much had happened over the last three days. I had become so completely engrossed in the enormous task before me, I could hardly remember that night up in the Beauty Spot campsite.

Each night I had been working on a financial plan for the entire design/build process that considered all the important variables: materials needed, design features, quality, size, shape, heating, cooling, you name it. My aim was to create a printed estimate showing detailed labor and material costs. At the very least, I wanted to know if the project was feasible. I could hear my dad again. "John, consider this as an exercise in project feasibility. John, are you listening? One, identify priorities. Two, recognize trade-offs. Three, do cost/benefit analysis. Four, revise your cost estimates. John. What you're considering is not easy. You need to pay attention. Are you listening?"

I was listening. I was listening, and I was as nervous and anxious as I had ever been. These estimates were just the beginning. I needed to prepare a budget so I could understand and control costs. The total dollar amount of the funds available to me and the amount I needed to borrow could be broken into two categories: hard costs and soft costs. Hard costs include labor and material to build the hostel. Soft costs include everything else.

Ben carried me to Home Depot and Lowe's in Johnson City. I knew they had pamphlets about decks and picnic tables. Sitting in the Pinto, eating hot dogs with Ben, I studied these pamphlets and added their materials lists to the lists I had compiled for the bathhouse and hostel addition. Both companies said they would have an estimate in two days, that I could call and get the numbers, and that they would mail the formal estimates to my motel.

The following afternoon, I called and they gave me the numbers. The estimates were within 5% of each other. That was a good sign.

Now the big one. Tomorrow I would be talking to a banker. I knew exactly where I was going. I picked the biggest bank in Erwin. At least, I had assumed it to be the biggest. They were in the biggest bank building in town.

* * *

"Didn't even make eye contact," I groused to Ben. "He just waved his hand when I offered to show him the business plan." Ben jumped when I shook my yellow legal pad violently and smacked it with the back of my hand. "What's wrong with these people they won't even take the time to listen to you. I mean, Ben, that's his job, for crying out loud!"

Ben just sat there. We just sat there. A few minutes later, I had gained control.

"Ben. I need to walk around. I'm just going to walk around and think a bit. But Ben, I need to see another banker. While I was waiting for the jerkwad who wouldn't even look at me, I spotted this other guy; younger. I'm betting he'll understand what a hostel is. Understand the impact the Appalachian Trail hikers could have on his community. You just hang out here until I'm back. Might be an hour or two. I've got to work up my nerve again."

*   *   *

"I'm telling you Ben, I went in that bank with utter confidence. I walked across that lobby with the roll and stride of a man who had business to tend; full of the kind of assurance and enthusiasm that comes with knowing you're on the right path; knowing you've made the right choice after diligently examining all the options. I walked in there like Bear Bryant taking on Auburn.

"Crossing the lobby, I caught the eye of that guy I was telling you about, the younger guy. I could see on the wall behind his desk a Washington Redskins poster. I held up my hand and gave him a tomahawk chop. He smiled. He was alone at his desk on the other side of the glass wall that enclosed his office on two sides. He smiled at me as I walked in the door."

"Come in. Have a seat," he said pointing toward the only other chair besides his. "My name is Harold Dinkins. I'm a Vice President here. What can I do for you?"

When I said that I would be inquiring about a loan, a business loan, he responded, "I'm glad you came to me, Mr. Shores. I'm here to tell you, we are Erwin's hometown bank, big Erwin boosters, and mighty pleased you're opening your business here. We need people like you here in Erwin, Mr. Shores. Mighty pleased. Now, tell me what you got going."

I was happy to see that Mr. Dinkins was even younger than I first thought. Looked like maybe late 30s. Nicely-groomed blown-dry thick mink-brown hair. A banker's dark blue suit; red power tie. The tie was covered with tiny tan elephants in pale yellow circles; elephants with trunk up and mouth open.

"Yes, sir, I have my projected financials here." I lifted my yellow legal pad a few inches and then put it back on my thigh. "I have a description of the business here, a brief business plan. I'm hoping to borrow some working capital, it's all in here." I waggled the pad for a moment, then lifted my chin exhibiting supreme confidence.

"Well, Mr. Shores. Why don't you just give me a verbal rundown on what you have in mind. I'm sure we can work something out. We're mighty pleased you've come to us."

With this, I gave him a brief description of my history. My understanding of the world of outdoor adventure. The prosperous dive shop I had owned with partners. My success at running human resources for a major corporation. Then I launched into the business I had in mind with as much enthusiasm as I could muster. I made sure he understood what a hostel was and how it worked. I described the bathhouse with endless hot water. I characterized the potential clients as a captured audience like visitors in Disney World.

"What I need, Mr. Dinkins, is construction money. I'll be purchasing the property with my own assets. I need funds to cover construction and a little bit extra for start-up costs. It's all laid out here in my plan." And I waggled the yellow legal pad again.

"Well. Mr. Shores. We do like working with proven entrepreneurs, and your experience with your customer type, your hiking and river adventures, well, I'm sure you know your customers. I do feel confident of that. But, Mr. Shores, you said the hostel would have nine beds, did I hear that correctly…nine beds?"

The word "but" rang like a church bell in my ears. Not sure what Mr. Dinkins was implying, I repeated. "Yes, nine beds."

"And you'll be charging what, twenty dollars per night per bed?"

"Yes-sir."

"The standard figure, Mr. Shores, the rule of thumb is that after overhead, you'll clear about 30% before taxes…before taxes," he repeated. "Let's see, nine times twenty is $180, times 30% leaves you with fifty-four bucks, but what concerns me here is the other side. You're planning on running your business day-to-day with $126, right? And you have a mortgage? Maybe two mortgages? You have electricity and phone and insurance and…"

I held up one finger and Mr. Dinkins stopped.

"Mr. Dinkins, if you'll read my business plan, you'll see that we'll have other income streams. We'll be running shuttles up to the trail for section hikers, picking up folks at the bus station and the airport. That's like a taxi service, Mr. Dinkins, USA Raft is doing that now and making big money. We'll have a store, sell food, sell outfitter equipment, you know, tents and sleeping bags…and hikers can pitch their tent in the backyard for only ten………"

Mr. Dinkins is holding up his finger now.

"Mr. Shores. You'll be running a hostel, yes? That's sorta like a motel, yes? Now Mr. Shores, there's another rule of thumb in the motel business. You're doing real good if you average 60% occupancy. Now, if we take that $126 and take 60% of that, you'll be running your day-to-day with, what … $76.60? Right? Round that to a nice, even $76. You've got that overhead, Mr. Shores, and that's a constant, that overhead is not going……"

I'm holding up one finger. Dinkins stops, leans back in his chair, and his bland smile and genial demeanor began to change. He crossed his arms.

"Yes, Mr. Shores?" … he said.

"In my business plan, I explain that we'll be selling food, ice cream, sandwiches, forty-cent Snickers…hikers are addicted to Snickers … and ……"

"Forty-cent Snickers? What's the profit on that, Mr. Shores?" he said, fixing me with a steady gaze.

"Well, it's not … the Snickers … the … when…when hikers come off the trail, they're hungry. We know what they like most, and we'll be stocking all that stuff."

"It's a hostel, isn't it … Mr. Shores, not a convenience store you'll be running?" he said with a hard smile.

"Mr. Dinkins, if you will do me that favor, the favor of looking over ... of reading my plan carefully, I think you'll see we have a solid idea here. We are less than sixty feet from a spot on the Appalachian Trail every single hiker traveling either north or south must pass. At that point, hikers are three miles from the Best Southern, the only place to sleep in Erwin. We'll have a captive audience, Mr. Dinkins, and a pretty tight plan for making the most of that. If you'll just read the plan."

* * *

"And Ben, I held out the yellow legal pad. I held it at arm's length. And he simply ignored me. Acted like nothing was happening. He just got up from his desk, walked around to my side, shook my hand and said: "Thanks so much for coming in, Mr. Shores." Imitating the banker's voice, I grabbed Ben's hand hard, shook it, and said, "Very interesting idea. Very interesting ..." I said this with the smirking smile and transfixing stare of Dinkins ... "eyes like a snake, Ben," I said, and continued in Dinkins's voice. "But we can't help you. We're not speculators. Our bank is not set up that way. I'm sorry, Mr. Shores." I continued to pump Ben's hand. "I wish we could help. You seem like a really nice guy."

Ben just looked at me. No reaction. I released his hand.

"I tell you Ben, it was like somebody hit me in the stomach. My trip back across the lobby had neither roll nor stride. I wanted to run."

* * *

The next day, Ben carried me to the Erwin branch of the Bank of Tennessee, based in Kingsport. I did not stride into the bank this time. One might say I slipped in quietly and looked around. Everybody was busy. The room was small and it seemed to be closing in on me. I wanted to leave, but just as I started to turn, I saw a stout, energetic young man whirl through the door on the other side. He entered a small alcove, picked up the phone on his desk, said three or four words, and hung up. He was alone and writing on a legal pad. I quickly crossed the lobby and stood quietly. He felt my presence and looked up.

"Do you need help?"

"Well I ... I'm ... Are you a loan officer?"

"Come right on in." He stood. We shook hands, and I introduced myself. "Have a seat, Mr. Shores. Sit right there," he said, pointing to one of the two chairs on the other side of his desk. A seat close enough that I put my yellow legal pad down on his desk.

"I'm Bubba Evely. I'm the branch manager here, and my key role is business development so, yes, by golly, I'm a loan officer. What can I do for you?"

"Well, Mr. Evely, I ..."

"Call me Bubba, and with your permission, I'll call you John." Before I could say another word, he continued. "I used to be Mayor, I'm a former Mayor and Alderman for the town of Erwin, and I'm a member of the Unicoi County Industrial Board. So, John, if there's anybody in Erwin can help you, it's me." Across the desk was a framed family photo. Seeing my glance in that direction, he reached for it saying, "That's my wife, Leanne," he said, picking up the frame and moved it closer, "and my two sons, Benjamin and Thomas."

"A lovely family, Bubba. You're a lucky man."

"I am. That I am. Now ... John, what can we do for you today?"

I started telling Bubba my plan; sixty feet from the Chestoa trailhead; turning part of the original house into a nine-bed hostel; the bathhouse with endless hot water; three shuttles into town every day ...

"Great idea, John. Great idea," he said. Studying me for a moment, he continued, "I read somewhere the number of hikers on the AT has increased exponentially ... that right?"

"Well ... yes ... almost, Bubba. Last year, 1,700 hikers attempted to hike the entire trail and approximately half of them reached Erwin. That compares to only 650 who attempted a thru-hike back in 1986 ... twelve years ago. Now ... Bubba ... this doesn't include the tremendous growth in the number of section-hikers, hikers from all over the world, a quarter of them are women, and ..."

"John, I had no idea the AT had become so popular. From all over the world? Man...and all this in our own back yard. You know, I have always thought the town of Erwin was missing the boat; you know, ignoring a great resource. We do almost nothing to accommodate those guys. I think what you are proposing is a step in the right direction. Now, let's get down to brass tacks. What kind of resources do you have? I assume you came in here to get some financial help, but what have you got going so far?"

"Bubba, I have property with substantial equity. It's located in Mountain Brook, a suburb of Birmingham, Alabama. Just for your information...I'm not bragging here...Mountain Brook is a very attractive, upscale community and houses there sell quickly. I estimate I'll clear forty, maybe forty-five thousand. I'll buy the property from Mr. DeHaven and use it for collateral, and borrow, say, forty thousand on a ten-year loan."

"John, that would work. We'll run a routine credit check, of course, but we'll need two things from you; a survey of the property proving all buildings will be outside the Nolichucky floodplain, and a sales contract signed by Mr. DeHaven." Saying this, Bubba Evely got up, came around to my side, and gave me a firm handshake. "You do that, John, and we've got a deal."

* * *

Ben was on time again. Ten o'clock on the dot. We had a deal going without speaking a word about it. Arrive on time and breakfast is on me. Unwrapping the second egg sandwich in his lap; coffee in his right hand; Ben was steering with his knees down Chestoa Pike when he asked, "How'd you get in the newspaper business?"

I liked Ben. He had cleaned up a bit. His wild, auburn hair was pulled back neatly under his ball cap. When he arrived yesterday, he was clean shaven. Without the straggly goatee, he was actually handsome in a scrawny, tough-guy way. I had rafted many rivers and knew the river-guide type. They were of all sorts, and Ben represented one of them very well; wiry thin, self-indulgent, and free of all responsibilities. He didn't particularly like his junky car, his thrift-store wardrobe, or the meager income, but he understood the tradeoff; the deal he had made with himself. He never said a word about this to me, nor did he ever speak disparagingly of his counterparts who came from wealth, drove an enviable car, and wore Patagonia shirts. He was not content. No, he was far from being content, and the restlessness came through in spite of his casual demeanor, but it didn't take long for me to see Ben as a survivor. Smart and well-read, Ben will score someday. I would bet good money on that.

"I started out with the phone company climbing poles."

"No kidding."

"Climbing poles ... right out of high school. I was a small 145 pounds, but strong as an ox. Then I joined the Army, got out, and went to college. After college, I came back to Birmingham and the phone company. I worked hard, and became the youngest account manager ever."

"So, how'd the newspaper fit in?" Ben balled up his egg sandwich wrapper and flipped it over his shoulder into the back seat. "Where'd that come from?"

"The *Birmingham News* was my largest account. Getting it was a big deal. The insider political scrambling and back-stabbing was something else. I must have impressed my boss somehow. When he assigned the account to me he said ... look John, be careful. No screw-ups. Naturally, I spent a lot of time over at the *News;* got to know all those guys really well. One day they offered me the job. It was a great opportunity for me, so I jumped on it."

"Human resources, that's personnel; right? Your department did the hiring and firing."

"And training, Ben. The employees of the *Birmingham News* were its greatest asset. Managing that asset was my job ... developing employees so they become more valuable to the organization. When I arrived, we had 1,200 scattered through half-a-dozen departments. It was a major operation. I wasn't sure I could handle it, but I had the great, good fortune to be mentored by the best in the business ... Harold Wilson ... he was well into his 60s, a tough and gruff old Chief Petty officer in the Navy, been at the *News* thirty years or so, wanted to retire the day he turned sixty-five, so ... Mr. Wilson started asking around, must have got a lead on me, I don't know how, I didn't know him as well as some others, but I heard it was him that picked me. I ... technically, I was his assistant, but I saw my role as just tagged along. I watched and listened. I'm really good at that, Ben. Most of what I've learned in life I figured out on my own."

"Doesn't sound very interesting to me. An outdoor guy like you stuck inside all day. How'd you do that?"

"I like people, Ben. I like the science of managing people. Finding the right person and getting that person in the right place is fascinating; just as fascinating as when you find that perfect line through a Class IV rapid.

"Yeah, I get that, I get that."

Driving in his intense way, wary of the roadway, Ben had his eye on an approaching UPS truck. I could tell he was thinking about what I had just said. I waited for him to say something.

"Now that you're gone, what's your best memory? Where does your mind go when you think of your old job?"

"Interesting question, Ben. Interesting you would put it that way."

Ben didn't comment. He slowed for a car turning left, then mashed the accelerator, all the while mindful of keeping the old Pinto within the 30-mile-per-hour speed limit running the entire length of Chestoa Pike.

"We had a managers' meeting every morning … hold on. Let me start over. First, Ben, for this story to make sense, you need to know there was a time when hardly anybody knew the Appalachian Trail existed at all. So, we're back then, we're back in that time, and the story I'm about to tell happened at a *Birmingham News* managers' meeting. I had worked for the paper for a month … little over a month … and was being groomed to take over HR. Let's see, it must have been about … well, it was right in the middle of the Watergate thing. Before you were even born. Are you familiar at all with the Watergate fiasco?"

"Of course. I read *All the President's Men*, and saw the movie. So I have a good idea how the story evolved in the newspapers. But, I'm still a little fuzzy on what those people did that was so historic and shocking."

"Well, it was right in the middle of it … '72? … '73? and Ben, in the early '70s, compared to today, there were very few hikers on the trail, keep that in mind. So, it was during one of our managers' meetings this took place. Victor Hanson II, the son of the founding publisher, was the general manager at the time. He took his seat at the head of the table. My boss sat to his right, and I sat to the right of him. On that day, the meeting included, in addition to Mr. Hanson, my boss, and me; there was Jim Jacobson, the Managing Editor. He always sat at the other end of the table. Jacobson was at the meeting representing the editorial division ... representing ... okay, Ben ..." I looked at my watch. "I'm early just in case JM Harris is early. When we get to DeHaven's place, just pull into the back yard. I don't want to disturb Don. I'd like to talk to Harris ..."

"Sure, John. No problem. So ...." Ben tossed the empty coffee cup over his shoulder. Ben didn't often take his eyes off the road. He was holding out one hand in my direction getting ready to say something. "So, these meetings ...?"

"They included all the key managers. Andy Smith, from circulation; Harris Emerson, from advertising with his assistant, Bill Ward. Anytime you saw Emerson you saw Ward. The two of them were joined at the hip, were so good ... advertising's the key to the newspaper business, Ben. Even though Emerson was getting up there ... seventy or something ... Mr. Hanson would have kept him on if he lived to be a hundred. Then there was Mickey Townsend, public relations, son of the assistant publisher; and Jim Payton, the production guy --- he was in charge of printing both newspapers; and Ross Peeples from accounting and the business office. And that was it."

"So, these meetings ...?"

"I was by far the junior person in that room."

"And these.........?"

"This particular meeting started out with a ruckus over column inches; you know, the amount of space the editors would allow for stories and photographs, or for this, that, and the other ... the editors and the advertising guys were always at each other's throats, but once this territorial struggle over the allotment of space had calmed, the subject shifted to pressing issues that would affect all departments. Shortly before the hour, Mr. Hanson looked around and asked if anybody had anything else to say. After a pause, Andy Smith, he was the circulation guy, cleared his throat. Mr. Hanson, he said, I've got something that might interest our readers. And he glanced over toward Jacobson, the editor. Not Jacobson, nor anybody else, could ruffle Andy's feathers. He was circulation. He knew what sold and didn't. He knew his readers and he always stood on solid ground. OK, Mr. Hanson said, Go ahead, Andy. So, Andy said one of his guys had a son. The circulation guy he was talking about was Lenny Stabler, and his son's name, I believe, was Paul ... yes, Paul. The kid was preparing to hike the Appalachian Trail, the whole damn thing, he said, that's the way he put it, actually, he said the whole damn thing from end to end. He said it was way over 1,000 miles. I almost choked on my coffee. Now, he had that wrong, of course, and that's going to be the point of my story. Lenny, said it would take his son five months or more."

"Yeah?" Ben glanced at me and back to the road. Then the rear-view and back to the road.

"Silence." I said, leaning forward, trying to catch Ben's eye. "Not a peep. They didn't know what he was talking about. Andy was looking at the managers, one by one, back and forth. They weren't looking at him, not one of them, but he plowed on saying how he believed it would make a good story and then he allowed as how he had promised Lenny he would mention it in the meeting. More silence, Ben. Then he stopped. Now everybody is looking at him. Andy was calm, but I could sense his struggle. I knew what was happening. I knew these guys were totally oblivious to what he was talking about. Somewhere someone whispers to the one sitting next to him ... Appalachian? Mr. Hanson, looking at Andy, spreads his hands and says ... What's the story, Andy? The manager across from Andy asks, What's the Appalachian Trail? Poor Andy, he didn't know what to say. I was watching Andy's struggle, so I raised my hand."

"You were going to explain it; tell about the trail."

"I was. I thought it would make a great story, and they were missing it. Mr. Hanson recognized me. John, he said. Then I turned my chair slightly so I could see Mr. Hanson better and told him how I was very familiar with the Appalachian Trail. I told him I had hiked portions of it every summer as a kid. Up in the Smokies. The Appalachian Trail is over 2,000 miles. It's the longest hiking-only, continuously-marked footpath in the world. It runs right through the Smoky Mountains National Park the long way. The thing runs through fourteen states. It runs up and down the ridges and peaks of the whole Appalachian Mountain chain from Georgia to Maine. Then I leaned forward a little, spoke directly to Mr. Hanson, and made my strongest point. If this kid intends to hike the trail end-to-end in one season, that's a monumental undertaking, Mr. Hanson. It would be like climbing Mount Everest. If someone in Birmingham was making plans to climb Mount Everest? … I think our readers would find that story fascinating."

"So, what did Hanson say?"

"Well, Ben … he didn't say anything. That was all he needed. He was ready to end the meeting. So, he looked at me and said, John? Will you put something together about this, give us a little report? Then he paused and said, Tomorrow? … You know, Ben, that word tomorrow shot through me like an arrow. I'm a slow writer. I had to prepare an oral report, and I'm used to having days if not weeks to put together such things, so I said something of that sort to Mr. Hanson and he just looked at me steady, not blinking an eye. I said Tomorrow? Mr. Hanson nodded, and, of course, I told him I'd do it."

* * *

By then we had arrived at the DeHaven property, and I had a lot of story to go.

"Just turn here, Ben. Just beyond the neighbor's driveway. Pull up into the back yard there. We're early. The septic tank guy said he'd meet me at eleven. Do you want to hear the rest of the story? I mean, am I boring you to death?"

"No, not at all. You're in a pickle. Looks like you got yourself in the hot-seat there."

"Right. At first I was wishing I had kept my mouth shut. Then I got an idea. I figured I'd just go to the morgue and look up some articles about the Appalachian Trail. Surely the paper had already published something on the AT. It would be effective, I thought, if my report came from our own paper."

"Wait a minute ... the morgue?"

"As far as reporters are concerned, old newspapers are dead. But past issues are valuable for research. The *Birmingham News* had every issue since 1850 stored in a room somewhere. Newspaper guys call the place the morgue, get it?"

Ben grinned and nodded, then opened his door wide. It was getting warm. The car had filled with exhaust. I opened my door. The old Pinto looked like a cormorant in bat-pose drying its wings.

"So, I went looking for the morgue. I had to ask somebody for directions. Found it on the second floor. Out-of-the-way alright, an interior space, several rooms between two hallways. The door had a window and I peeked in. Nobody around. I pushed the door open. Not a sound. Not a soul. Just inside was a lounge-like space, with a comfortable-looking, brown-leather chair next to an oak table and a lamp. Against the wall, a good-sized rack of newspapers from all over. On the oak table by the chair, I could see the *Paris Review*. It crossed my mind that this would be a great place to bring a bag lunch and catch up on the news.

"A high counter ran across the room separating this entry space from the main room. Over the counter, I could see long tables, and to the right of the tables, I could see the endcaps of rows of grey metal shelves holding, I presumed, reference material and other books reporters would need for research and fact checking. A little gateway led through this counter, and I shoved it open. Suddenly, a stern voice stopped me mid-stride ... *Sir! ... Sir. Can I help you?*"

"Yeah? Let me guess. The mortician!"

"Right on. You nailed it. Then I heard the scooching of an office chair on casters. When I looked, a tiny little lady with auburn hair caught up in a scruffy bun nearly the size of her head was staring at me over drug-store reading glasses. Black eyes, in fact. Very big black eyes, like an owl, looked at me through wisps of auburn and gray hair."

Ben laughed. "The mortician," he whispered.

"Yes ma'am? I called out as politely as I could. And Ben, as I backed back through the little gate, she just stared me down. Her chin tucked. Her mouth open ... like an owl-eyed Gerber baby."

Ben laughed again.

"I'm standing on the other side of the counter now, and she says ... Sir, please take a seat. I'll be with you momentarily. She had all the charm of a viper. Stung and confused, I retreated to the brown-leather chair and picked up the *Paris Review*. I had not been seated five seconds when she scared the crap out of me once again by her sharply-spoken Sir! Ben, the lady was not five-foot tall and from where I was sitting, only her head was visible above the counter ... the bunched up auburn hair and owl eyes seemed to be part of a severed head sitting on the counter. I got up and walked over, whereupon the little lady returned to her desk! She just sat down again with stacks of books and dozens of folders and binders and went back to work!"

"Did you leave?"

"No, I stood there not knowing what to do. She was hunched over her work, and without looking up, she asked what I wanted. I said I was wondering if she could make copies of all the articles we had run on the Appalachian Trail. This lifted her head. She stared straight ahead for a moment, then turned. Using her feet, she scooched her office chair in my direction. Down went the chin. The fifty-year-old Gerber-baby mouth opened. The owl-like eyes peered over reading glasses and through sprigs of graying auburn hair. Without moving one iota she asked ... What is your name young man? John Shores, I said. Do you work here? she asked. Yes ma'am, I said, surprised she would ask that, I'm in Human Resources. Human Resources? she says to me. She almost whispered it like a bewildered little girl. Human Resources? Yes ma'am, I said. Human Resources? she asked again, with a rising, edgy tone. You're not a reporter? Now it's beginning to dawn on me her problem. No ma'am, I said. Then, Ben, she stared at me for what seemed like three minutes and finally, in a very irritated voice, she said, young man, do you have any idea how busy I am right now? I said, no ma'am. She said, have you heard the word Watergate? And of course I had, so I said, Yes ma'am."

"So, here's where the Watergate thing enters the picture," Ben said, looking at me and nodding.

"Yes, and she goes, Well! in a huffy tone, and just looks at me again. Then, Ben, emphasizing every word one at a time, she says, I-have-had-four-reporters-in-here-ev-ry-day-for-a-week. See this? she says, and she turns and waves one hand at her desk. See this! she says again shaking her out-held hand. And Ben, she holds her outstretched hand and gives me that dipped-chin, owl-eyed look again." And I sit forward and imitate the look for Ben.

"Oh, my God!" Ben laughs.

"Well, she recovers a little. She takes a deep breath and lets it out like a quiet sigh. She turns away from her desk and scooches her chair ten inches closer and says, I suppose you know how to run a microfilm reader, she says, and this time she seems resigned to the fact that I needed help and she is looking a little kindlier at me. No ma'am, I said ... down goes the chin again."

I'm laughing too, now. "The Gerber mouth opens. The owl-like eyes peer over the reading glasses. Ben, I'm backing away. Listen ma'am, I said, stepping back and back again ... uh, uh," I imitate my fumbling for Ben. "I can see you are very busy, I said. Maybe I better come back another time." Ben and I both laughed hysterically.

When we settled down, I picked up the story. "So, Ben, I went to Plan B. It occurred to me the Forest Service would have a ton of information on the Appalachian Trail, and I was somewhat miffed I hadn't thought of that right off the bat. I went back to my office and looked up the number of the Forest Service and discovered there was an agency office in Birmingham. I called them right then."

"So, now you think you're getting somewhere."

"Well, Ben, if I did, the feeling passed. I heard this young, sweet, very southern voice saying ... Where exactly is the Apple-lay-shun Trail? I was stunned. This was an office of the U.S. Forest Service. It took me a few seconds to recover. In the Apple-*latch*-en Mountains! I blurted out. Yes, she says, I guess that makes sense ... but sir, the Apple-lay-shuns aren't in Alabama. Oh, but they are, I said. The most southern part runs into Cherokee County, up west of Piedmont...Bear Mountain? Ever heard of Bear Mountain? She comes back in that soft southern accent." I imitate this for Ben ... Sir, the Apple-*LAY*-shuns? ... Ben, that pronunciation, you know, Ben, I don't know why, but it irritated me so, and I said ...

"It's pronounced Appa-*latch*-ians."

"Sir? ..."

"It's pronounced *latch*, like a door latch; Appalachians."

"Sir? ..."

"You pronounce the word...it's an Indian word. You pronounce the ... would there happen to be a Forest Ranger in the office right now?"

"Sir? ..."

"Do you see anybody in a green uniform? And she goes, no-sir, it's just me and Pam here right now."

"Oh, my God!" Ben laughs; and he's pounding on the steering wheel, stomping his foot, about to knock another hole in the floor of the old mint-green Pinto. And I'm laughing too.

"Now, Ben, I'm down to Plan C. I put the phone back in the cradle and dropped my head. For a long moment I just sat there rubbing my head. Anyone nearby would have heard me whispering the word "tomorrow" a couple of times. I wasn't actually praying, but something I did got answered. I remembered Chief...Zack Chief Cross. He was Mister-Boy-Scout in Alabama. Everybody, from the President of the United States to the youngest Scout, called him Chief. During all my teenage years, I spent summers ... I spent time with, was led by, and made it a point to linger within the inspiring presence of Zack Cross. I picked up the phone and dialed his number."

Ben punched my shoulder. "And you got the information you needed from your old Boy Scout leader."

"Oh, yeah, oh yeah. I had a long conversation with Chief and took a bunch of notes. My first thought was preparing a handout for the next day's manager's meeting. I could have placed one in the seat of each manager. But, I thought the better of it. I got one of those long, gray, reporter's notebooks that fit in your back pocket. Every reporter carries one. These were newsmen. They would appreciate this gesture.

"At the meeting, I opened the notebook, and thanked Mr. Hanson for the opportunity to talk to them about something important to me personally. I said, Andy Smith is right. Lenny's son's Appalachian hike would make a very interesting story. I suggested that it be in the Sunday edition with pictures, and a map showing the trail from end to end. Then I took about fifteen minutes to tell them what I knew about the Appalachian Trail.

"That's my favorite memory from the whole time I worked at the *Birmingham News*. But Ben, think about it. Those were some of the smartest men I had ever met. It was the 1970s. People had been hiking it for over forty years and not one of those men was aware of the Appalachian Trail."

* * *

About that time, we heard the heavy, rattling, chumma-chak-akk-a-chick; chumma-chak-akk-a-chick; chumma-chak-akk-a-chick sound of a diesel truck. The noise roared through our open doors, as a gleaming white 1995 three-quarter ton Dodge Ram 4-door crew cab with shiny built-in aluminum tool boxes backed slowly by and eased up into the yard facing us.

"Holy cow! Check that out, John."

"Yeah, for someone who spends his day mucking around in sewage, he keeps a clean truck."

"That design rocks! I read about this. Chrysler picked up the idea from those hunky-looking Studebaker pickups from back in the early 50s. Big grill. Prominent headlights and all. Damn, he sure does take care of that thing. Look at that wax job. I'll bet he ......"

"Excuse me, Ben. I've got to go talk to Mr. Harris."

* * *

As I approached, Harris climbed down from the cab and shut the door, turning to me. He was a big man. Not fat; just big and powerful-looking. A man in his late fifties. He was neatly dressed for a man in his occupation. Clean khaki pants. The sleeves of his pale green Carhartt work shirt carefully rolled two notches. Steel-framed glasses. No hat. His expertly barbered hair showed streaks and flecks of grey.

"Mr. Shores?"

"Yes-sir. And you're Mr. Harris?"

"James Harris but just call me JM. What you got going here, John?"

"Well, JM, I'll be buying this property and building an Appalachian Trail hostel for the hikers that hike the trail past here." I turned and pointed back and forth along the line where the trail ran the horizon beyond the trees.

"They come down out of that mountain and cross the bridge ... right there." We couldn't see the bridge for DeHaven's house, but we both knew where it was. "Building a very big bathhouse, right over here, endless hot water for maybe twenty, thirty showers every day. You know David Sullivan? ... of course ... well, here's the plan he sketched out. Needs about 400 foot of field line."

Harris took the drawing and looked at it. He looked up, and turned around surveying the property as if he questioned Sullivan's decision. Seeing the stake Sullivan had driven in the ground, he nodded approvingly, walked over and kicked it lightly as if to say, "tank right here;" then rested his clean, bison-brown Carhartt work boot on top the stake as he glanced here and there and down at the drawing and back up.

"Best thing you've got going John ... no trees. Trees are a pain. All your lines can run in that plot right there," and he pointed.

"I understand rocks can be a problem around here."

"Not for me, Mr. Shores. I've got the biggest backhoe excavator in the county. My baby. She won't have any problems with rocks in your leach fields, I'll guarantee you that." We talked on for a few minutes and Harris gave me his price.

"Hey Johnny ... JM"

DeHaven was coming across the yard. "How's it going JM?" he said. He had known David Sullivan too, like they'd been grammar school buddies. DeHaven seemed to know everybody. The two of them talked for a bit while I stood looking back towards the house.

Turning when DeHaven called out, I had noticed for the first time a canoe stored under the shed. By its distinctive red color, I knew it to be an Old Town canoe. Lots of Old Town canoes are out there, and they last forever. If this thing had a serial number less than 200,000, it would be a valuable find. As I approached, I could tell it wasn't canvas. It looked like the

Guide series. Standing there looking at this canoe, half covered with DeHaven's junk, I couldn't help but remember the 1972 film *Deliverance*, which featured seven of Old Town's Guide canoes. Build records exist on every canoe going back sixty, seventy years, and the serial number is located on the upper face of the stem. I made a mental note to uncover that thing and see what it's worth.

On my way back, I saw Harris climbing into his truck. He waved in my direction as the truck thrummed and rattled away, its diesel engine sounding like a bucket of loose bolts.

"Well, Mr. DeHaven, that's going to cost me a pretty penny. He didn't measure. Didn't do anything but look around. Gave me the price and said it was firm regardless of the rocks. You know, I called five contractors. Got bids from just two of them. Harris was the only one who didn't talk about rocks. I'm going with him. I don't know … there was a way about him, I guess. He looked confident. Didn't ask a lot of questions. I got the feeling he's a hard worker who knows his business."

"Hard worker alright, and got a head on his shoulders. Lives in a small brick house on Chestoa Pike. Frugal. Plows all his profits into property. Got something like thirty rental houses scattered all around the county. Knows how to buy them right and fix um up. Every rainy day, he's got an inside job somewhere improving his net worth. His wife, she drives two Corvettes, one of um is that classic white, the other's a newer job. Canary yellow. You see her out in the yard almost every good day. Prettiest garden you'll ever see. Nice-lookin woman too."

* * *

"You like Dodge Ram trucks," I said to Ben, as I climbed back into the old Pinto, its doors still wide open.

"I do." Ben said, putting his book on the dashboard. "I keep expecting Chevy and Ford to pick up on the macho inclination of truck enthusiasts. They're still building those flat-looking sedan-type trucks and getting their tail kicked by Chrysler … selling two to one, according to *Truck Trend*. Did you see *Twister*? … you know, *Twister*, the movie? Came out last year."

"Yes, I did. Loved it, in fact."

"The hero in that flick was the truck, John, a '95 Ram just like Harris's but a two-door club cab. It was red. Remember that?"

"I remember. The thing had nine lives."

Ben laughed, banging on the steering wheel. "Yeah, yeah, right! Got sucked up in that F5 tornado," he said, still laughing.

"Well, Ben, I think that's when the hero died … the truck died in that scene, Ben. I'm thinking of the scene where the farm house is sliding across the road and the truck runs right through it and out the other side." Now I'm laughing at the absurdity. "A funny movie, Ben. Remember the cow flying through the air?"

"Yes, and how about the fireball from that exploding tanker? The truck survived a trip through hell; paint job unscathed. Oh, and the tailgate was bent all to shit in one scene and brand new in the next … a self-healing truck. Whoo, whoo, whoo, whoo-oo needs an unlimited warranty if, if, if your truck can do that?" Ben shouted through his laughter.

"The Laura Dern character, she was …"

"That's *Jurassic Park*, John," Ben said, sitting back and taking a deep, clearing breath. He whewed a second time and said quietly, "The meteorologist in *Twister* was Helen Hunt."

"Oh, right. I always get those two mixed up. Not *Jurassic Park* though. I'm thinking *Rambling Rose*."

"Oh, lordy, lordy," Ben said. "Imagine having a nanny like that."

This image got us both into an introspective mood. Isn't it odd how when you've been laughing your guts out and finally settle down, you tend to just sit and think a little bit. I heard

Ben chuckling to himself and just then, I saw someone walking across the yard.

"Bet that's No-Drip."

"No-Drip?"

"Al 'No-Drip' Higgins. He's a plumber. Must have parked out front.

"No-Drip?"

"The plumber. Hang on Ben. I think that's him. Just sit tight. This won't take long."

Those words, in reference to Al "No-Drip" Higgins, I would come to eat.

* * *

"Mr. Higgins?"

"Yes-sir … Shores?

"John Shores, Mr. Higgins. Thanks for coming out. That stake is where the septic tank will go. I'm thinking of putting the bathhouse over there." We both turned and looked in the general direction of my future bathhouse. "Big. I'll be growing this business and I want to build now for future needs. The building will be thirty by fifteen over all, with separate areas for men and women. The two bathrooms will be divided by a laundry room. Each side will have two showers, two toilets, and a long vanity with two sinks. And Mr. Higgins, we have town gas and water here."

"Then you'll want a gas water heater for sure … a big one."

"Yes-sir, a big one. Biggest I can get. Hot showers will be one of the main attractions here. I want to advertise endless hot water. When hikers ask me if they can take a shower, it's endless hot water. That way, when the hikers are back on the trail and somebody asks about our hostel, they'll say, great showers. Endless hot water."

"You say you're building a hostel." Higgins had pulled out a spiral-bound notebook. "I've heard of hostels. What is a hostel, actually?"

"A hostel, Mr. Higgins, is a safe, supervised place providing inexpensive lodging, particularly for backpackers … like here. People hiking the Appalachian Trail"

"Like those tourist homes you used to see before motels?"

"No … more like a cowboy bunkhouse; a big room with bunk beds." I pause, letting Higgins catch up. He's scribbling fiercely putting my words into his notebook. "At a motel you rent a room. Here you're renting a bed. Low budget. No sheets," I say. "Every hiker has a sleeping bag. The guests share the bunkhouse, the bathhouse, the front deck, grills, you name it. Hostels are for backpackers, primarily. People who are hiking or biking long distances. You'll see them along hiking trails in our country …" I pause and watch the Bic wiggling across the page … "but in Europe and other countries, they're in the cities as well; anywhere tourists are attracted. There's a hostel in Hot Springs, and one in Hampton. Both are profitable … doing well, actually. It's a booming industry, Mr. Higgins, world-wide, but not so much in America. That's why you haven't heard of them."

Higgins put the pen into the spiral of the notebook. "Here. Follow me to the van. I've got a business card like a letter, tells about my service and has references."

I followed Higgins toward the front of DeHaven's house. He was at least sixty; an older man, not youthful; but fit. Tall and slim. A talker. A talker for sure. After noting my answers to several of his questions, he had commenced telling me about plumbing a bathhouse at a summer camp near Elizabethton. I got the picture down to the last detail. Now, walking ahead of me, he said something about his uncles and moonshining.

"That's interesting," I mumbled in response to Higgins' rambling on and on. "Your uncles … they were those moonshiners up at No Business Knob?"

Higgins had parked his old blue cargo van in DeHaven's spot. DeHaven must have gone out soon after our chat. Higgins opened the passenger door of the van and dug a battered old thin brief case from under what looked like three jackets and a pair of coveralls; arms and legs entwined. This and two pairs of rubber galoshes, both bright yellow, were tumbled on the passenger-side floorboard with several empty beer cans. It was the typical contractor's truck. Receipts littered the dashboard. Several styrofoam coffee cups stuffed with crunched cigarette packs and the wrappers from his breakfast filled the console's cup holders. The ashtray was open and overflowing. Higgins was on his fourth cigarette since we started talking. He unzipped the briefcase and was fishing through the contents.

"Here's that card. Tells all what I do. See there? Got several good references. I ain't lying to you, I'm the best around these parts."

"I have no problems along that line, Mr. Higgins. I got your name from the Chamber of Commerce, and you did work for my lawyer, Bob Manuel. He said you did great work."

"That's right. Did the boy's kitchen remodel; plumbing and electrical. Put in those high-efficiency toilets in every bathroom. Done lots of stuff for him and his neighbor, his grandmother, half the people on his street."

I took the card. It was a five by eight business card with Al "No-Drip" Higgins in bold type across the top, followed by twenty or so bullet-pointed services, and under that, five or six one-line accolades by various people. One of them, I noticed, was Bubba Evely.

"Let's sit on the porch here," Higgins said, as he turned toward DeHaven's house. "I'll make a little sketch and you tell me what you want in that bathhouse." He lit another cigarette with the butt of the one he was smoking.

Higgins took his place on the three-seated porch glider. I pulled DeHaven's rocker around so we were more or less facing each other and I handed him the sketch I'd made several days ago. It was on graph paper, so it was somewhat proportional.

"That sketch is for you," I said. "I made a copy."

Using his briefcase as a lap board, he smoothed my drawing and muttered, "Well, Shores, this looks pretty good. Four showers. Four toilets. You've got that washer and dryer in with the water heater. Okay, I see, yes, good use of that space between the men and the women."

For the laundry, I had drawn a six-foot by fifteen-foot hall-like space through the middle of the building separating the men's section on the left and the women's on the right. I indicated a big double wash-up sink on the exterior back wall next to the entry to the laundry. Xs and arrows marked where the water service entered the building and where the waste water ran out toward Sullivan's stake in the yard.

"So, you want the bathhouse plumbed ... how about the hostel?"

"Just the bathhouse. Need to bring the main service line from the street ... and the gas. The gas company will dig the ditch. The septic system will be installed by the time you get here. You'll plumb and install the toilets, the vanity sinks, and the double wash-up sink out back ... that, by the way, will have a pre-wash sprayer." Higgins had the Bic out and was writing furiously. "I'll purchase the walk-in shower stalls, have them on hand, you'll need to stub those out for me. As soon as you do that, I'll put them in so you can install the faucet sets and connect the drains. I'll buy the water heater, but of course, I'll need you to install it and the gas lines. Install the water heater and outlets for the washing machine. Run the waste-water drain to the septic tank."

"I see you have the electrical outlets indicated here. I'm a licensed electrician too. You want me to run the wire? ... install the service box and all?"

"Yes, I'll need that too. Now, Al," I emphasized. "I'll be selecting and buying, I'll take care of the service box and the breakers, the electrical boxes, the receptacles and switches, the light fixtures, I will select and buy the toilets and sinks, and as I mentioned, the water heater. I want you to be responsible for the copper, the valves and fittings, the gas line, and the wire." My plan was to be the gofer. I didn't want Higgins to charge me for an infinite number of trips to Home Depot over in Johnson City. My goal was to make his job simple and straight-forward.

Higgins was making a column of numbers on a page in his spiral-bound notebook. Watching him work up the estimate, I remembered my father. I'd seen him do this dozens of times. I could tell Higgins had a ballpark price for each unit ... four showers, four toilets, five sinks, counting the one out back. The water heater. Washer and dryer. Electrical service box. Light fixtures. He seemed to be figuring the wiring by counting the walls, just like my dad.

He stopped and looked at me. "Temporary service. You're going to need juice when you start construction. You need to arrange temp-service with Erwin Utilities. Tell you what, I'll lend you the box, you put up the pole, a four by four post with at least eight feet out the ground. The power company will make the connection. There'll be a fee for that." And he looked back down at his notebook and drew a big circle several times.

Christ. Another damn thing not in my budget.

"Alright, Mr. Shores. This is my figure." No-Drip turned his notebook around and in large numbers circled several times was the price with two exclamation points after it. The man had a flair for drama.

"Okay, Mr. Higgins. That looks good to me. We have a deal."

When I saw the price, I was floored. I tried not to show it. A damn decent price. Way below my estimate, which was based on figures from the service department at Lowe's, specifying all plastic pipe. "I ain't running nothin but copper,"

Higgins had told me when we first talked. I reached out and shook his hand.

"Deal," Higgins said, and started putting his stuff away.

"Now, Mr. Higgins, I want to make sure we're on the same page here. Like I told you on the phone, I'll start construction around the first week in January. I'll have the bathhouse closed…framed-in and roofed by March 1." I said this eye-to-eye, nodding my head with the words. "I know it's winter, but regardless of weather, I'll have that building closed-in first of March," I emphasized again. "I want to open the first week in April. So, you'll have just one month. There can be no delays. Can you confirm that for me?"

"Mr. Shores, I'll have my work done and inspected by end of March. You can count on me. You have my word on that." And Higgins stuck out his hand again.

* * *

Backing onto River Road for the return trip to the motel, Ben said, "People actually call him No-Drip?"

"That's what he calls himself … Al 'No-Drip' Higgins, Plumbing and Electrical Fully Licensed and Insured. Introduces himself that way. My lawyer recommended him. Said he does beautiful work. All copper. Do copper right, Ben; and it never fails. No leaks."

"So how'd it go? You're about to wrap this up aren't you?"

"Getting close, Ben."

"You like negotiating deals, John?"

"I do, and that was a good one. No-Drip gave me an excellent price. But, yes, I like negotiating. That was my job at the *News*. Constantly negotiating. Convincing good talent to leave what they're doing and come with us; convincing a department head one of their guys has a better fit in another department. Convincing a poor performer that he'll live a better life working for some other company. You don't just fire people, Ben. It's a type of negotiation. You help them relocate somewhere else. Human resources is, well ... a lot of negotiating."

"What's your secret, I mean, after a lot of years, what's the trick; what works?"

"Simple things. Common sense."

"Like ..."

"Number one, Ben. Don't paint yourself in a corner." Ben glanced at me expectantly. I realized this wasn't an idle question. For whatever reason, he was looking for a real answer. We rode in silence for a moment while I gave it some thought. "Three things, Ben. Be careful what you demand. Leave room to maneuver. Know the deal breakers ... it's a little dance you're doing; all of it about the other guy. Put simply, you've got to know what the other guy wants and doesn't want. Those three things boil down to that one thing. That's the primary skill. You work off that. Knowing the guy. The other side of that coin is leaving room to retreat and reorganize ... and Ben, if the guy ... the secret ... if there is a trick, Ben, it's this ... if he pushes you out the back door, the deal is never dead unless you let it die. The deal is never dead. That's the trick, Ben. Believing that. Do it right and you can come around the house and in the front door again."

"You've got the eyes for it."

"Eyes?"

"Icy eyes, John. When you're serious, they pierce like knives."

"Humph ... don't know exactly how to take that, Ben."

"That's a compliment, John ... Huizenga ... Wayne Huizenga. Know him? "

"The Miami Dolphins? "

"That and ten or twelve other things, like Blockbuster Video and Waste Management. Built those two multibillion-dollar companies from scratch. When he started, in his twenties, he had one garbage truck. Down in Fort Lauderdale.

In the 1960s, South Florida was growing like crazy and Huizenga couldn't keep up. All his credit lines were maxed. So, he took the company public. That's another story, but he did it well and had lots of cash. In ten months ... ten months, John ... he bought out 133 other garbage companies. Took over all of South Florida from Palm Beach to Miami. You know how?"

"Nooo ......" I said, laughing. Ben was some character. I was thinking, where does he get all this stuff? Then I remembered. Appalachian State. Ben had majored in business.

"Wanna guess?"

"Nooo ......"

"With his eyes...like you, John. I read that Huizenga had ice-blue eyes like daggers, and they were devastating to the little mom and pop owners when they sat down to negotiate the sale of their businesses. Some of them became...literally...speechless. Of course, all of them became millionaires. The deal included cash; but just enough to close out current debts. The rest was stock in Waste Management. That was a hard sell. They couldn't see it then, but you can guess what happened to the early stockholders of a company doing billions today."

"Yeah, yeah, I know. You see those green Waste Management trucks all over the place."

"Like, thousands of those suckers. One of the largest trucking fleets in the country. Then he turned around and did exactly the same thing all over again with Blockbuster. Bought out hundreds of little mom and pop video rental stores and made those folks wealthy. Did it with his eyes, John."

"Well, Ben...I don't know. I think he had a little bit more going for him besides his eyes. Anyway. Listen, Ben. I've been meaning to bring something up. Got an idea the other day ... got a neat proposal for you. What would you say if I were to buy a couple of rafts, something like a sixteen-foot Hy-Sider, or a NRS Otter, and hire you to recruit some guides ... sort of run the operation."

"Heck yeah, if you could do that, but John, those things cost like five-grand each, and that doesn't count the personal equipment you'd need ... the helmets, paddles, life vests and the PFD's. The Forest Service stipulates that rafting the Nolichucky requires a Class V PFD ... you know, with the high collar that supports your head if you go into the water."

"Well, I understand all that, Ben. It's an invest ..."

"And wetsuits. Spring of the year, you've got to have an assortment of wet ..."

"It's an investment, Ben. Would it require a significant investment? ... sure, but you get that back. It's all considered in the price. The customer pays for that stuff. In the end, it's OPM, Ben. Other people's money."

"But there's a snag you might not know about ... the permit. A license"

"Yeah, yeah, I get that. I would imagine I'd need a permit."

"Oh, yeah. Big time. National Forest. Got to have ... got to get a permit from them. But see, they have limited the Nolichucky to just five permits. Only five permits, John, and they've all been issued. There're only four active. Only four companies are running the Nolichucky right now. One of um wants to sell. So, John, two permits. I overheard Jake Tapper talking about it couple weeks ago. They're willing to sell but they know the value of what they have in hand. The figure I heard was a quarter-mill."

"Quarter? ... quart? ... of a million dollars?"

"Right."

"Quarter of a mill ... ...?"

"Right."

"What did they pay for them ... the original ... "

"Who knows John, maybe like fifty bucks or something. Couple hundred."

"Damn." And we rode in silence for a bit.

Permits, the cost of permits. Something I had failed to consider when working out my budget. Back when I met with

David Sullivan, he had given me a stack of rules and regulations. I looked at that stack ......

"Christ!"

"Huh ... what, you okay??"

"Sorry, Ben. I'm just thinking. Sullivan, remember? David Sullivan? The environmental guy? He's in charge of licensing campgrounds, RV parks, rafting outfits, hostels like me, and other such places, like motels and bed-and-breakfasts. I can understand the bed-and-breakfast, they feed people. That's understandable. But hostels, Ben; hostels! It's just a plastic mattress, Ben. A bunk bed! I'm not feeding ... there's a fifty-dollar fee; an annual fee. You got to get a license to run a hostel. I'm being nickeled and dimed to death here. Looked at my checking account yesterday. Four-hundred-dollar deposit for gas connection. Thirteen-hundred for a floodplain survey. You wouldn't believe how I'm running through money. Like water gurgling down a tub drain the last ten days. But what I'm saying ... Sullivan gave me the rules and regs for running my hostel. Damn thing was half-inch thick ... single-spaced. And then No-Drip ... Christ! ... No-Drip tells me I have to pay for the water meter. Damn, Ben. I'm paying for the water. You'd think they'd supply the thing that measures how much! 1,120 bucks, Ben. And freeze-proof faucets. Forgot all about that. No-Drip mentioned ... cost like fifty, fifty-five bucks each. Telephone. Every hostel's gotta have a pay phone so hikers can call home, call around town looking for things. Who knows how much that'll cost? The shuttle ... Ben, I've got to find a big van seats twelve or fifteen people. I'll be running a minimum of three meal shuttles per day. What's that going to cost me? And ... and ... mattresses? I can't buy just an ordinary mattress. A hostel needs a special, waterproof job. I'll need nine ... custom ... made ... mattresses! I haven't a clue where to start looking."

"Well, John. That's an easy one. I'd call the Nantahala Outdoor Center. I'm living in the guide lodge at USA. We have those mattresses. But NOC has dozens of places. They must have purchased a hundred of them … got um somewhere."

"Thanks, Ben. Good suggestion. Bet they cost like a couple hundred bucks each. Then I got to get them here, probably from Toronto … or China."

* * *

Pulling into the motel parking lot, I saw Montgomery's dog Smitty coming to greet us; nose in the air sniffing. I whistled, and climbed out of Ben's Pinto. Smitty was a shaggy, mixed-breed mutt. Great dog, though. Trots around the parking lot not twenty-five feet from the highway. Never went near it. As if there were an invisible fence. I squatted and gave him a good rub-down with him licking my face. "Good boy. What you been up to today? Keeping that mean ol' black dog away from here, are you?"

"Hey, John. Don't let that pup pester you." Frank said, striding through the parking lot toward me. I stood and we shook hands, and Frank continued. "Warm for this time in June, isn't it? How you coming along on your land deal?"

"Just fine, Frank."

Frank Montgomery and his wife had just come from their quarters each carrying a stack of towels.

"You've reminded me. I've got another load of wash. Okay if I drop it off in the office?"

What a handsome couple. If managing rental property is Frank's second career, I bet he won't be in this dinky place very long.

"Sure, anytime. Debbie will be in the office tonight until around nine."

* * *

"Hello, Bob. John Shores here. Bob, I'm calling about … the bank requires a contract … Bob, I'm going to need a contract. Need for you to work up a basic contract. Bank's gonna want a signed contract me with DeHaven before they'll grant me a line of credit. Can you put something together on that for me? … great … now … here's my problem. I'm going to need that thing pretty … oh, thanks Bob. Friday would be great. Just something simple signed by me and DeHaven … notarized you know … one … one hundred dollars? …sure. Thanks, Bob. Nice round figure. A single-page? Nice. Thanks. I'll see you on Friday."

Two days. Just two days. Sign my life away in two days.

I sank into the motel desk chair still holding the receiver in my hand. During the call, I had paced around holding the cradle portion in one hand and the receiver the other. From the chair, I put the phone on the floor, still holding the receiver. Then I hung up.

What the hell am I getting into here? Debt, that's what. Sell my house and put everything I've got into this project and it goes down the tubes. What then? I'd have nothing. A life time squandered for a silly dream. Sell my house? So proud living in Mountain Brook. I had arrived. The most beautiful community in Birmingham. Just to say the address raised eyebrows. And what a deal! Diving couple. Sudden transfer. Had to move. Quick sell. Twenty grand in cash and assumed the mortgage. The cash got that banker's attention. So happy. Sat on the floor leaning against the wall of the empty living room, just laughing. Look at the size of this room! The furniture I had would fit in one of the closets. Good life living in that house. Roger and all those guys. Boaters and divers. Barbecuing in the back yard. When the recession of the early '80s resolved and the real estate boom began, the value of my home shot skyward. Now, I'm on the verge of blowing it all in one shot. The best investment ... the best move of my life and......

BANG, BANG, BANG.

"Mr. DeHaven! You gave me a heart attack. I was deep in thought when you knocked. You want to come in? Sorry. This place is a mess. I'm so focused, I can't ..."

"Naw, Johnny. I'm heading over to the Rendezvous. Thought you might want to come along."

"Damn right, Mr. DeHaven. I sure could use a cold one right about now."

* * *

When we entered the Rendezvous, the music was up a notch. I didn't see a single one of DeHaven's friends. Same as the last time I was here. The afternoon crowd is younger; louder, a little rough around the edges. Hanging out in a bar every afternoon means they're not working. Idle hands are the devil's playthings. But, I haven't seen much of that in Erwin. DeHaven led the way to one of the booths. I got the notion he wanted to talk. He had come by for a reason.

"How's it going, Johnny?"

"I'm hanging in there, Mr. DeHaven. In a rough spot right now. You know, when an idea comes to you ... in the beginning ... it's all so clear. You think it's more simple than it is. Just do this, and then do that, and after that, you do this other thing ... you know? You're working a list. You make a list. It all looks so simple. Then you do the first item and it starts to fall apart."

"What's falling apart?"

"...... I don't know ... it's the money. I drew up a budget. I was careful. Spent a lot of time thinking and drawing up that budget. I missed a lot of things. It's ... this project ... it's going to take everything I have, Mr. DeHaven. I'm not a rich man.

I've got a good chunk of equity in my house in Birmingham. I've got a little cash laid away. I'm running through that like crazy. Bubba Evely can issue a line of credit equal to what I'm putting in, but, Mr. DeHaven, if I can't make this work, I'm bankrupt. I'm......"

"But, Johnny. You've been in this spot before, haven't you?"

"Before? ... what do you mean?"

"The dive shop. You told me you owned a dive shop."

"Yes, sir. I owned a dive shop with two partners. We did well. We did very well."

"Then you've been here before. That's what I'm saying. You just don't remember. But you've been in this same place, feeling these same feelings. I'm bettin the list you created when you were puttin that thing together fell apart also. Bet your budget missed a lot of things back then too. Right?"

"Well, it was a long time ago. I don't remember."

"Johnny, I'm an old guy, and I can tell you this. We keep dealing with the same things over and over. When you're young, you get impatient or angry every time a problem comes along. When you get old like me, you just say, well, hell, there's that thing again. So, I can tell you something about this. What you're talking about is risk. You're about to risk everything, bet the farm, as they say. Cuttin off the limb where you're sittin. But Johnny, there's risk and then there's risk. The first one is reckless. The second one is thoughtful. Most people when they try their hand at business end up shuttin the door and walking away. But, the rest of um manage to keep going and a few of um get rich. Now, what's the difference? Those that loses has quit. Those that win, just keep going. They don't give up. A problem comes along, a big ol' problem comes along, and somehow they get past it. You been doin that all your life. Like waves on the ocean, problems just keep a-comin. So, Johnny. What I'm saying. You're a smart guy.

You're just lookin at a bunch of tough problems right now. Just push your way through um."

"Mr. DeHaven, I tell you, I don't feel very smart right now. I feel like I'm about to make the biggest mistake of my life. You know? ... I had a great career going. Mr. DeHaven, I'm very good with people. I ran human resources for the *Birmingham News* ... the personnel department, for seventeen years. Now, it wasn't me that went down, it was the newspaper. I could get a great job in HR tomorrow. I could go back to Birmingham and get a great job ... I could pick and choose, Mr. DeHaven."

"I'm sure you're right. I'm sure you could. But Johnny ... you'd be back in a place you've already been. The same ol' same ol. Wouldn't you? You want that? You want to go back instead of forward? Listen to me, Johnny. You go back to Birmingham; you might make a lot of people happy. You might be important to a lot of people. But, you build an Appalachian Trail hostel here in Erwin, Tennessee and you'll become famous. You do a good job with that? ... you put all your people skills in that? ... and there'd be folks all over the world sayin your name."

"You really think a hostel would work here?"

"Oh, Johnny. I know it would work." DeHaven said this softly; looking at me in the kindest way. "I been sittin on that porch forty years. I know it would work. Ain't no mystery to me. A million times they've been tellin me the hardships of stoppin in Erwin. Johnny ... it would work. But son, if you want something new, you got to stop doing something old. That's a rule of life. You can't get something new without giving up something else to get it. And when you do that? ... you don't know where it will go. Can't predict the future. Only fools think they can. What you do is create it. You can do that. You can make your own future. Look around you. That's what everybody's doin every day; taking up new things and changing um till they work."

"Well ..."

"Look, you're sixty feet from where the trail crosses the bridge. I measured. I know. You can't miss lookin at my house. You can't miss. You come down the trail either way and my house is what you see. Now, you put up a big ol' sign says hostel over here, cold drinks, hot showers, clean beds, by damn, Johnny, a bunch of um gonna stop and inquire. I'd bet my life on it."

"Well, that's exactly the bet I'd be making, Mr. DeHaven."

"Now, Johnny. That's not true. See? That's what happens. You get to imaginin things ain't zactly true. Runnin a business ain't like opening a box of tricks, I know that. There ain't no certainty. Nothin is guaranteed. But, Johnny, the smarter you are, the harder you work, the more you think hard and persevere, you cut down on them odds. There's things about you that makes the risk less and less. Don't go imaginin there's a big-ol'-green, fire-breathin dragon out there about to eat you."

"Mr. DeHaven, you're being very helpful. I want you to know ... I want to thank you for your encouragement."

"Well, hell, Johnny. I'm just securin my sale. You lookin all wild-eyed; I don't want you boltin on me." And DeHaven laughed and reached across the table and patted my hand. We sat quiet for a moment, then DeHaven got up and went to the head. I waggled my empty bottle at John, the bartender, and motioned with the neck of it toward DeHaven's bottle. John held up two fingers and I nodded an affirmative.

Man. What a mess. What to do. Like holding the reins of five horses and I don't know which is which. Pull on this one and the wrong head turns. Got to get this together. Got to get this on paper. Losing track. Losing control of this deal. Got to talk to ... Roger ... Mickey ... Charlotte. Got to talk to Charlotte.

"Come on Johnny. You got that look again. What's going through that brain of yours?"

"Mr. DeHaven. Let me run something by you. Tell me what you think. What concerns me is potential cash-flow. I'm most worried about income from the hostel. Nine beds at twenty dollars. Tents in the yard at ten bucks. Maybe not enough. Yes, I'll have hiker shuttles; slack-packers and all that. They pay big bucks for USA drivers to drive them up to the trail. I'll be selling snacks and drinks. I'll be selling equipment; run a little outfitter store. But will that be enough? I want you to know that I've had a lot of encouragement ... Bubba and Anjanette ... others I've met in Erwin. Wonderful people here in Erwin. But I've had some let me know I'm nuts in no uncertain terms. Telling me potential income won't ... winter ... it's a seasonal business with a long winter and nothing coming in."

"Of course." DeHaven drew out the word softly, throwing his hand to the side. "They'll be people tell you that. Lots of people can't see nothin but negative. They relish bringing people down. Ain't nothin pleases them more than to mess up your day. So, what you thinking about? Got another angle?"

"There's a big asset running by the door out there. The Nolichucky River. What I'm thinking, Mr. DeHaven is getting into the river adventures business. A side-line to the hostel. Start off with a couple of rafts. And Ben...you know Ben, the guy driving me around? Well..."

"Yes. I met Ben. Nice kid. We had a little chat when you were out that day measurin the property. A little raggedy, but young folks are like that today. Got no sense of manly pride. I get a haircut every Saturday. Shave first thing every morning. Like my shoes nice and shiny."

"Yeah, I know, but Ben is a great guy. Has helped me a lot. Couldn't have done it without him, actually. Surprisingly interesting and fun to talk to ... well ... what I'm thinking ... Ben is a river guide and he ... Mr. DeHaven ... that shed on the back of your house? What's the size of that?"

"Exactly eight foot by twenty. Me and my brother built it. Solid as a rock. Ain't going nowhere soon."

"Yeah, eight by twenty. Well, I'm thinking of closing it in. Building a high fence maybe fifteen feet out from the house creating a storage space fifteen by twenty. Gate on the road side. Door on the other end looking out at the bathhouse. Getting a couple of Hy-Sider rafts, paddles, personal equipment. All that stuff, and going into the whitewater rafting business. Lot of hikers take a zero coming off the trail at a hostel. Hang around three or four days and ... a zero is ..."

"I know what a zero is. Days off the trail don't count. They're zero days. Rest days. Sick days."

"Right. And after resting a day or so, some of them want to do something different. Something interesting and exciting; like whitewater rafting. We've got one of the most famous whitewater rivers in the country running past our front door. Seems to me a no-brainer."

"Big investment though. Where you gonna get the money? You're saying you're not a rich man and building the hostel will take all you have. What about ..."

"Two things, Mr. DeHaven. First, Bubba might extend my line of credit. If he sees this as a positive, as a for-certain expansion of the hostel's cash flow, a low-risk addition of another income stream, he just might consider it. Secondly, there are experienced river guides who come from wealthy families. And I have a couple of wealthy friends. I could put together a partnership."

"Well, Johnny. You'll wanna give all that some serious thought. Do this and you might be biting off more'n you can chew. You ain't expanding one business. You're talking about two entirely different businesses and startin um both from scratch. Well, I don't know. I don't know ... oh, hell, Johnny! Something just occurred to me. You got to have a permit. Forest Service. You need a license, and there ain't none left. You know that? ...!"

"Yes, I do, in fact. Talked it over with Ben just this afternoon. He said there's a couple of permits for sale though."

"Yes, but you know how much?"

"Heard that too."

"Ol' Paul. You met Paul ... remember?"

"Yes. In fact, I sat next to him here the other night. Really nice guy. Telling me all about his son living in Las Vegas."

"Yeah, I've known Jeremy since he was knee-high to a grasshopper. Smart kid. Lawyer. Did really well in Vegas. But ... well ... Paul, he was in here one night, some time ago, telling us about folks trying to start up a new raftin outfit. From what I understand, they had a shot at one of those permits. Seems one belongs to an outdoor adventure company with only secondary interest in the Nolichucky. That permit is for sale for ... for two-fifty? That what you heard? two-hundred fifty-thou? ... yeah? and the other one belongs to that little outfit, can't think of the name, but they're not doing so well. Over-spent building a fancy restaurant on their property, Paul said, and ran out of money. They let it be known they'd sell, same price. Maybe the two of um got together and fixed the price, who knows. Anyhow, what I'm gittin at, Paul was saying several people have inquired but nobody's interested ... at that price."

"Well, of course. Neither am I. But I'm thinking of approaching the Forest Service. Ask if they would consider issuing a sixth permit, seeing as how two of the existing five are practically dormant. Seems the Forest Service would be willing to exert that pressure for the good of the local economy."

"Well, Johnny. I think you got that backwards. What Paul said was they're not interested in more traffic on the Nolichucky."

"Where'd he get that idea?"

"He knows somebody tried to get the Forest Service to issue a sixth permit. Baxter family. They got more money'n God. One of their boys, James, I think ... got a lawyer and spent months and lots of dough trying to get the Forest Service to expand the permitting. They even got a Senator on their side, ol' Fred Thompson, now that's a powerful guy, that Fred Thompson. But he couldn't convince um. Couldn't move um an inch. Pulled lots of strings in Washington, too. Couldn't do it. The wrench in the gears was the fact that the Forest Service had no interest in it. They've got their hands full with what's on the river now. Don't want more traffic out there. Said if there were six active permits, they'd have to expand operations, and Congress cuttin their budget every year, trimmin'um back left and right."

"Oh, lord. Unbelievable."

"No siree, Bob!" DeHaven said, shaking his head slowly. "It's lucky for you Johnny, you just don't know it. You can't aim at two rabbits even with a double barrel shotgun. You got one good rabbit in your sights right now and, you oughter give it both barrels. I'm tellin you ... I'm tellin you, it's a winner. The hostel's a slap winner."

* * *

DeHaven drove me back to the motel. Climbing out of the van, I said my good-byes and turned to see Frank Montgomery coming out his office door waving a pink call slip at me.

"Hey, John. You got a phone call a little bit ago."

We met in the middle of the parking lot and Frank handed me the call slip.

"No name, do you know who called?'

"Sorry, John. I was out of the office and the housekeeper took the call. She didn't get a name, but it looks pretty urgent."

"Yes, I see. Call ASAP it says here in big letters with two exclamation points. Can't imagine who this would be. Is that the Erwin prefix?" I offered the slip to Frank.

"Yes, it is," he said, without looking.

"Can't imagine who in Erwin would have an urgent need to talk to me, but I'll return the call as soon as I get in the room."

"How's that rafting thing going, John?"

"Dead in the water, Frank," and Frank chuckled at my unintended pun. "I would need a permit, and, long story short, ain't none available," I said, making a goofy face looking at Frank under the brim of my Tilley hat.

"Too bad. I thought it would be a very good addition to the services of your hostel."

"I'm really disappointed. I thought I had a sure thing. Got to come up with something, Frank. I need to strengthen potential cash flow. I'm giving a lot of thought to marketing ... the outfitter store, for instance, building some cabins on the property, got this wild idea of maybe sponsoring a bluegrass festival, but nothing solid.

"Listen, John, while I've got your ear, got this question that's been bugging me. I get whitewater people staying here all the time. I don't know much about it, but I get the sense that the Nolichucky is a big deal. I hear these guys saying they're here in Erwin because the Nolichucky is running high, that the gorge is up to class five or something. What the heck does that mean?"

"Has to do with the rapids in the Nolichucky Gorge, Frank. The river's actual classification is three and four, but at flood stage, it's unofficially a five. Whenever the western flank of Mount Mitchell gets a lot of rain, the tributaries that fork around the mountain there pick up the runoff and all that water gets squeezed into the Nolichucky Gorge. That water running through the gorge becomes some of the best whitewater in the Southern Appalachians."

"And class five, that means something special?"

"Yes it does. Means it's as good as it gets. Class five is ... let me back up a little bit, Frank.

"A river ... a good whitewater river might drop 40 or 50 feet per mile, even more. Over thousands of years, the river cuts through and loosens a lot of rock, and this rock, during periodic ... during massive flooding, gets pushed into piles here and there down the river. Water surging through these rocks absorbs a lot of air bubbles. The frothy water appears white.

"Any river, like the Nolichucky, that has a lot of these points where turbulent water is flowing over a pile of rocks is called a whitewater river, and boating on rivers like this is called whitewater canoeing or kayaking. Boaters also refer to them as steep creeks or rivers."

"So, class five is a high rating, like measuring the difficulty of the river?"

"No, just the rapid ... the classification is given to each specific rapid. Each of the rapids along the river is classified. The Nolichucky, for instance, has rapids class one through class four, officially, but boaters see it as a five during high water. The classification changes depending on a number of factors, but the flow of the river is most significant."

"So, the classification system is one through five."

"Well, there are class six rivers ... class six rivers and rapids. That classification is for a stretch of river that's extreme in every sense of the word, some have never been successfully run. If a number of people do run it and survive, the rapid is reclassified to five...five-plus, some people might say. Yes, there are class six rivers and they are deadly.

"Like Niagara Falls," Frank said, with a chuckle.

"Yeah, like Niagara Falls."

* * *

Roger had sent me the mail he had collected at my Birmingham home. I had gone to the post office to pick it up. On the way back to the motel, I made a call on Anjanette Harris at the Chamber. Turns out, she was the mystery caller with the urgent message.

She was busting at the seams to tell me her new idea. She had been thinking, she said, about my plans for starting up an outfitter store, not realizing that my store would be located at the hostel. She took me outside and pointed down the street at a building for rent. That would be ideal, she said, beaming up at me. Erwin needed such a place, she said. I thanked her and promised I'd look into it. She went back inside and I started across the street.

I was interested, but not for the reason Anjanette suggested. A vague notion had entered my mind days ago. I should have run that past her. I should have mentioned the bicycle shop. Erwin did not have a bicycle shop. In spite of that, the Aldermen had been chewing on the idea of a bike path through town. There were federal and state grants for that purpose, and they were itching to get their hands on the people's money.

Standing at the plate glass store-front, I cupped my hands to block light and peered into the store's interior.

Narrow, but very deep.

I stepped away, walked to where, looking through the window, I could estimate the location of the northern interior wall. Then, stretching my normal stride a little, I walked to the approximate position of the opposing wall.

Seven paces. Twenty, maybe twenty-one feet. Pretty narrow for a commercial space. But man, that building goes way, way back.

I walked to the corner and turned left down to where I could look into the alley. I could see the rear wall of the building down the alley from where I stood. Placing my foot where I thought that would come out, I strode the distance back up the street to the corner of the first building. All of these fronts lined up down the block.

Thirty-six paces. Roughly one-hundred and ten feet. Long; long and very narrow. Twenty by one-hundred-ten. But what the heck. It's bicycles. Put them in a long row facing the south wall. Put helmets and accessories on the other wall. Modular wire shelving along that wall. Hang an especially good-looking bike in the front window. Set-up the repair-shop toward the back. Sales. Need some sort of counter, maybe an island towards the front.

I stepped backwards and looked up.

An apartment?

If I were to open a bike shop, I'd need a place to live. I had a place in DeHaven's house. If I build a hostel there, I'd live on the property. I was starting to get that feeling, that rush of discovery. I looked up at those dusty windows with different eyes.

Three tall windows. Is that all? These store-fronts join along the sides. No windows down the side. Skylights?

To get a fuller view, I jaywalked across the street and stood for a little bit imagining my bicycle shop in that space. The town had a good feel. Not much traffic for a downtown commercial area—there were some empty stores here and there—but it didn't look rundown like so many other small towns.

"Can I help you ... are you looking for someone?"

I turned to see a man about my own age striding down the sidewalk toward me. "No, sir. Just looking at that building over there, looking at the town...comercial."

"I'm coming back from the post office, I see you standing here in front of my shop, I'm coming back and for a whole block you didn't move an inch. Thought you were lost, or something."

"No, I'm thinking about moving to Erwin, maybe doing business here. Just wondering how these downtown merchants are doing."

"You won't find a better place. Lived here all my life."

"Oh, I like the town for sure, nice people, great people, I'm just wondering how the town is doing, businesswise."

"Clinchfield Railroad is keeping us steady. Coal production in the Central Appalachians doesn't fluctuate much. They're hauling about the same amount of coal today as in the late 70s."

"That's surprising. I had the impression the coal industry was in trouble."

"Well, it might soon turn the other way. Coal's share of energy production has surged nearly 20% in the last decade. I'm no expert, but from what I understand, coal production out west has nearly doubled."

"And you think this might have a positive effect on business here in downtown Erwin?"

"Certainly hope so; think it will, yes ... in the long run, but it's the young folks here's gonna make the difference. Some of the younger merchants started talking about getting together, form some kind of a renegade group to challenge the Mayor and Aldermen."

"Okay ... that's interesting."

"Yeah, the town's missing the boat, they all think. Since highway 23 was turned into Interstate 181 up there, all the new business went to Johnson City. Well, the same highway runs right past us, doesn't it? So, the young businessmen around here want the town to start thinking like we're in the 21st Century instead of the 19th. We can't afford the backward thinking any longer. Not a single restaurant around here can serve you a cold beer. Who's gonna stop in Erwin if you can't get a cold one with your pizza?"

"Well, you certainly have a point there."

"I'm sorry, look at me, up on my soap box again. Sorry bout that, just gets my dander up. Hey, my name's Jay Blevins," and he stuck out his hand and shook mine vigorously.

"John Shores. I'm from Birmingham, Alabama. I'm here considering some business prospects."

"And you're interested in that building there," he said nodding toward the building across the street.

"I am, sort of, yes."

"Well, by golly, I've got the key. Do you want to take a look at it? I'm a friend of the owner, and I have a key in case something happens over there. You want to take a look? I can take an early lunch break and ..."

"Sure, if it isn't too much ..."

"Naw! Com'on. I'll show you the place. Got a renovated apartment upstairs. You'll like it. Really nice. Here, I'll just step into the shop a minute, tell Doris I'm going to lunch, and get the key."

* * *

I entered the room that evening entirely new, excited, bounding with energy. A bike shop here in Erwin appeared to be the greatest of opportunities. I felt nothing but profound relief; and once more, and finally I believed, I had struck upon a thing that mattered. My life had been that way. Every time a door closed another opened even better than the one before. Every new adventure had brought vigor and potency, transporting me into a new understanding of the meaning of my life.

I had already determined that Erwin was a great little town. Everybody I had met seemed so friendly. I had no problem imagining myself in this town for the rest of my life.

I kept telling myself, who wouldn't want to do this? A bike shop! The simplest of businesses. One basic product. You sell them and you service them. A cakewalk compared to the dive business. I counted five reasons why someone would want to own a bicycle. I couldn't think of another. Simplicity itself. Selling them would be a simple question. You want this one, or that one? The whole idea made me feel good. Bicycles have an aura; whizzing along on two wheels, you just feel good. They epitomize freedom. They symbolize good health. It's a return to nature, about as eco-friendly as anything can be.

Not only that, the building was perfect. Downtown Erwin. Plenty of nearby parking. A place to live. Only $600 for the whole thing. Just amazing. I reckoned the owner was desperate to rent a property sitting vacant for who knows how long.

I called for a pizza delivery, and by the time it came and I had finished the last slice, everything had changed. A dozen problems related to the hostel on DeHaven's property had crept back into my consciousness. In spite of my efforts to set them aside with the same confidence and excitement as I had felt earlier, every problem that popped into my mind brought with it a sense of doom.

I had lost my grip on the bicycle shop idea. The thought of switching my focus away from the hostel brought anxiety, but neither could I simply dismiss it. I kept asking myself, why am I hanging onto this? I wanted to dump the hostel idea and get on with the bicycle shop, simply let it go, but I couldn't. I was in a quandary. If ever there was a time in my life that defined that word, it was this one. Perplexity, uncertainty, dilemma.

What to do, I kept asking; what to do? In just two days I would meet DeHaven in Bob Manuel's office and sign away every asset, every penny I owned.

It came to me that my problem was making a decision. Just weigh the advantages and disadvantages of these two business ideas and make a decision. With that, I remembered a decision-making tool I had recommended to my staff and certain department heads at the *News*; the old pro/con T-chart. Take a sheet of plain paper, draw a line down the middle, label one column the positives and the other the negatives, look them over, assign relevance on a scale one through five, and make a decision. Simple.

My room had a desk, and I sat there and began drawing up the chart. After drawing the line down the center of the page and writing "cons" on the left and "pros" on the right, I stared at the empty page.

Simple. This problem can be cleanly divided into two opposing views. I'll need two of these charts. First, the hostel.

Across the top I wrote: "Do I build the Hostel?" I scratched that out and wrote, "Is Building the Hostel the Best Use of My Time and Resources?" I gribbled that sheet and hovering over the trash can, dropped it like bombs away. I got out two sheets of paper and drew the lines. On one, I wrote, simply: "Hostel?" The other I titled, "Bike Shop?"

This is a major decision. Facts versus various opinions. Advantages and disadvantages. Strength and weaknesses of my plan to build a hostel in Erwin, Tennessee. And if not? ... A logical alternative?

After several hours, much of it spent pacing around the room, I had two T-charts, one in each hand. I set them carefully side by side on the bed and stood looking at them. I reached down and gently tapped the edge of one into a perfect parallel with the other, more anxious now than before I started.

This did not help.

* * *

One thirty. Crap! Five hours till morning. One day. One day to go. Man. Man, o' man. I need some sleep.

I had awakened with a start. Had heard my father call my name; heard my name spoken loudly like a shot in the dark. My ears were ringing. Looked at the clock glowing blood red on the night table. Got up. Opened the cooler and fished through the melting ice for a Mountain Dew.

Hot night for June. Almost July. Been here nearly two weeks.

Pacing around holding the unopened can against my head, I stopped and parted the curtains with one finger. Looking out at the silent parking lot, the highway oddly pale, empty, and foreign in the hazed lights from across the street, I felt like Martin Sheen in Francis Ford Coppola's *Apocalypse Now* waiting for his assignment in a cheap Saigon hotel.

Pacing back and forth, I finally turned and sat in the upholstered chair in the corner with the cold can against my forehead.

Air conditioner's not much. More noise than air.

I pulled the cooler over with my foot and, sliding down, propped my legs; put my head back against the wall, the dewy can against my temple; one side...then the other.

Man! One day to go. Do I really want to do this? Like getting married. Like standing before the preacher; whole damn rest of the world; and I'm saying forever and ever amen. Need somebody to talk to. Roger. Got to call Roger. Solid as a rock. Great guy. Listens to you. Hears what you're saying even when you're not sure, not sure what you're trying to say, miss him, miss Stallworth, miss Mickey. And I miss Charlotte. Wish you were here, Baby. I need to talk. Need your head on my shoulder where I can tell you the mess I'm in.

Just as on the trail, I unrolled my sleeping bag over the sleeping pad, and using my laundry bag as a pillow, I lay down, I slowly came back to normal. Wasn't so hot after all. Must have been me. Been in that bag under all kinds of circumstances. Felt like home. As soon as I crawled on top that bag, I began to think more clearly.

Just call my friends. How simple is that? Sometime tomorrow, the decision will suddenly become easy. Hostel or bike shop? As DeHaven said. People decide and then they make it work. The decision is not nearly as important as the resolve. Just call my friends. Stallworth. Roger. Charlotte ... just talk it out. Simple. Simple consensus.

One thing I had learned as manager of HR at the *Birmingham News*, the harder the decision, the less likely it is you'll make a mistake. Get the facts, make a decision, then go with it. That's what my grandfather used to say. Bogie. We called him Bogie. Imagine the worst-case scenario, Bogie would say. Do that, and you discover, even given the worst possible outcome, you'll survive. Just knowing that'll calm you down. One time ... I was eleven, had to choose between football and the trumpet. Play for Coach Ross or play in the band. Coach wanted me. I was small, but I was tough and loved the game. A hard decision for a little boy. I was so nervous I cried. Couldn't sleep. First get comfortable, Bogie had said. He had knelt by my bed, was patting my hand. Lie on your side, he had said. I was just a kid. Put your hands under your face, then smile. Actually close your eyes and smile, he had said. Then concentrate on your breathing. Feel the air entering your nose. Concentrate on that. You can't think of two things at once, Johnny, Bogie said. So, think about your breathing. Just breathe and listen to it. Pay attention to it.

Breathe ...

Breathe ...

Breathe ...

Bogie liked to sing. He sang to me that night. I was just a kid. He sang, I remember, Softly. He had a rough, growling voice that would break on the high notes. Just above a whisper. I loved to hear him sing. His favorite was a hymn. He sang it all the time. Something about sparrows.

How did that go ... sparrows?
Why should I......
Why should I feel discouraged, why should the ...
Hmm, hum...His words I hear
And...something...something
Should the shadows come
Hmm, humm ... hum
I lose my doubts and fears
His eye is on ......
His eye is on the sparrow ...... (That's it.)

His eye is on the sparrow
And I know he's watching me.
I sing because I'm happy
I sing because I'm free
He watches me
I lose my doubts and fears
Just one step … one step
His eye on the sparrow
He watches me
His eye
He watches me
His eye is on …
The sp…
Sparrow
Sp

* * *

"Anjanette? Hi, this is John Shores. Fine, thank you. Listen, Anjanette, I'm sorry to bother you at home so early, but I'm wondering if you'll be in your office this morning. Yes? Could I pop in for a little bit? Sure. Thanks. Well, about nine thirty? Great, Anjanette. Good, good. I'm running out of time on … well, I'll explain when I see you, but I need your opinion on something that's come up. Promise not to take much of your time. Well, I know, but you're a busy lady and I'm just one of your … thanks, Anjanette. I really appreciate your interest. See you in a bit."

Anjanette, what a sweetheart. Wish to hell I had her energy. Could use a transfusion about now.

After grabbing a couple of egg sandwiches at JD's, I took a large coffee to go and started off toward town. Reaching Spring Street and making my turn toward Carolina, I spun right around and retraced my steps. I had forgotten my folder.

I had returned to Dollar General and picked up a thin accordion folder. All my notes, plus my pen and legal pad were back in the motel room. Wasn't sure I would need that stuff meeting with Anjanette, but it didn't feel right leaving without it.

Now, with notes under arm, a coffee from the motel office, and my Tilley hat, which I had also left behind, I pushed off toward town once again.

Think, think, think, Shores. The T-chart on the hostel didn't look good. Not at all. As many cons as pros. Nothing was outstanding. Just ... when you looked at that thing, the feeling wasn't good. Not good in the gut where it counts.

* * *

Reaching the Chamber, I crossed over Main Street and continued to the alley. Don't know why, but I wanted to walk through the alley. Just take a look. I stopped at the back of my building and looked up.

Not much to look at. Rear entry. No exterior stairs to the second floor. No delivery back here. Alley too narrow. Deliveries ... through the front. Swell.

As I entered the Chamber of Commerce building, Anjanette called out a cheerful hello.

"Hi Anjanette, thanks so much for seeing me."

"No problem, John. That's my job. I'm here for you."

"Cutting to the chase, Anjanette, I've run into a couple of snags in my plans for the hostel, and I've come up with an alternate idea. I need some advice. Now ... about the hostel, basically, a couple of potential income sources seem not likely. I ... actually ... I don't want to get bogged down explaining those problems. Basically it's a feasibility problem. But ... that building you showed me the other day. You know Jay Blevins?

Jay ... really nice guy. Jay happened to have a key. Showed me the place. We walked through the building. He showed me the apartment. Have you seen it?"

"No. the work was done before I came to the Chamber. You'd never know the place was available. There's never been a sign in the window. I heard about it from another member. I understand they converted the upstairs apartment into loft space, and that it's really nice."

"Yes. It's great. Really. Perfect for me. Would be a great place to live. Right here in town. So, Anjanette, I'm thinking about a bicycle shop. Putting a bicycle shop ... sales and service ... putting that in there. Erwin doesn't have one, and what I'm wondering is if Erwin has the demographics to support such a thing."

"John, I ...."

"Before you answer, Anjanette, let me ... let me explain something. Back in Birmingham, I owned a dive shop. For quite a few years. Had two partners. We did well. So, I've had that experience. There are certain similarities between a bike shop and a dive shop. We did repairs. We sold a wide range of accessories. We were dealers for certain prominent manufacturers. We successfully wrangled those dealerships. I know how to work with manufacturers. I can do the same with cycling gear. In one sense, there's not much difference between selling and servicing ... say ... ScubaPro regulators or Schwinn bicycles. There's no one-size-fits-all with either of those products ... you know, regulators or bicycles. You don't put your customer on any old bicycle any more than you would strap on a tank and say, there you go, sir. You have to know what the customer wants to do. How he or she is going to use what you're selling. I'm good at that. I was damn good at the dive business and I feel certain what I learned and experienced there will transfer here. So, what I'm saying is, I'm not a newbie, Anjanette, I'm not ..."

"John, I can just look ... people can just look at you and feel confident that you would be excellent at anything you chose to do."

"Thank you Anjanette. I didn't want you to think I was being naïve in this. Lots of people think all you have to do is open your door and people come pouring in and you make millions. I would never consider a flower shop or an antique store, but a bike shop is something I know I can do."

"Well, John, let me answer your question; your concern about demographics. There are only six thousand people in Erwin. But John, there are eighteen thousand residents in Unicoi County. It is the fifth smallest county geographically in Tennessee. Although the county is long and narrow, this part of downtown is nearly the center. This means, with the shape and size of the county, no one would be more than fifteen minutes from your door. And you are right, we don't have a bike shop here, yet you see kids riding bikes all over. You see older couples riding for the exercise. Where do they get those bikes repaired? In Johnson City. Nearest place."

"That's enough right there to keep someone from buying a new bike. Something happens, got to take it all the way to Johnson City. I'd say there's pent-up demand right here in Erwin."

"And that backlog of potential buyers would kick start your business, John. Now, you said you had success in talking to Bubba, that he would grant you a pretty substantial line of credit. Have you talked to him about the bike shop idea?"

"Won't have to do that, Anjanette. I won't need to borrow money. Just like the dive shop, I can finance the operation by floor planning the bikes and, for accessories, most of the manufacturers will extend a line of credit. I'm sure my dive shop experience will enable me to swing that. And regarding floor planning, I've got enough money coming in monthly to cover the interest. Whichever bank handles the deal will be encouraged by the fact that I'll be getting the dealership for top-of-the-line bikes. With no other nearby competition, I'm sure to get the attention of the top manufacturers."

"Well, John. Honestly. I don't know what would stop you. This is a no-brainer."

"I'll still sell my house in Birmingham. That'll provide startup funding. But think of this. If I were to do the hostel, I'd be pushed to get that thing sold by the first of the year. Got a lot of little repairs need doing. Some painting. Clean up the landscape ... curb-appeal, you know? But with the bike shop, I'm under no specific time frame. No deadline."

"Well, John, like I say ..."

"One more thing, Anjanette, I've got a close friend in Birmingham owns a bike shop. Taught him and his wife to scuba dive. We've become good friends, spent lots of time together on trips. I called Riley and Sue. They loved the idea, were really encouraging, offered to help me any way they could, said they'd speak to manufacturers on my behalf, in fact, they invited me to come live with them for a month or so, would even pay me to come work with them in the shop, said they'd draw up lists of accessories, pointing out the more popular lines, and so forth. I'd spend a month or six weeks with them, come back here and get the space in shape. Install modular shelving myself. I'm thinking of getting an art major over at ETSU to paint a mural on the south wall where I plan to display the bikes. Anjanette, I think I can get all this done in time for the holiday season. Plenty of time to sell my house. I figure I'd get something like ten-grand above what rushing the sale would bring me."

"Shorter hours, John. The hostel would be round the clock. If I owned a bike shop, I'd be closed Sunday and Monday. Not open, like, till ten in the morning."

"November and December would be the busy season, off-season for the river guides. They are great personalities. Perfect part-time help. And when I ran the dive shop, we had high school kids doing regulator repairs. Kids would kill for a part-time job like that." I began ticking off additional advantages on my fingers. "Won't need the fifteen-passenger van. Won't need to borrow money from anybody. Jay said the owner won't be asking for a deposit. Rent, he believes is something like $600. Unbelievable. Includes the apartment. And, Anjanette, I've got a ton of furniture. I can make that loft look like a million dollars."

"John, we'd love to have that business on Main Street." Then Anjanette leaned forward a little and cupped one hand around her mouth and went, "Pssssst," with her eyes all wrinkled up. "Let me tell you something," she whispered. "You're the first to know. A little serendipity for you, John." And she stood back, beaming. "A bike path, a cycling-walking path winding over five miles through Erwin will be announced before the next Alderman and Mayor's election."

* * *

Even though the conversation with Anjanette could almost be described as thrilling, it had not cemented a decision. Or, maybe anything close to decision was simply deferred due to my plan to consult close friends that I valued and trusted.

Earlier that morning I had sketched out a list of topics and questions. Somewhere in the process, I thought of Mickey Townsend. I had determined that Mickey ought to be my first call. Mickey was older. Well, so was Stallworth, but Stallworth had that buoyant boyishness. Like me, Stallworth tended to have an ear for the unusual; a penchant for innovative thought; a leading-edge recklessness in his concepts or propositions. It was the seriousness of Mickey Townsend, his serious demeanor, his no-nonsense approach to everything that caused him to be generally venerated as wise; to be looked up to for his judgment and experience.

I met Mickey on the day I started work at the *Birmingham News*. I didn't warm to him quickly, though. He was the public relations director, and our roles at the newspaper rarely crossed paths. But, like everyone else at the *News*, I came to value his opinion on almost everything. Soon we were having lunch together once a week. I discovered he had a keen mind and a willingness to discuss any issue that interested or bugged me. We became fast friends. So, he was at the top of my list.

Mickey had retired several months earlier. He had suffered a serious heart attack. After a few visits my own circumstances kept me away and unaware of his current condition. I had called Andy Smith, the circulation director at the *News*, to make sure Mickey was fit to receive my call. He and Andy were best of friends. I was astonished by Andy's description of Mickey's surging health and intriguing activities. When I got Mickey on the phone, I praised his spirit and strength. We talked about the good times back when the newspaper was leading Birmingham's response to the civil rights movement. Together we had represented the newspaper at the opening of the Birmingham Civil Rights Institute, and the following year, at the opening of the Alabama Jazz Hall of Fame Museum.

After this pleasant conversation, which we both enjoyed, I brought up my dilemma. I explained how I ended up in Erwin, Tennessee, how I had stumbled upon the opportunity to build an Appalachian Trail hostel, and how that had led to the discovery of a great, inexpensive location for a bicycle sales and service business. Mickey, God bless him, was no help at all.

He thought both ideas were risky and the whole idea that I was facing a dilemma, fringed on insanity. Those were his words. In a voice bordering on anger, he told me in no uncertain terms that I belonged in the personnel business. He spent a great deal of time telling me how successful I had been, how others had thought me genius, and finished his rant by insisting that I return to a human resource position right away. Then came the only valuable thing in his whole spiel; and I must admit, it gave me pause. He said that if I waited so much as another three months, my value as an HR department head would begin to decline. I understood his point. He was right. The key to success in my field was keeping up with the myriad rules and regulations swarming down on you from three directions; local, state, and federal governmental agencies. And when I say "agencies," I mean dozens, including some I had never heard of before getting into the business. These regulations changed, it seemed to me, on a daily basis. If I were to return tomorrow and get a job heading some big corporation's HR department, I would spend the entire first year playing catchup.

I thanked Mickey, and it was a heartfelt thanks, for his time and his interest in me. We ended on pleasant terms and with promises that we would get together as soon as I got back to Birmingham.

I dialed the next number from memory. Clarke Stallworth was, no question, my best friend; a wonderfully good friend. I was disappointed by the voicemail message that informed all callers that Clarke was out of the country and would return calls on the fifteenth, so please leave a short message and phone number. I had so looked forward to what Stallworth might have to say about my adventure. He was a brilliant man, and I had imagined our conversation, had used the imagining of our conversation as solace during my darker moments in this struggle.

So, Roger and Charlotte, I hung up thinking; it's between us. My fate lies with you guys. Please be home. Please be in a mood to talk. I decided to call Charlotte last. I wanted to have all the details before I talked to her. She was my principal confidant. Her opinion counted by a factor of one hundred. I valued our relationship. It was the most precious thing in my life. I would not let anything happen to that. I would walk through a bed of white-hot coals if necessary. I adored her; she was my darling.

* * *

Okay, Roger. Please be home this time.

"Roger? It's me again. Did you get my message? Right. That's right, Roger. No, nothing new on the hostel. Exactly, Roger. That's what I want to do. So ... this'll take a few minutes. Are you sitting in a comfortable place? Okay, sure. Good idea, take some notes and just stop me if I get ahead ... right ... okay. So I'll just give you the rundown, get straight through it and then you ask the questions. Sure. Well, Roger, it's a great location. Right on Main Street. And, like I said in my message; no competition. And the apartment, the loft, man, you wouldn't believe."

So, I apprised Roger of the opportunity before me just as I had done with Anjanette. Pretty much the same story. I had it about memorized by now. Ben ... Anjanette ... I even spent an hour or so with Frank Montgomery one night. Everybody thought the bicycle shop would score big time. The loft was the cherry on top. Roger listened to my story. Heard the whole thing. When I stopped, he asked a stunner.

"Why did you leave the newspaper?"

"Roger, it just wasn't fun anymore. I had begun to hate my job, and I couldn't ... I can't live that way, Roger. I think we talked about that very thing back then, didn't we?"

"So, fun ... loving what you do, popping out of bed in the morning excited, that's important to you?"

"Absolutely. Couldn't have said it better myself."

"Every third weekend, it was your turn to manage the dive shop. Something like that?"

"That's right."

"How'd you feel on those mornings, John? You pop out of bed on those mornings?"

"Roger .... I ..."

"Before you answer that, John, I want you to think about something else. I want you to get an equation in mind. Got that? We're looking for asserting the equality of several quantities. Here goes. You might want to imagine a pie chart. Get the image of a pie chart in your mind. So, okay, John ... how much time have you spent cycling as compared to hiking, canoeing, kayaking, whitewater rafting? No...no, John. It's not that. I'm not getting at that. Let me finish. In terms of the people, John. How many hikers...compared to cyclists? So that pie chart. Slice up that pie proportionally. Hikers, canoeists, kayakers, rafters, and cyclists."

"Roger ... I really don't..."

"I can see that pie, John. I've known you for a long time. I think if you sat on one side of the table and me on the other drawing that pie chart, when we compared them, they'd look remarkably similar. I know you, John. On our canoe trips, I see how you interact with the other people. You have charisma. People like you, really like you, and do you know why? You are very good at what you do, and you share. You help people because you like people. I think you have a sense of all that, but there is something I'll bet you're missing. You interact so well with these people because you, and all of them, are in your element. Whether it is canoeing, rafting, hiking, it takes place, for you, John, in a very special place. There is a spiritual dimension...John, nature means something to you. When you are on the trail or on the river, you are in a spiritual place."

"Roger, I'm ... yes, you're right. I see that."

"John, you're not going to get that higher energy and consciousness in a bike shop. It may become the best business in all of Erwin. You might make a lot of money. But, is that what you're looking for? Will you hop out of bed all excited because you have a hot lead on selling an expensive bike? No, you don't need to answer that John, because I know the answer. Our emotions are determined by how we feel about ourselves and about life in general. It is imperative that we make sure we are in the right place doing the right things. Now, that's a very vague thing, John, when said that way, but every single person in the world knows what's right for him and what doing the right thing means. Discover your purpose, John, and you become and remain healthy, happy and fit. It's a spiritual thing. That's why you hit the trail. We had that talk, remember? You needed to get outdoors, get on the trail, get that feeling, and breathe that air. And look at you. Look what it did. You became so packed with energy, you invented two powerful new opportunities in less than a week!"

Then Roger hit me with something totally unexpected. He said that ever since I'd called him, on that first day in Erwin, he'd been thinking about how he could help. He needed a little spiritual energy himself. What would I think, he said, about his coming to Erwin, driving the long-bed pickup, pulling his popup camper.

"John, I've got a friend you've never met. Richard. We used to paddle a Grumman sixteen-footer. Fifteen years ago. First trip we ever took was down the Ocoee. A tandem. Aluminum. I don't think you were canoeing back then, but a Grumman tandem was the big thing back in those days."

"Oh, sure, Roger. I've paddled tandem. Owned that Grumman once."

"Yeah? Well, Richard's a carpenter. Darn good carpenter. I think Richard might be interested in a new adventure. Got all the necessary tools. Good draftsman. Can help you draw up a complete list of materials. He's good, John. Good friend. Been friends for years."

Roger went on to say they'd help me build the bathhouse. Live on the property with me. Said he would, in fact, do all the cooking. I don't know if it was his offer to help or his offer to cook that clinched the deal for me. Roger was a terrific cook, and my mouth watered thinking about barbequed pulled pork, ribs, salmon, and his magnum opus—Cajun red beans and rice.

"Absolutely," I said. "Absolutely."

"Great, John. I'll see you day after tomorrow. Are you in a double, or will I have to sleep on the floor?"

"Hey, buddy. You know I'm looking after you. I'll reserve a room other end of the building. Your snoring, Roger. Remember? Remember how you'd come off the river and find we'd moved your tent fifty feet from everybody?"

* * *

"Hi Baby. How've you been? ... I know, I know, but I've been through a bunch of ... no, I don't blame you. I'd feel the same way had you ... but baby, just listen ... okay, okay ... now baby, you ... no, I'm not in Damascus. No ... that's right ... no ... Yes, that's it. I'm still in Erwin. That's right. Still here because ... well, I can explain that, baby, you just have to stop a minute and let me talk. Okay, I will. I'll do that. But first ... yes, baby. That's ... No, you are exactly right. I am sorry ... yes I am. I'll make it up to you, I promise, but right now, I need for you to listen ... okay? ... okay."

I told my story to Charlotte. I explained everything that had happened since the day I had stepped onto DeHaven's porch. I took a good bit of time describing the property, the house, and what I planned to build regarding the hostel. I told her the AT passed not sixty feet from the front door. I told her about the Nolichucky. The rafting and canoeing on the Nolichucky. I described Erwin. That I felt really good about Erwin. Erwin, I said, is the friendliest town I had ever had the pleasure to visit. Low cost of living. Bunch of nice rental houses less than eight hundred. Less than one-half hour to Johnson City, and that JC had everything, just like Birmingham, including a huge regional teaching hospital--a great job opportunity for her. Less than an hour to the fantastic town of Asheville, North Carolina. And for her daughter, Claire? Erwin's got one of the best school systems in Tennessee. I described Anjanette. I described Bob Manuel and Bubba. Told the story of Bubba's enthusiastic support and willingness to help financially. Then I described the building on Main Street. I described the loft apartment is glowing detail. I ran through the particulars that made opening a bicycle sales and repair business in Erwin such a great opportunity. Then I explained my problem, the agony I had experienced trying to map out the remainder of my life and how important it would be for her to be in it with me. That I missed her terribly. Then I asked the big question. I want to be with you, I said. I want to spend the rest of my life with you. So, Charlotte, I said, where do you want to be? Will it be Birmingham, or Erwin? And if you came to Erwin, how would you see me? Which of these scenarios fits me best—me running a hostel, or me running a bicycle shop like Riley, back in Birmingham? I finished by explaining that Bob Manuel had drawn up a contract, that on Friday ... tomorrow, I would be meeting with DeHaven and signing that contract, there would be no turning back. And that was my worry. A big, big commitment. She had not said a word the whole time I talked. It made me nervous. I was surprised by her answer.

"John, you've been a busy man."

"Yes, baby, I have. I'm so sorry. I'll ..."

"Which of these two entrepreneurial efforts interests you the most?"

"Well, baby, I was leaning toward the bicycle shop until I talked to Roger and he ..."

"You talked to Roger?"

"Yeah, just hung up. Roger said ..."

"You talked to Roger ... today?"

"Yes, baby. I ...."

"You called him, but you didn't call me?"

"I called you baby ... we're talking right now."

....

"Charlotte?"

Charlotte?

.... (sigh)

"Listen baby. I called you last because I wanted to know as much as possible before we talked. You ... believe me Charlotte, your opinion is the one that counts. I intentionally waited until after six to call you tonight. I wanted you to be home and settled in. You would have been ..."

"John. It's okay," she said softly. The most wonderful three words I had ever heard. "You just don't know how much I worried. You called me when you got to Erwin, what? around the tenth? and now it's the twenty-third? I had a dream last night you were eaten by a bear. No...wait a minute. You've been talking. Now it's my turn. John, I like the hostel opportunity. The primary advantage from my point of view...you'd be building a tangible asset that could be sold when you retire. Acquiring and improving a piece of property. Can't do that with a rented store front. And there are a couple of other things you haven't mentioned. You say there is about an acre of open land? You could build some little cabins like those in Hot Springs. Remember that? When we canoed the French Broad? You could offer fishing ... what would you call that? guided fishing on the Nolichucky? Out-of-town fishermen come in, stay in your cabins, spend a weekend or a week fishing the Nolichucky. You could teach canoeing and kayaking lessons. Knock out a wall or two in that house and expand on your outfitter store idea. John, an Appalachian Trail hostel is you. That's, you baby. Your background in scouting? You could position yourself as a mentor to hikers."

"Baby, what am I going to do tomorrow?"

"Sign the contract, John. I can't see you in a bicycle shop. It's not like the dive shop. You're wrong there. You were in the dive business because it financed your own passion for diving. You got to dive the Caribbean and Australia for free. Don't you remember how cramped you felt when you had to man the store on your weekend? Inside all day, John? That's not you. You'll love the hostel. Running a hostel's more like managing human resources. An AT hostel? It's half negotiating and half consulting. What you're good at doing. You'll love every single second, those hikers coming in, asking you for advice, the fact that you are a critical component to a successful hike. John, that's you. Sign the contract, baby."

* * *

"Excuse me John, I'm about coffee'ed out." And with this, Ben reached and emptied his cup into the football-sized hole in the floorboard and tossed the cup over his shoulder into the back seat. A newly organized back seat, I noticed. Ben had a system going. Laundry day was also trash collection day. The back seat, except for the coffee cup and a balled-up empty brown-paper bag from this morning's trip to JD's, was free of trash. A stack of neatly folded shirts and cargo shorts took up only about one-third of the space on the back seat. For the first time I noticed two cardboard boxes. The one behind the driver's seat was closed, its flaps interlocked. The other, which was larger and open, held an assortment of rafting gear; a throw-bag, a tangle of tie-down straps, his helmet, and a shorty wetsuit. Except for what appeared to be dried white paint, the back seat looked neat and orderly.

"Thought I'd better clean up a bit, since we'll have another passenger this morning," Ben said, having noticed my appraisal of the rear compartment.

"Nahh, Ben. I think DeHaven's gonna drive his truck. I'll be riding with him. I'll still pay you the twenty," I said, as we glanced at each other. "You're relieved of duty this morning." Even though I had said this cheerfully, Ben looked stricken by this change in plans, and I felt the need to explain. "It isn't the space that's the problem. It's the exhaust fumes leaking through the floor."

"Yeah, yeah. I been meaning to seal the floor back there with roof coating. Just can't seem to get around to it."

"Well, Ben, who knows? It might be coming through the trunk, or from under the seat. You probably need to replace the muffler and tail pipe. Tail pipe's rusted off under there nearly to the muffler. That's probably the problem right there."

"Replacing the muffler's more than the car's worth, John."

"Well, Ben. You need to maintain your investment here."

This led to an intellectually-stimulating attempt to solve a mystery we had discovered. With exhaust fumes seeping up through the car's porous flooring, you would assume rolling down the windows would help. In fact, it made the situation worse. Of course, keeping the windows closed was not an option either, but the question remained; what principle of physics brought this on? The solution was obviously based on valid principles. In short order, we were contrasting Bernoulli's conservation of energy with Newton's third law. The car created drag in the volume of air we were moving through; a kind of air-foil, Ben insisted. When the windows were rolled down, it must create a vacuum inside the car, he explained. The same, the exact same vacuum phenomenon that lifts an airplane into the air. In terms of a wing, this physical effect was undisputable, but my pointing out that the car didn't look like a wing to me did not quell the debate, and the issue had not been resolved by the time Ben pulled in behind DeHaven's old white cargo van.

* * *

Ben backed out into River Road and turned to cross the bridge. DeHaven backed out and followed. At the end of the bridge over the Nolichucky, the mint-green Pinto with its orange fender and steel-gray passenger-side door turned right, heading back to Ben's bunk at USA Raft. The old, dirty-white, Ford Econoline van turned left onto Chestoa Pike, heading for downtown and Bob Manuel's office.

"Bob put together what I asked," I said. "Simple, one-pager."

"Well, it's a waste of your money, John. Like I told you, my word's better'n a contract you could unroll down Main Street."

"It's the bank. Not me. You know I trust you. The bank says we got to do this. It's procedure."

"Bubba knows me. Knows my word's good as gold."

"It goes beyond Bubba, Mr. DeHaven"

"Waste of time in my opinion."

* * *

"It always works out. It always does... ya know."

Over the years, I had heard Roger Perrin say those words exactly that way twenty times. He had been the president of the Bama Back Paddler's Association, and the leader of countless canoe trips. In his leadership role, he always projected a positive attitude. Roger was a big man, powerful looking, a big man with that serious, gritty look you see in certain bikers, which he had been in an earlier life. And for an ex-Harley rider, he was remarkably self-disciplined and moral; uncompromising in his standards. These qualities gave Roger stature among his fellow canoeists. He was solid as a rock. I don't know if Roger was religious. He never mentioned it. But he was spiritual. Not deliberately. No, you got none of that from Roger, but his calm, fatherly demeanor told you he was a little higher and a little more self-conscious than your average person. People behaved themselves around Roger.

"Yes, it worked out, Roger. I'm very happy. Settled ... you know? This is one of those moments in my life where everything seems connected. I can't wait to see Charlotte. I'm gonna hug her for ten minutes. Having her on my side now…that feeling? … it's indescribable, Roger."

"John, you're a lucky man. Charlotte is a great gal. Been on many trips with her and never for a moment was she ever anything but her true self. An open book. Patient. If I had to pick a single word that describes Charlotte, it's patience. Kind and compassionate and all that, but patient."

"Can't wait to see her. We've only been dating for a little over a year, but she hit me like a ton of bricks. I've met my soulmate, Roger. This is the person I've been looking for all my life."

Roger had arrived with my car the day after DeHaven and I had signed the contract. Of course, the first thing Roger wanted to do was see the property. DeHaven gave Roger the tour, and I described how an extension of the front bedroom would become the hostel. Outside, I pointed to the addition on the side of the house that had been DeHaven's brother's room, and described the rental space it would become. Then the three of us walked the yard. I described the bathhouse, and pointed out where the fence would run; an eight-foot fence separating the property from our grumpy neighbor. We stood by the stake David Sullivan had driven in the ground marking the site of the new septic tank, and I described JM Harris and his beast of a truck, and the problems of putting in a septic system in the basin of the Nolichucky. Roger pointed to the shed on the back of DeHaven's house and allowed as how he would enclose that for storage, and his description was almost exactly what I had imagined. Then, with nearly clairvoyant precision, he described what Charlotte had suggested, a number of small cabins, very simple cabins, along the River Road side of the property. Roger stopped. Looking at DeHaven and back at me, he hesitated for a moment. Then, with a couple of thoughtful nods, said he was certain an Appalachian Trail hostel on this particular spot would be more than successful. It would become a landmark, a beacon of light on the trail. I can't tell you how much that kind of affirmation of my ideas about the hostel helped. Roger's stamp of approval had put to bed every remaining qualm I had.

* * *

The Appalachians are part of the oldest mountain range in the world, rising up due to a series of geologic events creating the Euromerican super-continent. Beginning around 450 million years ago with the collision of an arc of volcanic islands with Canada and New England, and ending 200 million years later with the collision of Africa along the eastern continental shelf, a mountain range was created that included all of the current Appalachians, the Atlas of northwest Africa, the Scottish Highlands, and the Scandinavian Caledonides.

The immense force of this series of tectonic collisions pushed rock inland with nowhere to go but up; much of it the sedimentary floor of an earlier ocean. The marble and granite of the Blue Ridge and Northern Highlands, the quartz of the Kittatinny Mountains, the slate and limestone of Pennsylvania and Maryland, all of the volcanic and sedimentary rock heaped up in no particular order, pushed layer over layer, one upon the other.

Like compressing an accordion, the landform of what would become Virginia, North Carolina and Tennessee shortened by 200 miles, pushing the existing layers of sedimentary rock upward into folds running perpendicular to the direction of forces creating them. At the peak of this geologic cataclysm, the Appalachians reached three-mile-high heights comparable to the Rockies of Colorado and Canada.

Toward the end of this time, an ecosphere nearly equal to today's had evolved; a massive ocean, a huge, mountainous land mass, evaporation, and rain—250 million years of rain have eroded the once sharp, miles-high, and ragged Rocky

Mountain-like Appalachians into a softer, quieter version of its former self.

Today, views of the Appalachians from a Landsat satellite, appear as three parallel but dissimilar forms running northeast to southwest. The most distinctive feature is the folded area running through the middle: the Ridge and Valley Province that curves snake-like from Alabama and North Georgia up through Pennsylvania and into southeastern New York. Seen from high enough, this region looks sinewy and ropey compared to the smoother Appalachian provinces to the east and west. In reality, the ropiness is a parallel set of ridges, like corduroy; long, high ridges separated by narrow river valleys; parallel ridges measuring an average of twenty or thirty miles, broken here and there by gaps allowing land travelers to cross from one valley into another.

The Ridge and Valley Province, bounded by the Allegheny Mountains to the west and the Blue Ridge Mountains to the east, is filled with a succession of nearly impassible ridges. From the plains of southern Georgia all the way to Maine, a distance of nearly 1,500 miles, there are only three natural interior breaks. The northern break is the Mohawk Valley and the water gap created by the Mohawk River. Running east-west, the valley is a passage through the Appalachians between the Adirondacks to the north and the Catskills to the south. It can be traced today by following Interstate 90 across New York to Niagara Falls and the region between Lakes Ontario and Erie.

Two hundred miles south of the Mohawk Valley, the Cumberland Narrows provides the middle break of the three interior crossings. The Narrows is a water gap in western Maryland where Wills Creek cuts through the central ridge between Wills Mountain to the north and Haystack Mountain to the south. Seen from a rocky outcropping high above Wills Creek on the northeast side of the Narrows, this gap is one of the most stunning views in all the Appalachians. Photographs of this view show the river, the highway, and two railroads converging to pass through the gap, and in the distance, the highland plateau of Pennsylvania and West Virginia. Today's I-70 out of Baltimore and I-68 along the Maryland-Pennsylvania border provide a rough idea of the location of this, the middle of the three passages.

The southern break, 350 miles southwest of the Cumberland Narrows, is the Cumberland Gap, known by nearly every American as the gap through which Daniel Boone built the Wilderness Road. Indian hunters from as far back as 10,000 years had discovered the break leading north into the Ohio River Valley by following migrating bison from the Holston River valley through a series of three notches in the mountains. The third notch, leading into Kentucky, was the famous Cumberland Gap.

Slightly south of the Cumberland Gap is the Holston River system flowing southwest through Virginia into East Tennessee. The Holston River Valley connects to the Tennessee River Valley where the Holston flows into the Little Tennessee. This confluence of rivers provided another passage west. Although neither a break in the mountains, nor a direct east-west passage, and lying fully within the Ridge and Valley Province of the Appalachians, the Holston River Valley connects to a series of fourteen distinct valleys known collectively as the Great Valley running 800 miles through the center of the Appalachians.

Long before the first European hunters and explorers came to East Tennessee, a network of trails had been developed by the eastern Indians that exploited animal migrational paths through these passages, gaps, and river valleys. The Indians called the trail system Athawominee. Settlers translated that term as The Great Warrior's Path.

Two of the most important of the trails in the system were the paths from the upper Ohio Valley through Kentucky. through the Cumberland Gap, and south down to Georgia, and the one from upper New York that ran from ancient

Syracuse in the very heart of the Mohawk Valley, due south to the Shenandoah Valley, and then southwest through the Great Valley system into Tennessee.

This eastern leg, the most important of the two main routes of the Great Warrior's Path, split near Roanoke, Virginia at a place the Indians called Big Lick. Due to the many outcroppings of salt, Indian tribes had mined salt and fought history-changing battles at Big Lick for centuries. From there, the southern trace continued south across the Yadkin River Valley in North Carolina, and on down to Savannah, Georgia. The other trace out of Big Lick went due west, and followed the river valleys into Tennessee.

The two main branches of the Great Warrior's Path, the one from the Great Lakes and the Upper Ohio Valley, closely followed today by Interstate 75 south, and US 25E through Cumberland Gap, and the one from Syracuse following the western leg out of Big lick toward Tennessee, met at Chota, an ancient Indian village located west of Knoxville, Tennessee on the Little Tennessee River at the mouth of the Holston.

This historical coincidence, the merging of these two great trading paths at Chota, was probably the most important single thing affecting the settlement of East Tennessee. Even more important, from the perspective of the Indians of Eastern North America, is the fact that Hernando De Soto, visiting Chota, the nexus of the Indian trading system, set off the European disease pandemic that reduced the Eastern North American Indian population by 70%.

After this devastating event, Chota and East Tennessee had been resettled by an early Cherokee migration. The Cherokee, an offshoot of the Iroquois of upstate New York, had made their way south by following the Great Warrior's Path through the Great Valley, almost perfectly marked today by Interstate 81.

Here they lived peacefully as farmers, tending to pigs and turkeys and rambling, weedy patches of corn, beans, and squash, eating the occasional dog when winters got hard. They lived peaceably; that is, until the Europeans came.

The Europeans came, but it took nearly 100 years for them to make it into the upper Tennessee Valley. Confined to the coastal and piedmont areas of the Eastern Seaboard by the awesome, nearly impenetrable barrier of the Blue Ridge Mountains —no early colonial highways ran up and over these mountains —westward migration was delayed until all the good land had been settled, and the throng of new immigrants had nowhere else to go.

The first Europeans to reach the western side of the Appalachians traveled that alternate Indian trading route from Big Lick, the route that came to be known as the Wilderness Road. During the first 100 years of the Colonial era, over 100,000 immigrated from Scotland alone. The Scots-Irish migration, driven by famine and persecution, filled American ships that had unloaded imported goods in the Port of Ulster, Ireland's major seaport on the Atlantic. After unloading their goods, ship captains took on emigrant passengers creating a profitable return trip to the Port of Philadelphia. This deluge of humanity flowing from Ulster to Philadelphia and then southward and westward into the colonies, had a profound effect on the future nation and established the culture and society that would come to be known as Appalachian.

From 1710 to 1775, over 200,000 people from all over Europe emigrated from that single port in Ireland to the original thirteen American colonies. In 1748, Morgan Bryan cut the path for the first wagon to cross the gap south from Big Lick. Following the trace of the Great Warrior's Path, his goal was to move his family, and all their possessions, by Conestoga wagon to the Yadkin Valley of North Carolina.

When Bryan reached the mountain gap that stood in the way of his wagon, the 78-year-old Bryan and his many sons disassembled the wagon and carried it piecemeal up the last slope. It took three months for Bryan and his family to move a distance of about eighty miles over the gap and to their destination at the Forks of the Yadkin River south of Salem, North Carolina.

Daniel Boone's father, a close friend and former neighbor of the Bryan family, would make that same trip a few years later, and these two large families were the first Europeans to settle in Western North Carolina.

From the Yadkin Valley, from the South Fork of the Holston River at Chilhowie, Virginia, and from several other less important places, the settlement of East Tennessee by European pioneers began.

As the early settlers widened and improved the Great Warrior's Path piece by piece, the eastern leg came to be known as the Philadelphia Wagon Road. Tens of thousands traveled south by Conestoga wagon and some of these turned westward along the Wilderness Road in Virginia. Reaching Tennessee, this stream of immigrants splintered again, and trickled along the many Indian pathways following the creeks and rivers of the southern mountain valleys. Gradually, over the next 100 years, they took over the land in East Tennessee previously cleared and farmed by the Cherokee. The pioneer farm families, children included, produced all of the necessities of life from the soil and with their own hands. Food, shelter and clothing came from the acres they worked. Ax handles, rakes, and pitchforks were made from hickory harvested yearly from the forests. Sheep and fields of flax provided the raw materials for the linsey-woolsey clothing they wore.

* * *

Roger and I left the DeHaven property, and headed south out of Erwin on Temple Hill Road, which becomes US 19, the route running up through Spivey Gap close to DeHaven's new house, and onward into the region of North Carolina that many people call Little Switzerland. In a few miles, we exited right onto NC 352, the old road to Asheville, and for cyclists, an infamously steep and exhausting climb through constant switchbacks crossing over the Bald Mountains at Sams Gap and on to Asheville, North Carolina. But we were heading for Hot Springs, North Carolina, and a visit with the renowned thru-hiker, Dan "Wingfoot" Bruce. Old Asheville Highway forked left, and we continued toward our destination on 352.

During one of our conversations after Roger arrived in Erwin, he let it be known that he knew very little about the Appalachian Trail and even less about the nature and character of the Appalachian Mountains. These subjects had fascinated me since my Scouting days. On this trip to Hot Springs, we would be riding through a beautiful section of mountains new to him. So, as soon as possible after leaving DeHaven's property, I managed to pick up that earlier conversation.

"Roger, in a little bit we'll top the ridge here and cross over the Appalachian Trail. Believe it or not, we're still in Unicoi County."

"As in Erwin, county seat of?"

"That's right. Over the ridge, we're in North Carolina and the road we're on becomes NC 212, a route that travels through a fascinating assortment of the most beautiful and classic Appalachian mountain farms you'll ever see. Thoroughly modern today. There're new cars and pickups everywhere. Nearly every home will have a satellite dish. But the land was originally cleared by the Cherokee. The Cherokee, like their Iroquois ancestors, were farmers. Then the Cherokee were pushed off the land by European immigrants, primarily from Scotland and Ireland. It's the descendants of those early Scots-Irish, living the hardscrabble life throughout these hollows and coves, who got so much press attention back in the '60s. Remember that, Roger? Lyndon Johnson's war on poverty? Wasn't long before journalists discovered the deprivation up in these mountains. Even today, the word *Appalachia* conjures up visions of scrawny women and bug-eyed, starving children in worn-out Oshkosh B'gosh overalls."

Roger was sitting forward. "Imagine what this place was like before hard-surfaced roads. A muddy, rutted dirt road ran along this creek," he said, looking around. "Families living here were almost completely isolated. Lots of books about the people and the culture of these valleys."

"So, you've done some reading on this?"

"A little bit. Most of them full of myths and distortions regarding the lives and behavior of those people."

Roger sat back and bumped his seat back two notches, and continued his thought. "Writers just imagining how it must have been, sensationalizing the culture, writing about moonshine whiskey, about inbreeding leading to impulsive acts of violence, believing all the families up here feudin like the Hatfields and the McCoys."

"All through this part of the mountains, the roads follow streams. The one we're crossing over right now is Devil's Fork. They just improved the original dirt roads with gravel and macadam." I glanced at Roger who had angled his seat and his heavy body into more of a lounge-like position.

"And before that, I suppose ... an Indian trail ran along the creek?" he asked.

"Yep. By the time the Cherokee had been driven out of the Tennessee Valley, pushed up into these more remote valleys, an extensive network of trails existed all along this side of the mountains."

Roger was rubbing his eyes, and mumbled, "How long have Indian communities existed here; here in the mountains?"

"The earliest arrivals? ...10,000 years or more. From what I understand, there are arrowheads been dated that far back. Icehouse Bottom ... that's an archeological dig over in Monroe County...Icehouse Bottom is the site of a prehistoric Indian hunting camp dating back as early as 7500 BC. I read an article said artifacts uncovered there show evidence of an extensive trade network that reached tribal villages in Georgia, North Carolina, west along the Tennessee Valley, north through the Cumberland Gap into Ohio, the Great Lakes, the upper Hudson Valley, you know, big, big network of trading going on for centuries."

"The Ice Age had something to do with them being here, right? The theory that humans made that migration over the land-bridge up there in Alaska, following the food source...the big animals...hides for clothing and shelter."

"Not true, Roger. Not true for the North American Indians, well, hasn't been proven, there's no evidence, plenty of fossil evidence of moose and elk, even mastodon and woolly mammoths, but none for humans, same article I read about Icehouse said there's no archeological evidence of humans anywhere in America earlier than what they found at Icehouse Bottom. The speculation now is that North American natives came from Mesoamerica, ...you know, Mexico and Central America, probably by water across the Florida Gulf and over on the other side, the west side of Mexico, up the coast to California.

"Makes sense," Roger yawned. "If this was at the end of the Ice Age, ice extended all the way to the Ohio valley, was all over Pennsylvania, all across the northern tier. Right? Couldn't get through that stuff until after it melted. By then the land bridge was flooded by the rising ocean, least, that's what I understand ... about the rising ocean."

"Old Asheville Highway forks to the left up here and follows South Indian Creek. We're gonna bear right and travel along with Devil's Fork, pretty little creek, runs through this valley for some distance, we'll follow that all the way to its headwaters. Then, over the mountain up ahead, we'll pick up another water system and follow that through the next valley ... Roger?" I had glanced his way— "Am I boring you?" I said, seeing Roger, his head back, eyes closed.

"Heck no, man," Roger said, without so much as a twitch. "Interesting stuff. Love it. Keep going. Just resting my eyes."

"Well, buddy, You're missing the visual." I said. And Roger sat up, looking around.

"Beautiful country, John. Beautiful."

"This is a typical valley in this area. All through the western side of the mountains, the lower elevations consist of steep slopes, narrow valleys, and floodplains. Cherokee settled and cleared the floodplains, the flat, river bottom-land. Small plots in these steep hills, but rich, loamy soil from a million years of erosion. They were excellent farmers. You'll see this scenery all the way to Hot Springs. NC 352, you can imagine, was first an Indian path following along this creek. Right now on this trip, we're retracing the same route the early Cherokee settlers used."

"Floodplains? Floodplains ... huh." Roger said, looking around. "I understand how big rivers meandering back and forth over broad valleys for millions of years create...but these swift creeks running down mountain valleys, how do they ... they don't meander. They're eroding ... cutting deeper."

"Dams, Roger. Heavy rains wash debris down these steep slopes and into the creeks to collect at different points as dams. This creates a lake and heavy rains wash additional debris into the lake, eroding the hillsides, and when the dams rot or give away...well, over a million years ... what you see here, the flat river bottom-land kept getting wider and wider."

We went on in this manner, discussing the things we saw. I explained how the mountains were created half-a-billion years ago, about the extensive network of Indian trading trails and how an east-west pathway through the Mohawk Valley in New York connected ancient fishing villages around Long Island Sound with those around the Great Lakes region, how beautiful, colorful flint, mined by Indians in central Ohio ended up all over the northeast, how tribal warfare over the salt and copper mines of the central Blue Ridge had so damaged the political arrangement of the middle-Atlantic Indian confederacy that the English had little trouble establishing colonies, and how the flood of immigrating European settlers, using the Great Warrior's Path and its branches, gradually pushed the Indians westward.

* * *

"Roger, I ... Roger! Are you asleep?" Roger's head was over against the window. His open mouth released a quiet snort.

"No. Just resting my eyes, John. You're something else buddy. It's like we're traveling over sacred ground," Roger said, sitting up and scratching his jaw.

"Well, Roger, we are. There's nothing like this, anywhere. I have always been fascinated. Read lots of books. It's part of the attraction, part of the reason I'm so interested in the AT. When I think about the hostel, the thrill I get comes from the fact that I'd be living in the middle of all this. The AT? ... Roger, I'm telling you, the AT goes right through the middle of a bunch of history, not to mention the most fascinating geological stuff the world has ever seen. It's like a symbol of all that is great about our country, especially the beauty. It just takes my breath away to think that we're so lucky to have been born in the most beautiful county in the world. The Southern Appalachians, the history and culture, like nothing you see anywhere. The people, the isolation they experienced, their culture, the music, art, their religious practices, all of that got locked up here. Change was the constant in the rest of the world, but not here. Nothing changed for nearly two centuries. By the 1960s and LBJ's War on Poverty, many of the farms here weren't one whit different than they were in 1760. The communication revolution didn't reach them until radio. Just think about that, Roger. Think about that!"

"And radio was followed by the recording industry, John. Until radio and the record player, and, I should mention, the Sears Catalogue, which made both of those products available anywhere a postman could get his horse, the music in the more remote sections of the Appalachians had not changed since the 1700s. I'm going to get you to go with me to the Tennessee Valley Old-Time Fiddler's Convention someday. That's up in Athens, Alabama, the tip end of the Appalachians. Ten thousand people show up each year and several hundred musicians, playing nothin but that old-time stuff. It's the music style that existed in Ireland at the time they were immigrating to this country. Exactly the same. The same you'll hear today. Got locked into place by the isolation of those Irish families high in the Appalachians. That's a big gathering of ..."

"I know you love that stuff, Roger. That's the first thing I heard about you before we ever met—you were a big bluegrass fan. Got that pop-up camper. Since I've known you, off on a canoe trip or some bluegrass festival somewhere every weekend."

"Yeah, but what I'm saying, John, radio changed the culture of the mountains, it was radio drivin the recording industry. When old-time mountain musicians learned that their music could be recorded ... learned that they could make money singing into a can, and when those early music publishers and A&R people heard that music, BOOM, a whole new genre of music developed, country music, hillbilly, and bluegrass. You know, John, bluegrass music had its genesis in old-time fiddle ..."

"Comin up, Roger. When we go over this ridge crest, we pick up the Shelton Laurel Creek, We'll be going in the reverse direction. This valley was settled by the Cherokee moving up from the French Broad. When we come over the mountain, we begin ... we'll be traveling through what they settled last."

* * *

"Roger, up ahead you'll see a road sign on your right. Coppersnake Holler Road. It's the next road on the right.

How'd you like to have that address? Shortly after that, about half-mile, we'll take a left onto NC 208. I want to show you something."

Roger positioned his seat upright again. "Okay. What ya got?"

"See that sign? See that historic marker? On the left, there. Just before the turn."

"Yep. Got it. So, what's that all about?" His eyes followed the sign as I slowed for the turn.

"When we make this turn, Roger, you are only a few feet, maybe thirty yards from the site of the Shelton Laurel Massacre. Ever hear of that? One of the most disturbing events of the Civil War."

"No, doesn't ring a bell, John"

"Well, Roger, I don't think you'll be resting your eyes during this story. I just finished reading a great book, *Cold Mountain*. First novel by ... Frazier; something Frazier. Wonderful writer. Gonna be big someday. Anyway, the story takes place right here in the Southern Appalachians of North Carolina. People don't generally know it but a lot of the worst part of the ..."

"*Cold Mountain*? I don't think I've heard of that one."

"It just came out, I spotted it among the new book releases at Barnes and Noble."

"Okay, I'll have to look for ..."

"So, right around here, Roger. We've been following the Shelton Laurel Creek for some distance now. This is the Shelton Laurel Valley where some of the worst events of the Civil War took place. Like I started to say, people don't generally know it, but there was intense fighting between the Confederate Army, the Home Guard, and gangs of vandals, mostly escaped Union prisoners and deserters. They were joined by killers, rapists, and thieves taking advantage of the chaos and near anarchy the war had caused in these parts. From up in Kentucky, all the way down to Georgia, the mountains were laced through and through with Union sympathizers. Something else not many people know. About half the people in these mountains supported the Union, were against slavery, and did all kinds of nasty things against the families here who supported the Rebels. Jeff Davis, President of the Confederacy, and Governor Vance of Tennessee, and numerous Confederate officers heard incessant cries and pleas from the local mountain communities for protection against these unionists and the criminals they tended to support. That's what *Cold Mountain* is about. A great story, but tragic and chilling. I was riveted to the book."

"So what about the massacre?"

"The massacre took place early in the war. Took place right here, Roger. Confederate soldiers, and there were several battalions, worked up and down the west side of the mountains along here. Tried to maintain some sort of order. They fought an endless number of small skirmishes and a dozen or so major battles. The war raged all through here. It's just that certain events, like Antietam and Gettysburg, get all the attention. But, Roger, some of the most horrific fighting that took place during the war happened all through here, caused, mainly, by an endless influx of Union Army deserters joined up with those of the native population who sided with the Union and a bunch of plain old bushwhacking outlaws. Hundreds of terrible acts. Four or five of these outlaws would ride up to a poor, dirt-farmer's homestead, haul off his daughters, steal the horses, eat the cow, and kill the rest of the livestock they couldn't take with them. Just vicious acts of terrorism. The massacre that took place here began with a raid on the home of the Confederate Battalion's commanding officer. I read that Frazier, the author of the book, spent about a year traveling through here, researching the history, and he …"

"So, what was the massacre, some kind of revenge or something?"

"Exactly. The commander sent several corps of his men out to track them down. They searched the farms of known local unionists. They tortured people trying to get information. They tied one woman to a tree for hours, her baby in the snow, crying in the snow at her feet, but she wouldn't tell on her husband and sons. This really happened, and it was a scene in Frazier's book too. They would tie a farmer to a tree, seems that was their preferred method, then torture his kids, especially his daughters, in front of his eyes, or kill his animals one-by-one, trying to get him to talk. Finally, the solders rounded up fifteen local Unionists. Two of them escaped, but they marched three boys, teenagers, I think one was like thirteen or something, and ten men, and marched them into the woods. They were ordered to kneel. The soldiers wouldn't shoot on the first command, but when the officer in charge threatened to put his men on their knees too, they fired. Some of them, even at close range, didn't hit their mark, and you can just imagine the terror and chaos. I read that the youngest boy was shot in both arms. With his bleeding arms wrapped around the officer's legs, he begged to be sent home to his mother, but they shot him eight more times. Well Roger, that was the Shelton Laurel Massacre, one of the many tragedies that took place around here."

"Thanks, John. It's been a great ride up to now. Thanks, buddy. I'll let you know if I have nightmares tonight."

"Roger ... you can't be in the Appalachians without longing to know more of its history and culture. Least, I can't. This is a very special place to me. It's different here. The rift the war caused lasted longer in these mountain communities than anywhere in the rest of the country. You see Confederate flags, even today, all over the place; especially in the smaller communities further south; from around here all the way to Georgia. They hang like drapes on front porches. The other half of the community is silent about it, but those flags tell you the war is still on, just mentally now. Two proud sections of the Appalachian community still glare at each other across the street. The Shelton Laurel Massacre shows in a very clear way what happens when communities are divided and sucked into battles; continually threatened by a lawless society redefined by hatred. Any horrible act can be justified under these circumstances. An eye for an eye. They burn down your barn, you kill their cattle, they come after your cattle, your son gets killed, you catch and hang one of them, and the consciousness of the community, formed by marriage bonds and farming partnerships for centuries, just disappears in the blood."

* * *

"So, did the Birmingham newspaper ever feature Paul and the Appalachian Trail?"

"Yes, they did. Nearly a full page with a map of the trail from Springer to Katahdin, a photo of Lenny Stabler, and his son Paul; Paul standing by his father with his hiking poles and backpack and ... well, I was proud of the part I played. I've still got that issue somewhere."

"Why do you suppose the existence of the Trail was so little known back then?"

"I've given that a lot of thought. I've read dozens of books by hikers and outdoor enthusiasts. This is a common question that several writers have tried to answer. I think all of them got it wrong."

"Okay, so ... all of them ... then, you must have a pretty good answer. John. Let's hear it."

"Sure. First, think of the AT as a concept, Roger. An idea or a notion. And the concept ... the idea ... changed. Let me explain it this way. The idea of a long footpath got started with the famous Long Trail, a two-hundred and seventy-some-mile trail running through the Green Mountains of Vermont. Began building the trail just after the turn of the century. That was the first man-made trail in America." I glanced over at Roger.

"Built just for recreational hiking. Hiking trails before that were established by animals with American Indians following the animals, and modern Americans following the natives. The Long Trail was the model for what became the Appalachian Trail."

"Yeah, I think I know that story. A guy named McKay got the idea of the Appalachian Trail started back the twenties, or something. He was some kind of ..."

"It's pronounced like sky, Roger. Benton was his name. Benton MacKaye ... like spry or sigh ... pie in the sky."

"Got it, John. Benton MacKaye."

"MacKaye wrote an essay proposing the AT in 1921. Then he organized the Appalachian Trail Conference to build it. The first conference met in Washington, D.C. That was in 1925. MacKaye had been talking about his Appalachian project for twenty years. In today's jargon, we would call MacKaye a networker. He was brilliant at networking, at drawing powerful, deep-thinking people to his ideas. He invited the best of those folks to attend; foresters, public officials, social philosophers, lawyers, architects; all of them had embraced his goal of building a footpath along the entire Appalachian crest-line. I think there were about thirty people, mostly men and a couple of women. MacKaye named the event the Appalachian Trail Conference. He was not a leader; someone else took that role. He had himself appointed its field organizer. They all met the following year and the year after that. Nothing happened as far as actually constructing the trail until a guy by the name of Myron Avery came along and turned what amounted to a pipe dream into an ongoing project. In the fall 1928, Avery began organizing trail clubs all up and down the Appalachian range. These volunteers built the trail in about eight years. Completed it. Finished around 1937, and by then, Myron Avery had walked and measured every mile of the trail. He published the first guidebook in the early thirties. But Roger, they didn't see it ... nobody saw what they had just built as a single thing. The concept of the AT back then was of a trail linking the incremental parts of the Appalachian range. Today, we think of the AT as a single pathway from Maine to Georgia. They thought of it incrementally; as a pathway linking regional systems of pathways. All those clubs from Maine to Georgia. Each club was focused on a single section; a short stretch of the Appalachians they had been hiking themselves for years. A section of interlinking trails they all knew like the backs of their hands. They saw the purpose of their work as creating access to the mountains for tramping and outdoor recreation." I looked at Roger. His face was frowned, and he shifted uncomfortably.

"I don't understand, John. You're saying they built a trail from Maine to Georgia and they couldn't see ..."

"Let me explain it this way. A young man named Earl Shaffer was released from the Army shortly after the war ended. He was traumatized by the things he had seen and experienced. I believe it was his best friend died over there, killed during the landing at Iwo Jima. Today, we call his emotional state post-traumatic stress disorder, a mental-health condition triggered by terrifying events. Shaffer only knew he was suffering and needed to do something about it, so he decided to walk the entire Appalachian Trail from end to end. When Shaffer completed his thru-hike ... in forty-eight ... nobody believed he had done it. In fact, in the middle of his hike, the *Appalachian Trailway News*, not knowing Shaffer was making the attempt, published an article citing ten reasons why it was impossible for anyone to hike the entire trail. Shaffer had to show the officials of the ATC his journal and hundreds of photos he had taken along the way. Thank God he had packed a camera, or they probably would've thought he fabricated the whole dang story. Even with the photos, Myron Avery and others grilled him for over two hours before they were satisfied and ceded his victory. Now, Roger. Stop and think about that. The trail had been complete and thru-walkable for over eleven years. Nobody actually did it until

Shaffer, and when it was done, they didn't believe him. Why? Roger ... the question is, why didn't they believe him?"

"Because they thought it was impossible, like the four-minute mile or climbing Mt Everest."

"I don't think that's it, Roger. Hundreds of people attempted to break the four-minute mile and climb Mount Everest. As far as I know nobody...not a single person tried to hike the AT end-to-end in a single season before Shaffer."

"So here comes this guy, walks in the door and says, guess what I just did. He surprised them."

"Well, Roger ... I think they ... I think they looked at Shaffer like he was a nutcase. Who would do that, they were thinking. Why would *anybody* do that, they were thinking. Nobody had hiked the Long Trail from end to end. In fact, as far as I know, nobody anywhere in the world had ever made it a goal to hike a long footpath end-to-end just because it was something to be conquered. John Muir, for instance. In the woods constantly. Went into the wilderness just to be there, just to connect with his inner self. Thousands of people all up and down the east coast hiked the Appalachians for the same reason. So, when Shaffer showed up at the ATC headquarters making his claim, all the officials could say was ... huh? Why would anybody take five or six months out of his life and do something nearly impossible to imagine? Where was the reward?"

"Yeah, yeah. I see your point. Where was the reward? The four-minute mile and Everest were established goals. Lots of people tried and the ones who finally succeeded became instant heroes. The AT. Where was the glory? That's what those officials were thinking. They must have looked at him and said, exactly what did you accomplish, son?"

"Roger, I have the answer." I looked at Roger and he glanced at me. "The trail wasn't built for that purpose. That answers the question. And it also explains why the general public was unaware of the accomplishment. There were dozens of hiking clubs up and down the trail involved in the project before it was over. Each club had worked on a short stretch of the trail. There were connector trails everywhere. People hiked them for the diversion, for the exercise, or to simply, like Muir, to be in the wilderness. Everybody thought of the trail in that way. A pathway linking regional systems of pathways. Nobody thought of the entire trail as an ambition; an objective. Of course, the trail ran for over two thousand miles. It was a real thing. A fact. It existed, and they could see the whole trail in their mind's eye, there were maps of it, but they didn't think of hiking it in that way. They thought of it incrementally. The AT acquired an entirely different ... here's the thing, Roger." I tapped the dashboard a couple of times with my knuckles for emphasis. "The AT acquired an entirely new meaning when those thousands of volunteers ... when all those clubs heard of Shaffer's accomplishment."

"Yeah, yeah. I see it John. If from the beginning people understood the AT as ... as you said, an ambition, a trail to be walked end to end, somebody, or even everybody would have planned a thru-hike; would have been waiting for the day the thing was finished. Somebody would have said, okay, there it is. Let's go. Let's hike the thing. But they didn't. Not a single person ever thought of it that way."

I leaned over and rapped the dashboard with the word, "Exactly! And Roger, the other side of that coin is that nobody knew the AT existed but the hikers who built it. Here was the longest hiking trail in the world and it had attracted almost no attention. It's hard for people to understand that today. The trail has become an object to be conquered. Thru-hiking has become an alluring goal. Because hundreds have hiked the distance in a single season, have conquered that goal, people today see the trail differently. But just a few years ago, back when I delivered my report, when all those incredibly intelligent, totally-connected, and socially-aware newsmen were clueless about Paul Stabler's ambition, people were still thinking of the Appalachian Trail as a day hike, as a place where you might go for the weekend to experience the wilderness."

"You would think that Avery and MacKaye would have wanted everybody to know what they had done. Man, I mean that was a monumental accomplishment, so why ... I just don't understand ... it's almost un-American."

"Avery and MacKaye *were* uninterested in publicity. That's the usual explanation for why nobody knew about the trail. So, people point out Avery was not interested in publicity. MacKaye made no effort to bring his idea to the general public. Avery worked strictly with the hiking clubs. MacKaye worked entirely within the elite intellectual community; that was his groove. So, the consensus is, the trail received no publicity because MacKaye and Avery weren't into publicity. But look, Roger, thousands of people, real people...worked on that project and rejoiced when the trail was complete. Were none of those who actually built the trail interested in publicity? None? Not a single one? Thinking about that, you come to realize ... it was an inside job. They weren't building the Appalachian Trail for the general public. They were building it for themselves. Think of that."

"So Shaffer is responsible for the change. Now I have another question. Why *did* he do it?" And here, Roger threw out his hands. "I think the ATC officials posed a good question. Why'd you do that, son?"

"Shaffer was walking off the war."

"And walking the distance was a secondary consideration?"

"Yes, but it consumed all his mental and physical energy. That was the drug; the medication he was seeking. Apparently it worked. So there *was* glory in it. There *was* something to be conquered. But I want to correct something you just said. Shaffer was responsible for bringing the existence of the trail to public awareness, but only in this sense: his accomplishment was to inspire others. Shaffer was followed by Gene Espy in the early fifties. He became the second thru-hiker to complete the AT in a single season. But the most important of those inspired by Shaffer was Emma Gatewood. Gatewood hiked the trail in the mid-fifties at age sixty-seven. She had twenty-six grandchildren, so she quickly acquired the trail name, Grandma. I say most important because Gatewood became a hiking celebrity. Dozens of trail-town newspapers sent reporters out to interview her. Word spread like wildfire that hikers had come across a grandmother walking the trail with every intention of reaching Maine. The Associated Press did a national profile of her when a reporter tracked her down in Maryland. While she was in Connecticut, her story appeared in the August issue of Sports Illustrated. She took a zero to appear on the Today Show. These appearances made her a celebrity even before the hike was over. Afterwards, she appeared on TV with Groucho Marx and later that year with Art Linkletter, two very popular shows in the fifties. Roger, because of all that publicity, she is generally recognized as the person who saved the trail."

"And the trail needed saving?"

I paused and gave that some thought. "It did. Two devastating things happened in the decade prior to Shaffer's hike. First, in the fall of 1938, a hurricane, often called The Great New England Hurricane, killed hundreds of people and damaged or destroyed something like sixty-thousand houses. With that kind of destruction, you can imagine the uprooted trees and broken limbs all over the trail. Now Roger, gasoline chain saws weren't generally available until after the war, so we're talking two-man cross-cut saws, axes, and horses; teams of oxen; a mind-boggling, overwhelming situation for the local trail volunteers. The other thing was world war two. A number of key trail figures, including Myron Avery, belonged to the Reserves. With the attack on Pearl Harbor, they were called to active duty. Then when the war got underway, fuel shortages and rationing brought trail work to a screeching halt. It wasn't until 1951 that the trail was declared open again."

"Wait a minute. Shaffer hiked the trail in '48, right?"

"Yes, but he ran into problems all along the way. When he reached the northern end, the trail was such a mess, he could only guess his way through. He explains how challenging it was in his book, *Walking with Spring*. Even in the mid-fifties, Gatewood complained about the condition of the trail in every article and appearance. That's why she's credited with saving the thing. The Appalachian Trail community, seeing her on television and reading those articles, were awakened and motivated to do something about it."

"The Appalachian Trail Conference still exists?"

"Yes, still exists. Fully in charge today. Its mission is to preserve and manage the trail. This is interesting, Roger. Work on the trail is still done by volunteers. There are thirty official clubs, some of them quite large; thousands of members; and they all coordinate their work through the ATC. But oversight is a complicated partnership. The property, meaning the trail itself including wide buffers on each side, belongs to the National Park Service. Management is provided by the US Forest Service. But in reality, these two giant agencies defer almost completely to the ATC. But Roger, that's where the simplicity ends. The ATC's role is played downward through four regional partnership committees that function as communication links to the trail clubs and thousands of volunteers. Then there are the states. The trail runs through fourteen states and the ATC must work with a myriad of state agencies, environmental, land use, waterways, and who knows what else. And not only does the trail run through those states, it passes through dozens of parks, protected watersheds, and nature preserves, each with its own management structure. The ATC is a vast, complex partnership, a model of organizational efficiency."

"And what about trail towns, like Erwin. And your hostel. Will the ATC affect you in any way?"

"Well, they can help me. They can be a tremendous help, I mean, an indispensable help. In fact, as soon as I committed to the hostel project, I called them right away. Got this lovely person on the phone ... Laurie. She answered my call. Information Services Manager, I believe she said. Well, she was so encouraging. Wished me the best of luck in the project and said soon as I got construction underway, I should call her back. She would put me in touch with sales and set up a dealership ... you know, maps, guidebooks, and other ATC materials. They have a website now, she said, and she'd make sure my hostel was listed. Would list me in their next guidebook. Very nice person. Very sweet, so, you know, the ATC will become my partner too."

"Hey John, betcha haven't thought of this. It's 1997. Next year, when you open the hostel, '98. Exactly fifty years after Shaffer's walk. How's that for providence? You're opening your hostel in celebration of the most important event in the AT's history!"

* * *

North of the Smokies, the Appalachian Trail passes through Davenport Gap and runs along the North Carolina-Tennessee border. Weaving in and out of both states, it crosses the Pigeon River and climbs nearly 3,000 feet up Snowbird Mountain. From atop Snowbird, you can look back on the path you just traveled, way back to the Smokies. Running along Max Patch Mountain, it passes over Walnut and Bluff Mountains and down toward the French Broad River at Hot Springs, where it pops out of the woods and intersects with NC-209 just south of the Smoky Mountain Diner. The Trail was built right through town. It runs right down the main street of Hot Springs for over a mile. White blazes mark the path through town and over the bridge and along the river. Across the river, the trail climbs a steep ridge to a blue-blazed side-trail that takes you to the top of the famous vista, Lover's Leap.

A first-time hiker walking through Hot Springs is immediately struck by the close, historical association between the two very different communities. The hiking community needs, desperately needs, the services trail communities can supply. None has met that challenge with a better understanding of the partnership's mutual benefit and dependence. It is the first town the north-bounders actually enter full of enthusiastic expectation. For many, it is the favorite town of the whole distance. The success of Hot Springs illustrates the potential of other trail towns. The partnership between the town and the hikers will preserve a town's special qualities, its history and standing, while contributing to its economy and engaging its citizenry. This assessment is not imagined. It is proved by the fact that the population of Hot Springs is growing once again, growing because hikers with fond memories are retiring and buying property in Hot Springs, North Carolina.

* * *

"Who's this Wingfoot guy?"

"Wingfoot's his trail name. Dan Bruce is a legend in his own time, Roger. I'd say he's in the top five most influential hikers in the Appalachian Trail community. Completely dedicated. Thinks about nothing else. Least, that's what I hear."

"You said he publishes a guidebook. He's an avid hiker?"

"You bet. He's thru-hiked the AT seven times. First time was 1985, I believe. I've been told by those who know him well, he's been hiking since his college days, some twenty years by the time he completed the whole thing in one stretch. His second thru-hike took place in 1987, the AT's fiftieth anniversary. Wingfoot organized what he called the Golden Anniversary Expedition, a project he imagined would connect more than forty trail celebrations that were to be held in trail towns and nearby communities up and down the trail. Met with and talked to newspaper reporters every stop. A big shot-in-the-arm for the trail. The guy is indefatigable and totally devoted to the standards and traditions of thru-hiking and the wilderness character of the AT. In fact, he made a pledge. Get this, Roger ... two hours of service given back to the AT community for every mile hiked on the trail. He preaches this to every hiker he meets. Hiking any trail is a privilege you must recognize by paying it forward."

"Good grief, John. That's a lot of hours."

"Rounded down, that's seven times two times 2000. Maybe he meant that as a rule of thumb for the ordinary hiker. Not a repeat thru-hiker or a seven-time hiker like himself."

"Seven times! Is that a record or something?"

"I believe so, but Roger, you know how everybody has a personal reason for hiking the trail? ... Wingfoot's different ... his purpose was different from any other." I picked up Roger's glance. "He was hiking ... let me put it this way. He hiked it seven times, but each time, each time, Roger, it was to fill in the blanks of his knowledge of the trail ... to gather information and answer the questions the previous trips had inspired. Because, Roger, the trail changes constantly ... hostels come and go, get better or worse, as do restaurants and motels. Portions are re-routed almost every year. Mileage changes. Mileages between shelters change. Everything changes constantly. Wingfoot hiked it over and over to improve his knowledge and record these changes precisely because he had seen the need for a comprehensive trail manual. Before his, before *The Thru-Hiker's Handbook*, nothing like it had existed."

"Pamphlets, John. I'm not a hiker, you know that, but I've got a whole file drawer about outdoor activities, including hiking. Lots of pamphlets on the AT and other trails; day hikes. You can get them from the Forest Service."

"Right. Lots of pamphlets. I've collected dozens over the years myself. Nearly every hiking club produced its own, but that's just it. That's what I'm saying. What Wingfoot observed, I don't know him that well, Roger, but my sense is that he is taking a proprietary view of the trail community and could see that good, reliable information was the missing link. Back in the early eighties, the best of these publications was called an *underground guide* ... titled something like that."

"Wingfoot's?"

"No, sorry Roger. Darrell Maret, another avid hiker, not Wingfoot. Maret had been publishing guide books, *underground guides*, he called them, written specifically for thru-hikers. These booklets were photocopied and passed by hand from hiker to hiker. They were better than anything out there on thru-hiking the AT. This is how Maret's reputation was established. Back then, the most avid hikers belonged to clubs, and all of them knew Maret. He was an excellent carpenter and for years had worked with the Georgia Appalachian Trail Club maintaining shelters, clearing the trail, and such. He began calling his booklet *A Bootlegger's Guide*, for some reason, but the ATC got interested ... they got interested in offering a better guidebook, so Maret changed the name again to *The Philosopher's Guide to the AT* ... his trail name, Maret's trail name, is The Philosopher, well-known trail name among the more active hiking club members. He figured they'd know from the title who wrote it. Anyway, about five or six years ago, Wingfoot bought the rights to Maret's book and changed the name to *The Thru-Hiker's Handbook*. It's my preferred information source. An excellent guidebook. Still, it lacked important details and current, accurate descriptions of hostels, maps of trail towns, and so forth. So, Wingfoot hiked the trail with the aim of improving his book ... each time looking to make his guide more accurate. I doubt it's financially successful. Doubt that Wingfoot's concerned one way or the other. Based on our conversation, he just wants to get it right."

"What do you think your chances are of getting your hostel listed?"

"Well, Roger. I intend to get it listed. It will be listed. I'm a good negotiator, I'm pretty convincing when I have to be, and I *intend* to get in that book." I tapped my knuckles on the steering wheel for emphasis, looking at Roger.

"Well, you are that, John. Convincing. You nearly stole that canoe from me. I got home and thought, what the heck did I just do? An Old Town, no less. Two Extrasport life jackets, a fairly new paddle, your beer and the pizza. I picked up the check, remember? Like that Trisha Yearwood song ... When it comes to brains, got the short end of the stick."

"Now, Roger. You know that canoe wasn't ... that canoe had a pretty gashed up bottom, Roger. But, I'll bet you five I get in the book. And listed on his website...did I tell you he has a website? It's open now. You can go to it. Hikers are going to it already. You know anything about websites?" We glance at each other. "I'll ask him to show it to us when we get there."

* * *

Dan Wingfoot Bruce was medium height, slim and fit. A lean, mean, hiking machine. Today, he was dressed in cycling wear; black cycling shorts and a teal and orange T-shirt. Clean shaven with closely trimmed black hair. He carried a serious, even stern look on his face, but laughed easily. A no-nonsense kind of guy. You couldn't get him off the subject...adventure, nature, environmentalism, the Appalachian Trail, any trail, really, and you would have a good conversation. Bring up something else, and he became a blank wall. Except for computers. He had joined computers and the Appalachian Trail at the hip. Roger and I didn't know much about the Web. When Wingfoot ushered us into his spare bedroom office, we were so curious, it was the first thing we brought up.

"Well, in the first place, I've been very interested in computers from the beginning. I had an Apple II and when

IBM came out, I bought one of those and opted for the Microsoft operating system. Then I stumbled across a story about the Web ... around '93, I believe, and got a copy of Mosaic, that's an early web browser. Then Mosaic became Netscape Navigator, and when Microsoft came out with Internet Explorer, I switched to that. I started off with Mosaic in 1993. Spent way too much time. I was fascinated. Up all hours of the night."

Roger bent over and squinted at the monitor. "That's a nice-looking layout, Dan. Where'd you learn to design a website?"

"Spent a lot of time nosing around, collecting Web addresses. Looked at a lot of websites. Some were clean and easy to navigate. Others were messy and horrible. Got some books on graphic design, and typography. Right from the beginning, I was interested in building a site myself, about the trail, of course. Could see the value of that right away. Bought some books. Taught myself HTML and CSS ... html, that stands for *Hypertext Markup Language*, programming used to create webpages. CSS, that's ..."

"I'm telling you, Dan, I wouldn't have a clue," I said.

"Nothing wrong with that, John. I just had that interest. Subscribed to a couple of computer magazines. Bought some books. Looked at what others had done. Spent a lot of time searching out good sites. I have a long list of addresses that I collected. I started early. Ninety-three. Not many people had even heard of the Web. Read somewhere about Amazon, Jeff Bezos. That was two years ago. Ninety-five. July of ninety-five, in fact. Almost exactly two years ago. I remember because I was at home July fourth reading a computer newsletter. I accessed the Amazon website the day it launched. Read all I could find about Bezos and the programs he used. Nosed around his site trying to understand what he'd done, how it was done. You know, John ... look at something long enough, you understand. Hours and hours."

Dan Bruce's home was small and sparsely furnished. There was evidence of his outdoor passion everywhere. Maps on the wall. Gear stowed in odd places. Within moments of our arrival, he was showing us, giving us a demonstration of how his website worked. What it would become in the future. The main feature was trail journals. He was almost rapturous as he described how his goal was to get hundreds of AT hikers to maintain their trail journals on his website. How they could be accessed by anybody who had become a member of *The Trailplace*, his website.

"I understand what you're saying, John. It will take some initiative on the part of the hiker. And you're right. Most hikers keep a journal, carry a small notebook where they jot down experiences and observations from the day's hike. And you're right. You are. Most of them will stick with that, like you say, seeing the task of maintaining a website journal as a diversion from the plan. But I am confident a good portion will become excited about the potential of *The Trailplace.* When they reach a telephone somewhere, they'll call some significant other at home, read their journal to them, and have them email it to me. Or they'll use a library computer to check on other hiker journals and email entries for their own journal. It's gonna work, John. Guarantee. Might take time. Might build slowly, but it's gonna work."

* * *

The Smoky Mountain Diner is the primary goal of many hikers coming into Hot Springs. After you exit the trail onto NC-209 and follow white blazes down the hill, you round a slight curve, and there it is. If you are the typical hiker coming up from Springer Mountain, Georgia—twenty-five or thirty miles into your hike—you have been dreaming about pancakes, eggs, grits and gravy, cheeseburgers, French fries, meatloaf, creamy mashed potatoes, apple pie, ice cream, and hot coffee from a real coffeepot; been dreaming those dreams for three or four days. At this family-style, locally-owned diner, you get quick service, large portions, and an extensive, varied menu. Solid food. Good food. Southern comfort food. Just good ol' down home cooking offered in a casual, unpretentious atmosphere, served by friendly women.

"Hey, there, Wingfoot. How y'all doin?" sang out a large woman serving burgers and fries to a couple of men in overalls.

"I'm just fine, Mary. Got any grub left in here?"

"Plenty. Got plenty. You gentlemen just grab a table anywhere. I'll be with you directly."

Several hikers—we'd noticed their backpacks on the porch—jerked upright with the mention of Wingfoot. Several pairs of eyes followed as we walked by, turned the corner, and took a booth by the window.

"The handbook business has become very competitive, and I predict that in a couple of years, it will become brutal," Dan said as we took our seats.

"How many are being published now?"

"No idea, John. Clubs are still publishing, and every year another thru-hiker publishes his notion of how to prepare hikers to meet the challenge. There are several top publications and the competition between them is fierce but my book is still, by far, the most popular."

"When is your next edition coming out?"

"Around first of February. I'd like to be sooner, but dealing with editing and printers…it's just a monster, John. You have no idea. Those last few weeks. I'm working nearly twenty-four-seven."

"I need to be listed, Dan. Erwin will have a true hiker hostel for the first time. Hikers need to know. Next season's hikers … think about them, Dan. It's gonna be important to those hikers that my hostel is listed." I leaned toward Wingfoot looking him straight in the eye. "Lots of hikers skip Erwin. First, because it's a three-mile walk into town, and secondly because Jan Curran's denigration of the town has gotten around. Word-of-mouth has it Erwin's not good to them, and this is patently untrue, flat wrong, just wrong, probably the consequence of Curran's own personality and false assumptions. When hikers learn that I'm just sixty feet off the trail, it will make a difference. I aim to change the message about Erwin. So … Dan … you have an opportunity here to correct a wrong."

"I like what you have in mind, John. Twenty bucks for a bunk in the hostel and ten-dollar tenting. And your timing is spot on. In ten years…in ten years, if not five, traffic on the trail will double, so …"

"And that includes full bathhouse privileges and three free dinner shuttles into town …"

"I understand that, John. It's a good deal. You know, I've been telling hikers if they budget carefully, they can thru-hike for a dollar a mile…two thousand plus. You're in line with that, John…you're in line with that. I'm happy to include you in the book for that reason. But, that's not the problem."

"What's the … let's talk about the problem."

"The question is; can you be open by April? Early March is a popular leave date. A bunch of thru-hikers will hit you first of April. How do you know you'll be ready by then? You won't start construction until January?"

"Correct. That's right. But it's not a problem. Simply not a problem, Dan."

"Heck, John. Seems like a problem to me!" Dan leaned forward, matching my posture. "You can't just wave a magic wand. It isn't gonna happen just because you say so, right?"

"Won't take a magic wand, Dan. I know what I'm doing. I've built things. Been doing construction since I was a kid. Spent lots of my time banging nails. My dad was a contractor, a damn good one. I like learning things. I pay attention. Ask questions. Believe me, Dan. I can do this because it ain't the first time." and with that, I sat back glaring at him.

"John, I can't hang my butt on a clothes line for everybody to whack at will. This ... like I said, the guidebook business is fiercely competitive. They're all looking for blunders and I can't afford a blunder this year. My book has become very, very accurate. I've hiked the trail seven times looking for ..."

"Dan, did you ever hear the story about Chuck Yeager, the famous test pilot? The guy that broke the sound barrier?" I looked back and forth between Roger and Dan, both sitting across from me in the booth, per my instructions to Roger. I leaned forward on my forearms and continued, looking straight at Dan. "During the second world war he was one of the few pilots who made ace-in-a-day, downing five enemy aircraft in a single mission. Back on the ground his mechanic asked him how in the heck did he do that, and Yeager responded, You don't understand. There were five of them and only one of me ... I didn't have a choice."

I delivered that with precision and paused, looking straight into Dan's eyes. "So, Dan, that's me. I'm gonna get this done because I don't have a choice. I get the property in January, and here, look at this." I pulled out a folded copy of the contract from my back pocket, the contract I had signed in Bob Manuel's office. "See this, Dan? Right here. That's my signature ... right there." I held the paper between Dan and Roger and pointed to my name. "My signature right there, see that? ... commits everything I own to this project ... every dime Dan, every dime I own. So ... Dan. I'll be open first of April, because you know what? I don't have a choice."

Dan looked at me for a long time. Glanced at Roger. Looked back at me. "Okay, John. You're in, but don't make me look silly. You have to be open ... you have to be open first of April. Send me about 200 words describing your hostel. I'll put you in. But, please. Don't let me down."

"Dan ... when you're trying to win the Daytona 500, you don't concentrate on the car up ahead spinning out of control. You concentrate on the gap between him and the wall. Like Yeager said, you don't concentrate on risks. You concentrate on results. Dan, nothing's going to prevent me from getting the job done."

* * *

Late start. JD's for breakfast. More time spent with Roger at DeHaven's place than expected. Long visit in Hot Springs. Too long. Exhausted. Both of us. Going home. Birmingham Alabama. Home. All my life, even travel, extensive travel. You never forget home. Dived Cuba, most of the Caribbean, Australia, traveled to Mexico. Central America. Seen wonderful places. Nothing like Alabama. Cuba even. Clarke and me in Cuba. What a trip. Diving the Isle of Youth. La Evangelista, Columbus called ... named it second voyage. Became Devil's Island when the Caribbean pirates based there. Dived Avalon, Jardines de la Reina. You gotta be a shark junkie to dive Avalon. Stallworth loved it. Twenty-five meters, good visibility, not much underwater current, and maybe fifteen, twenty reef sharks. Clarke was in heaven.

Come on, Shores. Wake up! ... Isle of Pines. Isle of Pines. Think about the Isle of Pines. What a trip.

...............?

Isle of Pines? ... pines. What happened to the pines? Thing was like a field of corn. Castro's Isle of Youth. Changed the name. College kids working their butts off in tropical heat cuttin cane. Jeez, can you imagine? Been everywhere. Bonair. Aruba. Belize. Dived Ambergris Caye. Sharks. Talk about sharks! That submarine buoy. Three thousand feet of water. One hundred and ten down the chain. Communications, some kind of communications thing. Off the coast Ocean Beach. South Shore. New Providence Island. Submarine buoy one-hundred-foot dive. Love deep dives. Just comes natural. Easiest thing I ever did, Shores. Communications signals draw sharks. Lots of White Tip Sharks cutting all around. Look left.

Look right. Here they come. No fear. Fascinating. Stingray City north side of Cayman. Knew about that place before anybody. Fed Manatees. Stingrays, big like the hood of a car. Fed Moray eels. Man, those trips. So lucky to be ... so lucky. Met so many wonderful people. Met Jock Cousteau. Jacques-Yves Cousteau invented the Aqua-Lung. Explored the ocean on the Calypso. Met Cousteau. Came within a gnat's whisker of getting on that boat. The Sheraton New Orleans. The lobby bar. Oh, man what a bar. Closed that thing one night with Jean-Michel. Jean-Michel Cousteau. Yes, I did. Three in the morning ... we closed that baby down. What a night. Damn barge sank the Calypso last year. Still. Still. Still. Coming home ... nothing like home.

"State-line coming up Roger, here we go ... sweet home Alabama ..."

Sweet home Alabama. Comin home Baby. Comin home. Gotta stay awake. First thing, call Charlotte. Hi Baby. Let's go to Highlands for dinner. Drop Claire off at Gran's. Need to sit and look at you for an hour or something. We'll have wine. Ask Frank to hold that table in the corner. Just us. Want to just ... just hold hands. Just look at you for an hour. Gotta stay awake. Gotta stay awake. Talk about our future. Our future Baby. Talk about our future.

"Roger. First thing. Let's arrange to get Richard and us together somewhere, maybe grill some steaks at my place, you know ... have a planning session and ..."

"Roger?"

..............!

"Roger!"

Come on, Roger. Wake up you bum. Talk to me. Gotta stay awake. Okay. Okay. I'm gonna stop for coffee. King-sized Baby Ruth for the rush. Stop and open all four doors. Get you awake then, ol' buddy ... ol' buddy ... ol' buddy.

* * *

We had taken US 25 out of Hot Springs which travels along the French Broad for some distance to Newport, North Carolina where we picked up I-40, then I-75 in Farragut, Tennessee, and finally I-59 south into Alabama. It was late. Our planned two-hour visit with Wingfoot had stretched into five. We left Hot Springs, and as soon as we reached I-40, we exited for a quick drive-thru burger and refueling. We lost more time stopping for coffee. It was a long trip after a day filled with anxiety. But I had achieved my goal. I would be in Dan's book.

It was nearly eleven when I dropped Roger off at his house in Homewood, a short ten-minute drive from my house. The first thing I did, arriving at my home in Mountain Brook, was call Charlotte and make a date for the next evening. Then I stood for a long time by the phone thinking, what have I gotten myself into. I had until January, very early January to wrap up my affairs. I had to sell this house. This house. I remember saying this house and feeling nothing. So odd, I thought at the time. Scary odd. I had no feelings at all about leaving this house and starting a new life in Tennessee. I remember walking into the living room and from there into the kitchen. Turning a kitchen chair, I sat backwards resting my chin on the chair-back. Something was missing. Something was different. I was missing. I realized in that moment that I was different. It was me. The house didn't feel the same because I no longer felt myself there. It was barren. I could see in my mind's eye the empty house. The barren four walls of the kitchen. The cabinet doors standing open. The house emptied out. My stuff somewhere else. I realized that my life was that stuff, and wherever it went, I also went. I was somewhere else. I had left my soul, my heart and soul, back in Erwin, Tennessee. My future was in Erwin.

The next morning, I called everybody I knew, all the people who had been important in my life, and told them the news. I was cheerful. I delivered an upbeat message about my future prospects. It took all morning, but toward the end I had honed my delivery to the point I could get through the story in less than ten minutes. I longed to speak with Stallworth, but he was still out of town. I fulfilled my promise to Mickey Townsend. We had a long lunch, and by the time we parted he was complimentary and wishing me well. Of course, I told everyone I spoke to that my house was for sale. I would appreciate a little word-of-mouth advertising. If your referral becomes a buyer, I had said, I'll give you a finder's fee. A thousand bucks, I had said.

I asked everyone about real estate agents. Did they know a good one? Had I the time, I would do the job myself, I said. For sale by owner. Keep the 6% commission. But, that wouldn't be prudent, I told them. I needed to sell. Sooner rather than later. And it happened just that way. Mickey was the one who came through for me. His aunt was a top agent specializing in Mountain Brook properties. Walking through the house that day, she said to pack three-quarters of my clothing into suitcases, and store them in the garage. The closets would look bigger, she said. It was October by the time I scheduled the open-house showing. I Painted the exterior a beautiful dark green; blue-grey shutters; bright white trim. Fixed little things here and there. Reworked the landscaping. The place looked wonderful from the street.

Have a fire blazing in the fireplace, she said. Hickory wood makes the most attractive fire. Mickey's aunt certainly knew her stuff. Have soft classical music playing on the stereo. And did I have a bread maker, she asked. I did. I motioned, and we walked into the kitchen where I pointed to my Westinghouse sitting on the counter. It made beautiful bread. I usually baked at least twice a week, I told her. Cost me seventy bucks ... plus the gym membership. She laughed at my joke and immediately flipped serious. Time the bread-maker's bake-cycle to start just before your open house, she said. Let the soft, warm aroma of fresh-baked bread fill your home. Smart woman.

Two things made an easy sale possible. First, my house was a modest home in an upscale neighborhood. Mountain Brook is a small, intimate, prestigious community built on rolling, heavily forested hills. Beautiful, mature trees are everywhere. The streets meander in gentle curves up, down, and around those hills in beautiful fashion. The properties are very large, two and three acres for the larger homes, and these larger homes, at three to five thousand square-foot, are sprinkled all through the neighborhood. Two small, tastefully-designed shopping areas, peppered with boutiques, bistros, and specialty shops, complete the feel of a high-class, elegant community.

The second contribution came as a complete surprise. Following the housing slump of the early '90s, government agencies became involved in the housing market. Political candidates campaigned on their housing policies. This political movement culminated in the passing of the Taxpayer Relief Act. The act permanently exempted from taxation the capital gains on the sale of a personal residence, encouraging people to buy more expensive first homes. The new legislation was signed into law in August. My open house was in October. The family that bought my house knew the legislation was coming and understood the implications. They told me they had long dreamed of living in Mountain Brook, but lacked the financial resources. This was their chance, they said, and they took the leap.

* * *

Most people just say *Highlands*. Family and investors call it *Frank's place*. Frank Stitt had become a celebrity chef in Birmingham. Like a smash hit first novel, The Highlands Bar and Grill was Frank Stitt's first effort. A country boy from Cullman, Alabama, a little town at the southern tip of the Appalachians, mostly rural, mostly agricultural—a mix of commercial chicken, cow, and potato farms, as well as an assortment of small, family farms—he knew southern cuisine even if back then he didn't call it that.

Like most kids with a streak of genius, Frank did not like school. He received his primary education at Alice Waters' Chez Panisse in Berkley, California. Inspired by then-chef Jeremiah Tower, Frank moved to France where he worked in a couple dozen kitchens throughout Provence and Burgundy. At twenty-eight, he returned to Birmingham. With his mother's help, he launched his restaurant dream. Frenched-up Southern cuisine is popular all over the country now. Every upscale community has its quasi-French bistro. But, back in 1982, Stitt's vision was the original. And his success at Highlands has elevated the restaurant scene in Birmingham to nationally recognized heights.

* * *

The Highlands Bar and Grill is located down the hill from my home in Mountain Brook, and over near the University of Alabama, Birmingham. The area was not the best block in town back in '82. It is transformed today, largely due to Stitt's success. This is where I took Charlotte for dinner.

The stone and stucco façade, with over-large, square and palladium-style windows, emits a warm, inviting Spanish feel. We entered the elegantly-designed bar, and pushed through the glass doors into an even more elegant dining room, an open concept with a variety of seating areas embraced by walls decorated with French art posters. After an exchange of pleasantries, the hostess took us to our reserved table. In a moment, Frank came over for a short chat. And then, we were alone.

"Remember that long weekend getaway when I just took off in the Corvette ... after that unfortunate thing with Victor Hanson III? It was August; perfect weather. Beautiful day. Unusual for August. I had become sick of the newspaper. I knew it was falling apart. Salary cuts. Demotions. It was like senior management was lobbing hand grenades into the HR department. The paper was going down. Sure of it. And, Charlotte? ... it was impossible for me to keep going. My faith in the people I worked for had deteriorated so quickly.

"I spent Friday night near Chattanooga. I remember Saturday morning, went up Lookout Mountain, went out on that rocky point away from the main overlook. You've been there. The mountain. The city in the distance. The river below. The wind beautifully scented, and gentle, cool for August, and dry. The sun had warmed the rocks. It produced a feeling, all of it, the air, the sun, the proportions, the enormous view. Baby, I can't ... I don't have the words, but in spite of the grandeur of it all, I felt as low and dismal as I ever had. I sat on that rock numbed and vacant. In a few minutes, I pulled out my pocket journal, that little notebook I used to carry when I worked for the *News*, and you'll never guess what I wrote. I wrote ... One year from today, I will no longer be working for the *News*. One year from today, I may not be living in Birmingham. And I put in parentheses; Get ready for this change.

"That's okay, Baby. You don't have to say anything ... my prediction was off a little, but now I can look back on that point in my life and I know something inside was trying to speak to me, trying to tell me that my life ... the life I was living wasn't supportable. Trying to tell me that it was impossible to keep this up. The urge to escape. To run away. It was the urge itself ... that urge, Baby, that feeling was a message from my soul. Telling me I needed to pay attention, to wake up and look around. Up on that mountain, the darkness inside me, so stark against all that sunshine and vastness, it woke me up. Baby, I started … right then, I started paying attention. Something inside me set in motion. I didn't dwell on it. You know that. I never spoke of it. This is the first time you've heard this, but it never left. That attentiveness stayed with me. It woke up a feeling I used to have … that I could do anything, I could … when I make up my mind, Baby, you know this, I can do anything. I always knew … no, you don't have to say anything, Baby. When I got back from that little escape, I was different. Before … before, sitting up there in the sunshine as gray as I've ever been in my life, I was grieving, Baby, it was like my best friend had cancer, and I knew he would die. The *News*. Baby, I had loved it so much, but it was dying, and I was grief-stricken, that beautiful picture in my mind was fading, and it was like losing a family … how I had seen my life for years and years, like losing my best friend. I knew I had to let go. I had to let go and move on."

"John, I understand. I hope you know I understand. I'm in the grief business. You're talking to the expert here. If what you're doing is not feeding your soul, it does the opposite. It wears on you. It tears you down." Charlotte said this softly as she reached for my hands across the table.

"I'm sorry about being in Erwin so long without calling, Baby. In Erwin, I was just so …"

"I understand John. Forget that. I've already forgotten. I understand … John, I understood then, and I understand now. You know why?" she said, squeezing my hands. "I understand … you! That's why I'm here right now sitting at this table. I like what I see. You are strong, and you are so smart. You have been searching, but you know what?" she asked. "When one door shuts, God opens another. But you are so special, John … you walked into the room and there were ten doors open."

"Baby, I wish I had met you …"

"John, you are my man. I'm like you," she said, letting go and patting my hands. "You say you've found your soulmate. Well, I have too. This is what I want … what I've been looking for, too. I like how you've taken to Claire. That's so important to me. I love seeing the two of you together. Out in the back yard that day, you were teaching her to play croquet, how to hit the ball through the hoop and still be in play. It was so cute. I stood ... I was washing dishes. I watched the whole time. You are very good with her, and that means so much to me. Everything."

"You will like Erwin, Charlotte. It lies in a gorgeous valley. The people there call it the Valley Beautiful. Don't know who came up with that twist, but it's true. The Nolichucky river runs through it. We'll have plenty of time in the off seasons to canoe and hike the area. We're not far from the French Broad, the Nantahala. We can picnic up on Beauty Spot with Claire. There's a piece of flat water down-river from the hostel where we ... where you can teach her to paddle."

"John, that dark time you spoke of happens to people when disconnecting from old systems. Some people never get over the quandary, can't turn the corner, can't fill the hole when something they had come to bank on, to build on, suddenly shrinks to nothing. They're disconnecting, not fully out of the old world, not yet fully in the new. When things stop working like we've come to expect, then our ideas about how life works no longer explain things, and confusion follows. But you are different. You went through that tunnel and out the other side in a flash. You're in bright sunshine again."

"Baby, I'm hoping you'll come."

"Let's work on that, John. There's a lot to think about. I've got to consider Claire's feelings." Charlotte was patting my hands again, and took one in both hands. "I'm open to that conversation. I'm not going to rush into anything, but I'm open. I like your plan. I like that. I can see you talking gear with hikers. They're going to love you, John. Now look, I think that's our dinner coming. I can't wait to dig into those crab cakes."

"That's Paul. He's a runner tonight, but I heard he'll be assistant manager when Arnold leaves, heard that before I left for Hot Springs."

"Hi Paul! How have you been. I'm so delighted you're working our section. How was that trip through Little River Canyon?"

* * *

Roger, driving the largest U-Haul you can rent, towing a trailer carrying my Taurus, pulled into the new Holiday Inn, Erwin, Tennessee. I followed, driving the Corvette. I pulled myself achingly from the bucket seat and walked stiffly through a slush of snow toward the truck. It was about five in the afternoon and everything I owned had been hauled from Birmingham to Erwin.

My boats were tied on top the Taurus. The Old Town tandem I bought from Roger was nearly as long as the car. Next to it, my pride and joy, a Mad River solo canoe. And my Perception kayak, being shorter and thinner, was wedged on its edge between the canoes. It was December 28. During this transition period, DeHaven had given me permission to set up camp in his old house. After putting my furniture in storage, I would meet with Bubba Evely, get my line of credit established, and finalize the sale. This was scheduled to take place on January 2.

The snow began falling heavily as we passed through Chattanooga. By the time we reached Knoxville, we knew the more direct route, taking US 11 through Greenville and Tusculum, was out of the question. We stayed on I-81 and took I-26 to Johnson City, making a big loop back toward Erwin on the Interstate. Even though the snow was sticking to the road and becoming dangerous for a very large truck pulling a heavily loaded trailer, staying with the Interstate highways seemed the more prudent decision. Our seven-hour trip became nearly eleven.

Holding my hand high in the air, I got Roger's attention, and motioned to him that he should move the truck over and out of the way. Then I signaled one finger up, meaning I'd be back in a minute. Turning, I walked under the portico toward the entrance of the motel. Steadying myself by holding to the back of a convenient bench, I removed my Sebago Men's Classic Leather Weejuns one at a time and dumped out the snow.

At the reservation desk, I met a cheerful, bony-thin, woman in a denim dress wearing white galoshes who started explaining where we should park the truck and trailer. She spoke in a rapid staccato; a voice with a southern accent unlike any southerner I had ever met.

"He's pulling to the side, ma'am. If you don't mind us sitting out there for just a few minutes, all I need is to make a phone call. If you'll direct me to your ..."

"Where y'all moving to?" She asked.

"Here," I said. "Erwin, Tennessee."

"Oh? Well, I bet you're working for Nuclear Services. You look the type." she chirped.

"No ... No. I'm starting a business."

I needed to make my call to DeHaven, but my plans in Erwin needed attention too. It occurred to me in the moment, this person might be a good contact. It crossed my mind that hikers must call here all the time seeking information. Anybody who ever considered a business start-up knows the pride you feel, and the desire to tell the whole world what you're about to do.

"Oh? What kind of business? Erwin isn't the easiest place to start a business, but I guess no place is easy, huh. Y'know? I mean, for startin a business n'all."

"A hostel. A hostel by the Chestoa Bridge ... for Appalachian Trail hikers."

This stopped her. She blinked her blue-shadowed buggy eyes several times. She seemed not to understand. I started to explain just what all that meant, but she interrupted.

"Hikers! Wow! A hiker hostel!" The bug-eyed, chirpy woman said this using quick, little gasps and arched eyebrows as exclamation points.

"You know, my mamma, God rest her soul, my mamma used to help the hikers, trail angel they called her, used to pick them up hitchhiking, would drive up your way just to catch them walking to Erwin, pick them up and take um to Pizza Plus, all the pizza you can eat. They liked that. Helped them all kinds of ways, carried them to shower at the Y, you know? just cause she liked what they were doing. Wow! A hiker hostel!"

"Yes, now hang on a minute. I need to make that phone call. Where are your public phones?"

"Here. I can show you." She disappeared from the reservation desk, and popped out a door to my left all knees and elbows. "Follow me. Just down here, see?" She stopped about ten feet ahead of me, left-hand on hip, poised on one leg, the other out at ninety degrees balanced by the heel of her boot, her long, skinny arm high and pointing. "The sign right there?" she said, glancing back at me. "That's the lobby phone. You can use that." Then she whirled and whipped past me saying, "And I'll run out and tell your driver where to park. I'll be right back." Her long, bony legs had her halfway through the lobby when over her shoulder she called back, "You have a reservation? … I'll be right back."

"Ma'am, I just … I stopped just to …" and with that, she went out the door.

I was filling a styrofoam cup with coffee when she came back, Roger in tow. Like a ballet dancer, the night manager waltzed straight toward me, her denim dress making a sound like someone shaking dust from a rug.

"Mr. Shores. Will you be offering shuttles for the hikers?"

"Roger, you didn't have to come in. I'm about ready to …"

“He’s looking for the bathroom, Mr. Shores … go down that hall, Mr. Perrin. It’s to your right. You’ll see the ice machine” she said, hip ajar, boot-heel out, arm stretched high and pointing. “So, Mr. Shores, most hostels offer shuttles, and I was wondering.”

“Yes. We will, as a matter of fact. Yes.”

“Well, if you are, you’ll likely be needing drivers, and I want to put my name in the hat. I know all the roads around here, Mr. Shores. My momma used to take hikers up to Sams Gap and Flint Gap, Devils Creek Gap, Indian Grave Gap, Iron Mountain Gap, I know all the gaps. I know those roads real well, if you’ll be needing anybody. I can do that.”

“Well, Miss … ah … you are?”

“My name’s Randee; Randee Pander, but folks call me Miss Randee, you know, that southern thing. I ain’t married, but … aah … not yet, least ways.”

“Well, Miss Randee, write your name and phone number on a piece of paper, and we’ll let you know if we need anybody. Now, I need to make that call.”

* * *

“She was a nice lady.”

“That’s been my experience here, Roger. Everybody I’ve met has been very pleasant and helpful. Old time southern hospitality, I guess.” Saying this, I started laughing.

“What?”

“She was funny. Did you get a good look? The eye makeup? That was pretty intense … dark blue. But nothing else. Everything else about her was plain and simple. I think she was trying to hide her buggy eyes, but they stood out more.”

We were seated on DeHaven’s porch glider. Sitting down, we heard the clear, plastic covering over the cushions crackle in the cold. Both of us had our jackets zipped, arms crossed tightly, our hands stuck deep into our arm pits. It was Roger's idea to sit there.

"I'm getting out of this truck, John," he had said. "Been in this thing for eleven hours; eleven hours enough already." I heard the door locks pop. "If I sit here any longer, I won't be able to move for three days."

"But Roger, we've got the heater going. It's toast ..."

"That heater ain't gonna help my busted butt, John."

"How about the Corvette? You can put the seat back."

"The Corvette? Are you crazy? This body?" he had said, turning to me with both hands on his massive chest. "You'd have to pull me out on a gurney; hook a come-along on that tree over there and pull me out on a ..."

"Okay, okay, Roger."

So, we climbed down from the truck cab and took our seats on the glider. It wasn't bad. The porch was protected on three sides. A light wind was coming from the back of the house. And the snow was new, and beautiful.

"How long?"

"From the call at the motel? If he left right away, maybe another fifteen minutes."

We sat quietly for a while watching the snow blowing through the hazy glare of the streetlight at the end of the bridge. It was nearly eleven o'clock. The new Holiday Inn was only a mile or so back on Temple Hill Road. Due to heavier snowfall up on the mountain, it would take DeHaven at least forty-five minutes to get here from his place at Spivey Gap. But my call was thirty minutes ago. The big U-Haul and the trailered Taurus barely fit where the old Econoline van used to sit. DeHaven would have to park behind my Corvette on the other side of the truck.

"Was DeHaven upset you called so late?"

"No, I don't think so. I had called before we left Birmingham. Told him we were on the way. I guess he figured the snow would hold us up. First thing he asked was how's the trip. Told him it was pretty bad weather for driving a big truck.

He understood. I was worried about him driving down here at night in the snow, but he said he was used to it. Said he threw a dozen cement blocks in the back of his van when he heard the forecast. Said the old Ford would get him here and back alright."

"I thought DeHaven had moved out."

"He did."

"The house is empty?"

"Far as I know. Supposed to be. Can't see through the curtains." And I motioned toward the front door.

"What about this glider?"

"His wife didn't want it. Ancient. They have all new porch furniture, that plastic wicker stuff, DeHaven said. Flamingo pink. Told me I could keep this if I want, but if not, put it out by the road with a big sign saying yours free. Said it would be gone in twenty minutes."

"Ancient is right. My grandmother had one of these. Is this art deco? Must be from the '30s or something."

"Lattice-pattern three-seater, Roger. Pretty ordinary. My grandmother had one too, probably from the fifties. They made millions just like this one. I think gliders got popular after the war. Lots of people just wanted to sit, sit on their front porch and do nothing, heal maybe. You know, for them, it was the depression and right on top that, the war. I've never seen any but had a metal seat. I think these cushions were added later."

"Is that DeHaven?"

A familiar white cargo van eased to a stop on the roadway where one could see the porch between the house and the U-Haul cab. He had come down Chestoa Pike from the other direction. He was to our right peering through the driver-side window. The light from the bridge and the glare of the snow lit his face just enough to reveal a slight lift of the chin, another southern way to say hello, and confirm our presence on his front porch. The van eased off and in a few minutes, DeHaven came around the back of the trailer slogging through the snow, his pant legs tucked into a pair of ten-inch Wesco Fire-Stormer boots laced to the toe. Snow glistened in his raven-black hair. A striking man in silhouette against the snowy background.

* * *

DeHaven had lit the Warm Morning kerosene stove for us, and the place was heating up. There was a distinct old-house odor when we arrived that I did not notice before. That odor was being replaced with a kerosene odor. Between the two, I preferred the kerosene.

DeHaven's new house had been finished earlier than he had expected. He was quite pleased with the work his youthful builders had done. With his furniture gone now, this house, my future home, Erwin's future hostel, looked shabby, to say the least. It had the appearance of having been built in several stages. The exterior was a mixture of stone from the Nolichucky, some clapboard siding, and concrete block. Old-style cinder block. Probably made one at a time by a local workman in his back yard. The Sears Roebuck catalogue used to carry the Wizard block maker for $57.50. One man, working alone, could turn out 125 cinder blocks in a ten-hour day, so the catalog said, and the sales copy projected a profit of ten dollars. Ten bucks in one day was an enormous amount of money to a man making a dollar-a-day as a department store clerk. The big, heavy, steel-and-cast-iron machine came with twenty-five iron pallets. Each block was removed from the machine on one of those pallets, and by the time the operator had made twenty-five blocks, the first one was dry enough for its pallet to be reused.

Back at the turn of the century, concrete was a miracle product. One of Thomas Edison's inventions was a single-pour, two-story house with a grand front porch. Some of his houses still exist, but the company he started is long gone. In

1900, Harmon S. Palmer patented the first commercial machine that would be used to create concrete blocks. Back then, they were called cinder blocks. The aggregate used in the concrete mixture was coal cinders, the waste from coal-fired furnaces. Cinders were everywhere and free to anyone who would haul them away. Today the blocks are concrete and fine gravel, and called concrete masonry units, CMUs for short. The cinder blocks that Palmer's first machine produced, were 30x8x10. Since the blocks were so large, they had to be set in place by a hand-cranked machine. That was the year 1900. He invented the prototype of the Wizard in 1905. It produced a block 8x10x12. By the 1930s, masonry organizations set as a standard the block we use to this day; 8x8x16.

The house, part of it, at least, was built of Wizard-produced cinder blocks. The roof was of tin, real tin back in that day. I don't know exactly when the house was built, DeHaven said it was over a 100 years old, but metal roofing has a long history dating as far back as Jerusalem in 970 BC, the roof of a temple, I believe. This is something I remember my father talking about. He said the Romans used copper as roof covering for the Pantheon. Many medieval European buildings have copper roofs over 500 years old, he said. Dad preferred a metal roof, but, considering the cost, all the houses he built were shingled.

The DeHaven house had a standard, standing-seam metal roof of tin-coated steel. This kind of roofing came in rolls that would be cut to the full pitch of the roof. Once cut, the sheet would be run through a crimping device that prepared the standing seam. The fastening system was hidden from view and from rain and snow by the standing seam which would be crimped again to interlock the panels. Nails secured a side lap along one edge of a panel, which was then hidden by the standing rib, the seam of the next panel. This roof must have been poorly done, or maybe the problem was the poor quality of the tinned steel, but it was obvious to the eye that the roof had failed. Every seam was coated with roof tar, it looked to have been patched many, many times. Maybe the crimping of the seam had been done by hand, but for whatever reason, it had failed.

Part of the problem may have been the shape of the roof. It wasn't a standard gable or saddle-type roof. It wasn't your standard hip roof either. It was a hybrid of those two. A misshapen hip roof would be a fair description. A high-quality craftsman installing a standing-seam system on this oddly-shaped roof would have a dickens of a job on his hands. A poorer craftsman would make a mess of it. I suspect that was the case here.

The front porch was set in under the main roof, protected left and right by portions of the house. The porch floor was concrete, cracked concrete, and had once been painted. Three concrete steps brought you to porch level. My intention was to create an expansive deck across the whole front of the house level with this porch floor. A covered deck. The hostel's living room, so to speak. There would be a propane grill, a couple of vending machines dispensing snacks and beverages. Long, sturdy picnic tables. Deck chairs and maybe a bench or two. A place for hikers to congregate, grill their suppers, and engage each other. This was the kind of community I wanted to cultivate.

The front yard was a narrow, all-gravel parking lot. Around the left side, a little 10' x 10' shed hung on the side of the house. It was DeHaven's brother-in-law's room at one time. I planned to turn that into my first private rental unit. Further along, you came to an open back yard. No trees. And the lawn, if that is what one would call it, stretched beyond my property line into the neighbor's property with no discernable separation. Standing alone, roughly in the middle of the back yard, was one of those steel ramps you can get from Sears. You drive your car up on this ramp for front end work; like changing the oil. A sizable patch of dead grass told me that DeHaven took out the plug and let the old oil drain out on the ground.

The lot was small, just over one-acre and roughly triangular, bounded by Chestoa Pike along the left side and River Road along the right. These two roads forked off from the foot of the Chestoa Bridge, giving the triangular lot a rounded point. The house sat within that point. The new bathhouse would be located in the back close to Chestoa Pike, and I had plans for building a row of cabins along River Road sometime in the future. As soon as possible, we would build an eight-foot-high solid barrier fence along the back line of the property to spare my neighbor the anguish of being in full view of the coterie of hikers that would someday be camping there.

Stepping through the front door, one entered the living room. Old brown carpeting still covered the floor. The Warm Morning kerosene heater stood to the right in a little alcove, the portion of the house framing the right side of the front porch. Straight ahead was a framed opening to the kitchen. The walls were of painted wood paneling; a yellowed white, streaked from aging. During my previous visits, I had noticed that the paneling was wormy chestnut. Wormy because by 1940, four-billion American chestnut trees had been killed by a pathogenic fungus, and once dead, stood like white ghosts across the entire mountain landscape.

In the Appalachians, one in every four hardwoods had been an American chestnut. These magnificent trees had two distinctive characteristics, first, they were very large, having a crown up to fifty feet across in open fields. Longfellow's village smithy famously stood under a spreading chestnut tree. In the forest they grew straight and branch-free for fifty feet, attaining heights of 100 feet or more. A typical forest chestnut when mature would reach five-feet in diameter.

Once dead, they stood like this, at full height, limbs attached, and bleached white for years due to the second characteristic. They resisted rot. Being dead, however, they had no resistance to a tiny wood borer whose voracious appetite left the infested dead wood drilled with tiny, pin-sized holes. Even so, the standing dead chestnut remained an important, cheap lumber source for years. Millions of barns, sheds, and chicken houses were built with chestnut wood shot through and through with worm holes. DeHaven's living room paneling could very well have been a recycled chicken house.

Toward the back of the living room, a short hallway, leading from the far right corner, opened to the master bedroom. A similar hall to the left led to the bathroom. On the left side of this hall, a door opened into another small bedroom, its exterior walls framing the left side of the front porch. I planned on extending this bedroom into the side yard about ten feet to create space for the hostel. The bathroom had a standard built-in tub. No shower. A toilet. A sink set in a small vanity. The walls of the bath were papered blue with fist-sized orange fish. Cracked and dirty black and white linoleum tile covered the floor. Linoleum. Canvas-backed. The real stuff, made of linseed oil, powdered cork, and resin.

* * *

The next morning came with steel gray skies spitting snow. The bitter cold told me the roads were still rutted with frozen snow and ice. We had a truck load of furniture to unload, and, more pressing, we had a rented truck and trailer to return with contractual costs mounting by the day. First thing, I called the rental company in Johnson City and negotiated an emergency extension. They gave me three days to return the truck without further fees. I had already rented the largest storage unit I could find. Roger had a great idea. On the way, we stopped by the Rendezvous. In the early afternoon, a younger, rowdier crowd would begin filtering in. Flashing sixty-bucks in my hand, I had no trouble convincing two of these obviously unemployed men to help us unload the truck. Roger, with his take-charge, don't-mess-with-me demeanor operating in full, supervised the unloading and unit-stacking and packing. I stood watching the unloading progress, pointing here and there, having the men set aside the furniture and kitchen supplies we would need over at the DeHaven's house. Roger suggested we stop calling it DeHaven's house and start calling it The Hostel.

It would be nice to crawl into real beds. We had slept in sleeping bags laid out on the old carpeting in front of the Warm Morning heater. All the sundries we would need for a time had been stowed in the Ford Taurus, including a small selection of kitchen gear, my spice rack, salt, sugar, all the necessities. On our way out of Birmingham, we had stopped at Kroger to pick up some groceries, and Roger had asked if I had been mindful enough to set aside kitchen stuff for the house. After bantering back and forth over my snarky reply, he asked if I had brought along a large pot. Roger was going to cook, he informed me, a foregone conclusion, I had secretly hoped, and he proceeded to fill the shopping cart with supplies and his favorite condiments. The Corvette had been towed to Erwin stuffed full with grocery bags, and boxes.

By the time the house was in order, it was eight o'clock. Roger had a recipe for what he called instant chili. Several hours later, we sat in the living room with steaming bowls of chili, planning Roger's return trip to Birmingham. He would borrow the Ford Taurus, he said, and return with his big pickup and pop-up camper. Richard would drive my car. We sat on the couch, he with his sweetened ice tea, and me with my favorite IPA beer. Steaming chili notwithstanding, a chill ran over me.

Can this be done? Can it be done in time? This grimy old house. A hostel? Can this be done?

* * *

January 2, 1998. A new year. Brand new year; brand new start. Yesterday I had dutifully eaten my bowl of Hoppin' John, by damn, with cornbread. A traditional New Year's Day meal in the South. Brings good luck, the old folks say. Please let it work this time. Lord, please. I'm gonna need lots of luck.

"Mr. Shores? I can see you now."

"Hi Bubba, how ya been, how's the family?"

"Fine, John … finer than frog's hair split three ways. So, you're back. Did things go well in Birmingham? Take a seat, John. You can sit right there." Bubba pointed to the same armless upholstered chair where I sat the last time I was here.

"Sold my house to the fourth family that looked at it, Bubba. Easier than I thought. Housing market is flourishing in Birmingham. I'm quite happy with the outcome all around. Got my camp established at the old DeHaven place. Everything I own is stored in A-Z Self-Storage. I'm ready to go to work. Just need to wrap up the financials."

"Well good, good, good," Bubba said, shuffling through his desk drawer.

"John, I don't see your file here. Jean must have it at her desk. Sit tight and I'll be right back."

Glad Bubba suggested a line of credit over a straight-out loan. More control and lower interest rate. One of the lesser-known, lesser-used options a bank offers. Don't think I ever heard a bank advertise them. Lot better than taking out a loan every month or two, repaying it, and then doing it again. Perfect when you can't figure the funds needed up front, or dealing with unpredictable costs. Whatever the borrower wants, for whatever the borrower has in mind. Just need collateral or good standing. Here it's DeHaven's property. Mine when I deliver that thirty-six-point-five cashier's check.

"Here we go, Mr. Shores." Bubba bustled back into his office in his usual high-energy way. "I've marked all the places for you to sign and initial. This is a Cross pen, John. When you finish signing that thing, stick it in your pocket. A small token of the appreciation we have for choosing us as your bank. Now, while you are signing that, let me explain this is a revolving line of credit. Your limit is forty-thousand. When you pay it down, you can keep on writing checks. Interest is due only on that portion you have borrowed, the part you have spent, okay? Got that? Pay it to zero, you still have the capacity to borrow without returning here and applying again. We'll be here in your hour of need, John. If there's anything I can do for you ... ever ... you just let me know."

* * *

"Now, John. You can stop apologizin, I'm an expert drivin in snow. But, I been stuck up'n that house for four days. My wife's beautiful, and I'm one happy man and all that, but she's drivin me crazy with them honey-dos. Never seen so much stuff need being done to a brand new house."

I had parked the Corvette in the lot where DeHaven does his banking, and we were walking toward Bob Manuel's law office. DeHaven's blue Dickies work pants, lightly starched and ironed to a sharp crease, were tucked again into his laced-up mountain firefighter's boots. He was wearing a Stetson Newsboy style houndstooth hat that may have been fifty years old. Manuel greeted us at the door grinning his big lawyerly grin, and ushered us to seats near his desk. Giving attention to all the details, Manuel explained what we were getting ready to sign, pointing with his Bic pen to each blank line to initial, and date, and where we were to sign. DeHaven handed me the deed, and I handed him the $36,500 check, effectively ending my account in Birmingham. It was a sobering moment. I was profoundly aware that this transaction had ended one phase of my life and started another. In my mind, I was climbing a mountain with no idea at all of what I would find on the other side. After DeHaven had deposited the check in the bank across the street, I followed him over to the Rendezvous. I had just signed my life away, and I needed to chill.

* * *

"I know both of um," DeHaven was saying, shaking salt on his napkin-coaster. We had taken our seat in one of the booths. Business was slow today, shortly after noon, and only two other men in the bar.

"Good boys, but they both spend way too much time in here. The stocky one, think his name is Bob, Bob something, he works summers at the nursery farm. The Bruce place. They give him a tenant house, I don't know zackly where, but he does live in a tenant house with his high school sweetheart. Got married, I think he was seventeen. You can guess why. Got six or seven kids now. They all used to come by my place summertime; tubing the Nolichucky, you know. His wife would sit up on the porch with me, counting um as they walked back up the road with the tubes. Seem to be happy'n all. Kids, that is. The other one, he ..."

"His name is Bob Slagle. Something else, isn't it? Two Bobs. Roger was calling them Bob One and Bob Two."

"Well, Bob Two's mother ... Mildred? Millie, they call her Millie ... well she inherited all that money."

"They've got money?"

"They had money. That's the way it works, seems, all the time. Ol' man Slagle, her grandfather, made a bundle sellin his land to the pottery, then invested in the railroad just the right time. Millie's father, he got into real estate. Made a bundle when Johnson City bust its seams after the war, then lost a bundle when the pottery pulled out. He came out even, but still, Millie inherited a right good sum. Now it's gone and nothin to show for it. Don't know why Democrats so hard against people getting rich. By the time a third generation come around, they give it all to hairdressers and car salesmen. I think one time Millie Slagle had a lake house over on Davy Crockett and three boats or something. Your working-class man built all that stuff. All the while that money drained through Millie's fingers, bunch of ordinary fingers out there scoopin it up. For a Republican like me, that's what we call spreadin the wealth around."

"Well, Bob Two was a good worker. Both of them actually. I'm gonnna be using them again, sure of that."

"That Corvette you're drivin, yours?"

"Yes, sir!"

"You didn't tell me you owned a Corvette. What's the story on that?"

"1986 Indy 500 pace car. They only made a hundred of them that year."

"Just an investment, right," DeHaven said with a grin.

"No ... well, but it was a good deal. Got it from a bookie. The guy was a diver ... scuba diver. I got to know him pretty well. He came to me with a deal I couldn't refuse. Seems he lent a sizable amount of money to the owner of a certain car dealership. I don't know if you know this, Mr. DeHaven, but bookies lend money too, make most of their money that way, juice, they call it. What's the vig? they say. Vigorish is a gambling word, sorta means interest. Well, the car guy couldn't pay, bet it all on the Sweet Sixteen and lost. My friend had gotten himself in a bad spot financially too, same tournament, NCAA Men's Basketball tournament ... do you follow sports? Crazy to bet on ... well, they don't call it March Madness for nothing. You never know when an upset will happen. Brings out the best of them. Only guarantee is no guarantee. So, that's what happened, and when the car dealer offered to pay off his debt with the Corvette, the bookie had to sell it right away. He came to me. Like I said, Mr. DeHaven ... a deal I couldn't refuse."

"Always liked the Corvette."

"Me too. It's been a lot of fun. Not much help for a construction project though. I might have to trade it for a pickup truck."

"Speaking of which, when do you figure on startin?"

"Soon as Roger gets back. He's bringing an old buddy of his, supposed to be a great carpenter, guy named Richard. Can't remember his last name, but he's bringing all his tools. I'm going to give him the lead. I've done the work myself, but I'm not a professional."

"Well, John. That seems wise. Making Richard the lead man will keep him interested, but keep an eye on the job. Get what you're lookin for."

"Will do. Will do that, for sure."

"What you startin off with?"

"The bathhouse. That's the priority. Soon as Roger gets back with Richard, we're going over the list of materials. Roger says Richard is really good at figuring materials. And he's a good draftsman, can draw up an accurate design … the technical … you know, the blueprint. Richard can do that for us. Then we'll order the materials we need from Home Depot. They gave me the best prices."

"Using T-111 on the exterior, something like that, I suppose?"

"Oh, heck no, Mr. DeHaven. Using twelve-inch white pine planks. Vertical planking. I want a genuine rustic look. Same thing paneling the interior. Starting off with three hundred pieces, one by twelve eight footers."

"Getting that from Home Depot?"

"No, I looked around; found a lumberyard over in Hendersonville. Better price per foot than Home Depot. Delivered price at that."

"John, you should get the pine directly from the sawmill. You'll get an even better price. They'll deliver too."

"What sawmill?"

"Well, I don't know right off, but they're always cuttin pine somewhere."

"You're not talking green are you?"

"No, whoever's cuttin will be sellin dry lumber. That's all they do, you know; go from one stand to another; move the sawmill from one stand to another. They'll be dryin it somewhere."

"Do you know anybody with a sawmill?"

"Not right off, but if I was you, I'd contact Fred Price, the local Ranger. Forestry Service'll have a list of registered consultin foresters. Those guys know everything going on. They all know each other and keep up on things. They'll tell you zackly who's got lumber to sell."

* * *

Roger returned with his pop-up camper, Richard riding shotgun, and a young Birmingham boater named Bobby Bentley driving my Ford Taurus. They arrived during the afternoon of January 4. It was a Sunday. I remember the church bells. A real church bell pulled by a rope. There were two churches near me and both would announce the coming morning service by ringing bells.

Bobby was a shocker. A class-five paddler and well-known whitewater river guide. I knew his name. I'd also heard his reputation. Heard he went through women like clean socks. Of course, all of this was second-hand information to me, but now I knew, sort of knew why. He looked like your quintessential California surfer boy. Long blond hair. Strong and attractive. Had that boyish vulnerability so many women love. but unlike most men who have a tendency to be drawn to the same type women, blond or brunette, short or tall, buxom or thin, socialites, rich, poor, secretaries, maids, Bobby was totally indiscriminate so long as she was a beautiful, stop-your-heart knockout.

"It was almost embarrassing to see him in action," Roger said.

"How's that?"

"Well, I had him figured after a couple of group trips. He would swagger about looking strong, innocent, and full of river knowledge, and the minute one of the women would take notice, he'd take notice of her. Almost like he had silently announced, okay, gals, which one of you will choose me this time. Certain women would ignore his strutting and preening. He'd just ignore them right back. He would be drawn to the one drawn to him. There's a lot of work to be done in preparation ... well, look who's telling you ... you know that, John, inflating the rafts, gathering the equipment. The customers, they're all standing around watching. Most of the women would be watching Bobby. He would stand out, his blond hair flying, his boyish busyness, seemingly the expert among the experts. He'd look all distracted by the importance of the work, but you could tell, least, I could tell, he was watching all of them."

"In a sense, the woman he ended up with, had chosen him."

"Exactly...so long as she was beautiful."

We were in the yard watching Bobby dig post holes for the boundary fence. Roger and I had just spent the last half-hour showing Bobby how to break up the rock with the digger bar and scoop them out the hole with the double-handled post-hole digger. Bobby had no skills for construction work, so we had him digging post holes. He was strong as an ox. Finishing a hole, he would call us over and we'd set the four by four posts and prop them with two by fours. Then Bobby would mix and fill the bottom half of the hole with Sakrete.

We had a mountain of Sakrete carefully stored on wood pallets and covered with blue tarps. We had a mountain of everything, in fact. Almost all the materials required for the bathhouse and the hostel had been delivered. There were piles of carefully stacked lumber, shower stalls, toilets, sinks, and what-not in every out-of-the-way spot, and everything covered in blue tarps here and there across the yard.

Between setting posts for Bobby, we were working with Richard laying out the superstructure for the bathhouse. Superstructure meaning the rim joists and beams that would hold up the floor of the bathhouse. Both the deck at the front of the hostel and the floor of the bathhouse would be built the same way. The deck, the part you walk on, would be of treated five-quarter lumber. Five-quarter meaning the lumber was, before milling, an inch and one-quarter thick. The deck would be screwed to floor joists, with the ends of the joists attached to beams running long-ways under the floor and to the rim-joists that run around the outside edge. All of that rests on six by six inch posts set in concrete. Like I said, we had a mountain of Sakrete. Counting the fence, the bathhouse, and the front deck, we had 100 post holes to dig, and each would take from two to six or more fifty-pound bags of Sakrete.

While Bobby dug, Roger, Richard, and I measured the precise distances and drove stakes to mark the locations of those six by six posts. Eventually, Bobby would come along and dig the holes. As soon as the concrete set and these posts were rigid, the three of us would begin installing the beams and rim-joists.

Richard had done a masterly job in drawing up the layout of the bathhouse, the fence, and the front deck. From these plans, we derived the lists of materials needed and all had been ordered and shipped at once, a huge truckload unloaded by forklift and placed on pallets and concrete block in the yard.

I knew exactly what I wanted to build and how it would be built. I wanted rustic, all natural-wood rustic. I adapted the modified timber-framing style I had learned from my father, a structural system I had learned by helping him build dozens of boat houses along the Warrior and other rivers and lakes around Birmingham. The structure was quite simple, actually.

A system of lateral stringers set between posts would provide framing for the vertical siding on the outside and paneling on the inside. The strength of the structure would come from these walls, lined inside and out with vertical pieces of one by twelve pine.

When the deck of the bathhouse is screwed to the floor joists, the walls will be framed lying down on the deck and then raised into place. Builders call this *platform framing*. With the walls in place, the roof-system is framed in and covered with half-inch plywood roof sheathing. Then the five-vee metal roofing is screwed to the plywood. Once the structure has been roofed over and weather-proofed, the vertical exterior siding of one by twelve pine will enclose the walls. At this point, the building is ready for plumbing and installing the electrical system.

Sounds simple until you factor in the weather, which was horrible. All of January and during the part of February we were building the bathhouse, the weather alternated between days of bitter cold and warm days of rain. We got snow. Then we got rain. We got everything the skies could throw at us. But the worst thing was totally unexpected. I knew the weather would be unforgiving. After all, it was the dead of winter in the mountains of East Tennessee. But sunset at three in the afternoon? That I did not expect. Had no clue, was completely taken by surprise. But there it was. The ridge. The same ridge that guides the Nolichucky through the Gorge and on toward Erwin. The ridge with the eighteen switchbacks. The ridge that came down to Chestoa Pike along the west side of my property. A ridge as steep as the white cliffs of Dover. That ridge cut off the setting sun at three o'clock, and the temperature would drop ten degrees in five minutes.

I had expected to work ten-hour days. Had expected ten hours of daylight. We got seven, if the sun was shining. And three hours of bone-chilling dusk.

* * *

Shortly after Roger and the crew had arrived from Birmingham, there was a break in the weather, a warm night with heavy cloud cover and zero wind following a day of steady rain. The snow had disappeared from the yard. Roger suggested we build a fire and have steak-on-a-stick for supper.

Under the shed behind the house, almost lost in the pile of junk that DeHaven had left behind, Roger had discovered a dozen or so oak timbers, salvaged I suppose from some barn or shed. Before even mentioning steak-on-a-stick, Roger had dragged a few of these timbers to a flat spot in the yard and had a fire going. With the fire already ablaze and Roger talking steak, we found a couple of buckets and a small bench, and had gathered in a close circle around a cheerful fire. It was Bobby who brought it up.

"What's this I hear about Erwin hanging an elephant?"

"Well, Bobby … in the first place, it wasn't Erwin that hung the elephant. It was the circus. Some townspeople joined in, and some railroad people carried it off, but the idea came …"

"Circus? Why would a circus hang one of their elephants?" Bobby was looking back at me, then at Richard.

"She turned rogue," came a voice from the dark. "Killed her trainer. She was a huge Asian elephant named Mary, the principal attraction for the Sparks Circus. Big Mary some called her."

We all turned in unison, surprised. A man in a sheriff's uniform appeared in the circle of light, squatted down near the fire, and held his hands toward the warmth. "She was born in the 1890s when the Sparks outfit was still traveling town to town by horse and wagon. She was just a four-year-old calf when Charlie Sparks bought her, his first exotic animal. She became the family pet."

This was our introduction to Deputy Tom Handel. Roger was in the process of bringing out the little drop-leaf table from the kitchen. His second trip out to the fire, he set a big bowl of top round steak, cut on the bias into a mound of thin strips. He had split skewers from the oak we were burning and all of us soon had strips of steak sizzling over the fire. A few moments over hot coals and we were savoring delicious morsels of medium-rare steak. Roger had the process slightly wrong, and I demonstrated how simply laying two or three strips over the end of the stick not only cooked the meat sufficiently, but kept the stick from burning. Deputy Handel accepted our invitation to join the steak-on-a-stick fest, claiming an obligation to make sure we got the true story about the hanging, an event most folks in Erwin found embarrassing, if not in fact the worst moment in Erwin's history.

"Okay, I'm going to tell the story of Murderous Mary, but there are several things most people leave out. Very important things.

"The first of those things is the awesome impact the completion of the Clinchfield Railroad had on all of northeastern Tennessee. Between 1905 and 1909 the road was completed from Dante, Virginia, to Spartanburg, South Carolina. For the first time, a railroad connected Kingsport, Erwin, and Johnson City. At Bostic, North Carolina, it connected to the Seaboard Air Line Railroad. Further south, in Spartanburg, it connected to the Atlantic Coast Line. The northern end at that time reached St. Paul, Virginia, with leased rail links to the Norfolk and Western lines. St. Paul became a crossroads for points east, west, north, and south. Gentlemen, I want you to think about the effect of this change. The Clinchfield line became Erwin's link to the world. Someone living in Erwin in 1901 was completely isolated. Eight years later, people were pouring into town. They came from all over ... New York, Chicago, Atlanta; right through Erwin. From Birmingham, Alabama, heading north, right through Erwin. Heading to Houston, or over to Charleston, or Savannah, or down to Sarasota, Florida; they traveled right through Erwin.

"So, when people tell the story of the hanging in Erwin, they forget the fact that these little towns, Kingsport, Johnson City, Erwin ... had been blown wide open by the construction of the Clinchfield Railroad. Before construction started, Kingsport was little more than a telegraph station. Erwin had a population of something like 500 souls. By the time of the hanging, there were 2,000 people, several hundred living in tents, rowdy outsiders, many of them couldn't even speak English. But they had money and they were eager for entertainment and spectacle.

"This fact, the fact that these tiny hamlets, previously completely isolated from the civilized world, were suddenly thrust into the era of industrialization, is a primary factor in the frenzy that led to the hanging of Mary. Hundreds of families living in tents. Three out of four people were outsiders, come from all over the country; come from overseas, Russians, Italians, Poles, speaking little or no English; all these strangers new in town; unconnected; almost anonymous. All three towns were growing so fast they couldn't house the craftsmen swarming in for jobs. The streets were raw dirt, dusty in hot weather and a sea of mud when it rained. Hogs, cows, and chickens ran loose everywhere and foraged along the weedy vacant lots un-noticed and un-disturbed. Sidewalks were built of wood planking. Every man carried a gun, as did many women. All three towns were growing helter-skelter, like the wild, wild west.

"Into this primitive scene came the circus. Nothing like it had ever happened in Erwin. In 1915, the railroad line reached Elkhorn, Kentucky making a connection with the Chesapeake and Ohio line. By the turn of the century, every circus traveled by rail. Up until the completion of the upper line of the Clinchfield, most of the natives, the original citizenry of this region had never seen a circus. If they did, they had traveled over to Knoxville ... by the old road, gentlemen; 100 miles by horse and wagon. For people who had lived most of their lives with virtually no entertainment at all, this was an exciting change in circumstances. Nothing like it had ever happened in Erwin. But, seen another way, it could be called unsettling. When things change suddenly, important social bonds are broken.

"The Sparks Circus was in town for two reasons. First, those thousands of families brought into the area by the new railroad ... the fact that they were working good jobs and had money to spend. Secondly, a new route had opened. The Clinchfield was the only railroad that ran due south; a cheaper route for the smaller shows traveling down from Ohio or west through Virginia. The Sparks show had always wintered in Carthage, Ohio. With the completion of the southern line, they moved their winter quarters to Salisbury, North Carolina. So, the year 1916, the year of the hanging, was new and unsettling for the Sparks people as well. The circus had grown slowly but steadily over the last fifteen years. Traveling by rail, they did shows from Canada to Georgia. They came through Virginia and Tennessee in September, North Carolina in October, and Georgia in November, ending their tour with a show in Salisbury, their new winter quarters, around Thanksgiving.

"Back in that day, a circus coming to town was a big deal. Merchants up and down the main streets prepared for record sales. The Sparks show had been advertised by posters and in the newspapers weeks before they arrived. Every store had a billboard in the window. Charlie Sparks was a big advocate of creating Circus Day. He was often successful in convincing the town fathers to call for a worker's holiday.

"His show was preceded by a parade, a show before the show that was free to all. A grand parade led by the elephants, followed by two dozen or more colorful circus wagons carrying wild, snarling animals, and star performers waving to the spectators. About twenty clowns walked along, falling into the crowd, trying to kiss the pretty women, teasing the children. And last, but far from least, came the steam-powered calliope, self-contained, mounted on a carved, painted, and gilded wagon pulled by a pair of prancing white horses. A jolly clown worked the keyboard, driving steam through a set of tuned train whistles. Because the temperature of the steam varied, the circus calliope played wonderfully off-key, a unique musical sound that could be heard for miles.

"But an element the tellers of the hanging of Murderous Mary forget today, and this is a key point, gentlemen ... those who come to town on Circus Day with no money looking for fun and falling into trouble. For the mountain men and their families, this was free entertainment leavened, no doubt, by copious quantities of moonshine whiskey. In the towns where the Sparks show played, thousands came just for the parade. The streets in Erwin were jammed.

"Finally, there is one more important detail either left out entirely or twisted untruthfully. Charlie Sparks was a very fine man. There were twenty-two circuses on the road in 1916, and he had the highest reputation for honesty and fair dealing of them all. This came from the mouth of John Ringling. Nobody, Ringling said, ran a show more like a Sunday School than Charlie Sparks. He took care of his customers, his employees, and his animals, with more attention to detail than any other.

"Imagine that. Keep all these overlooked details in mind as I tell you this story."

Deputy Handel looked at us one to the other, and we just nodded; not knowing exactly what to say. Handel stood and picked out some steak strips and resumed his seat on the bench. We all did the same, and soon the sound and smell of steak filled the air.

"Well, Mary grew to become the largest Asian elephant in captivity. She was the star of the show. She could play the well-known parts of twenty-five different songs, songs like *Row, Row, Row Your Boat*, and *Mary Had a Little Lamb*. Clowns would set out a rack of horns, and Big Mary could squeeze the rubber bulbs that blew the horn for each note.

"Almost every circus had a version of clown baseball. For Sparks, Mary was the pitcher. She could toss a ball with her trunk as good as any pitcher's arm. If she struck out the batter, the crowd would go wild. When Mary was at bat, she would often knock the ball into the crowd, and they would go wild again. She is said to have had a batting average of 400, the Babe Ruth of elephant baseball players. Fully grown, she stood eleven feet, nine inches, and weighed four and a half tons. Big as she was, she could stand on her head, her back feet high in the air, or sit at a table drinking tea with a clown. It was 1916. People were easily entertained back in that day."

"So, why did they hang her?" Bobby asked. "I don't understand. An elephant like that? ... could do all that stuff, you know?"

"She killed her handler. She killed the guy just before the show in Kingsport, Tennessee."

"Oh. That's right. You said that. Okay, yeah ... okay."

"This was a tragedy, but worse for Charlie Sparks. He had just arrived as a first-class circus. Back in that day, you could judge success by the number of rail cars the circus required for moving from one rail town to the next. In 1903, when Sparks first switched from wagons to rail, he had just one car. He was basically a trick horse and pony show. By 1916, he had grown the outfit into a successful circus with clowns, acrobats, horses, lions, and elephants. During that time the Sparks Circus had gradually increased to fifteen rail cars, putting it into the category of a major railroad circus for the first time in its history."

"Wow! You mean it took fifteen railroad cars to haul the circus to the next town?"

"Well, Bobby, that was small. Sparks was a small outfit. Just for comparison the Ringling show required ninety cars."

"Holy cow! That's a whole train. It must have cost a fortune."

"The circus owned the rail cars. They just leased the line and rented an engine and engineer; the brakemen and conductors in the caboose. But the point I'm making is, Charlie Sparks couldn't afford any kind of major upset. He had been growing the circus steadily, and financially he was stretched pretty thin, and when the show arrived in St. Paul, their assistant elephant trainer had hooked up with an aerialist and they ran off together. Management was looking to replace him, and along came a hobo by the name of Walter Eldridge. Eldridge, who went by the nickname Red for his flame-red hair, had dropped into St. Paul from a Norfolk and Western boxcar a few days before, and had been working as a handyman for one of St. Paul's hotels when the circus promotional team came through town putting up posters and handbills for the show. Soon as the circus got to town, Red went looking for a job and landed the position with the elephants. Couple hours later, he was walking with the elephants down the main street of St. Paul. That night, he rode in the elephant car to Kingsport.

"As I said, Kingsport was a wild-west boomtown, springing from practically nothing in less than ten years. The building of Kingsport was a project of the Clinchfield Railroad Corporation. Hundreds of homes and businesses were under construction. In addition to the couple thousand people already there, a thousand more had come down out of the mountains for the circus. The town was buzzing with excitement. The afternoon show was a sell-out, and I heard if the show hadn't been booked for Erwin the next day, they would have stayed a couple more days.

"In the late afternoon, the elephant trainers walked their animals down Center Street toward a pond where they intended to water the creatures and let them play prior to the evening show. Elephants love to play in water. Each trainer rode his elephant and directed and controlled the animal with an elephant stick, as was the common practice. The story of what happened next has been told a hundred different ways, but the most accepted version is that Big Mary spotted a hunk of watermelon in the street, and went to pick it up with her trunk. Red, maybe reverting to how he might treat a mule under these circumstances, whacked Mary on the side of her head with his stick. Now, the side of an elephant's head means the ear, and an elephant's ears are very sensitive. Mary gave a powerful snort, and swung her trunk around knocking Red off her back and onto the ground. Falling from eleven feet up, and landing on his back, Red was struggling to get his breath and get up when Mary deliberately placed her foot on his head and stepped forward with all her weight. Red's head burst like a melon, and brains and blood shot in all directions. The watching crowd screamed in horror and ran terrified into the fields.

"When the trainers got Mary under control and calm, the crowd returned and began to shout, kill the elephant, kill the elephant. A blacksmith came out from his nearby shop and shot her five times with his pistol to no appreciable effect. All this happened only a few hundred feet from the circus tent, and some say Charlie Sparks himself ran to the scene. Hooking his arm around Mary's trunk, he talked her into a calm. In no time, Mayor Miller and Sheriff Hickman arrived, arrested Big Mary for murder, and staked her by the county jail.

"Addie Sparks, Charlie's wife, was responsible for the care of all the animals. Without doubt, putting Mary down was a difficult decision. They had no children. Like a couple loving their dog like a child, Charlie and Addie loved Big Mary. Part of their family for twenty years. She was the star of the show. Reported to be worth $20,000. Gentlemen, in today's money, that would be $300,000. No sane person would casually destroy something that valuable, much less a family pet. So, gentlemen, here is where the popular stories about the hanging of Murderous Mary run off track. Everybody in the circus world knew that you can kill an elephant by shooting her behind the ear canal with a small pistol. So the question is, who made the decision to hang her, and why?

"She had killed the man. Charlie and Addie Sparks knew that. Something had to be done. They had two choices. They could destroy her, or they could change her name, and sell her to another circus. The second was out of the question. Charlie and Addie were moral and decent people, they would not pass a dangerous animal along to another circus, and give her another opportunity to kill. I'm a sheriff's deputy. I'm in this business because I know people, I understand people, and I know people like Charlie and Addie Sparks. I think they were devastated. I think they held onto each other and wept like babies. And then, they just turned their backs and let events take their course. Regardless of tragedy and pain, the show must go on. They just let Mary go.

"The next day, the circus train, including Big Mary, traveled to Erwin. Mary did not perform for the matinee that afternoon. She was chained by her two front legs behind the tent to stakes driven deeply into the ground. After the show, Mary was trooped along with the rest of the elephants to the Clinchfield yards where a 100-ton derrick car stood waiting; Derrick number 1400.

"No one knows who ordered the crane to return from its assignment unloading crossties in Johnson City. No one knows who ordered Clinchfield workers to dig a hole up the track a little way, some said as big as a barn. But gentlemen, it is my opinion, and mind you, without any factual proof...the decision was entirely political. The dangerous rioting in response to the killing of Eldridge, the trainer, was in Kingsport, not Johnson City, or Erwin. Clinchfield owned Kingsport, the legal jurisdiction where the so-called murder happened. Clinchfield appointed Mayor Miller. Sheriff Hickman was on the Clinchfield payroll. Clinchfield owned the rail yard where the hanging took place. And finally, Clinchfield was the employer of those that hung her. So, gentlemen; go figure."

Deputy Handel poked at the fire for a moment, then tossed his skewer into the burning embers and resumed his story.

"Nearly all of the circus roustabouts and performers had left the circus grounds to attend Mary's last walk. All agree that the crowd numbered around 3,000 people. A procession of five elephants walking trunk-to-tail lumbered into the yard and up to the crane. While Mary's back right leg was chained to the rail near where the derrick car stood, the other elephants were led away, their trainers fully aware that the death of Mary would traumatize the other elephants; that elephants are known to grieve for months after the death of one of their own. They didn't go quietly. Mary was agitated and trumpeting. The elephant herd hesitated. The trainers were having trouble getting them to move. All of them were bellowing back at Mary. Witnesses say they are convinced the elephants knew what was about to happen.

"A tender threw a seven-eighths chain around Mary's neck, threaded it through a steel ring, and slipped the link-loop over the derrick crane's hook. It is said the operator hesitated. The crowd began to jeer and whistle, then he threw the stick. The reel took up the slack. Her head lifted. Her front feet came off the ground. She stretched taut; the roustabout had forgotten to free the chain from her back right leg. Then, with the crack of a high-powered rifle, the chain snapped. Mary fell to the ground. Injured severely, seated on her haunches, she could not get up. The roustabout scrambled up her back as he would climb a hill and attached a heavier chain. The winch began to scream again, the chain tightened, and Mary was lifted high off the ground, her legs paddling as if she were swimming through water. In a few moments, she was dead.

"Someone took a photograph seconds before she died, her trunk straight out in a windless attempt to bellow once more. The next moment, she fell limp. Immediately, the derrick car began moving up the rail where they dropped her into the hole. Twenty minutes later, it was as if nothing at all had happened."

We sat silently looking into the fire. In a minute or two, Deputy Handel rose, wished us well, and walked off into the darkness.

* * *

They were calling it the El Niño Winter of 1997/98, claiming it would be the granddaddy of all El Niños, a patch of unusually warm ocean water hundreds of miles wide stretching from Peru nearly to the Philippines. This force majeure caused winter temperatures across the south and southeast to soar upwards of fifteen degrees above normal. Winter temperatures like this will bring rain, lots of rain. But, past El Niños threw in a big snowstorm now and then, just to keep things interesting. Well it did rain, but up in Canada freezing rain killed fifty-six people, the worst ice storm on record, they say. Ice three inches thick on all the trees. Here, it just rained. Five days after we took occupancy, it rained four days straight. Over the first two days, we got five inches. They got nine inches over at Mount Mitchell. The headwaters of the Nolichucky branch off and wrap around the west side of that mountain, and the heavier rain there brought the river to a high water mark over on our side. Flood waters, roaring down the coves and hollows over on the Carolina side of the Unakas wiped out over 500 homes, and over here in northeast Tennessee, nearly 200 were severely damaged or destroyed. Well, how lucky can one be? I picked an El Niño year to build a hostel.

"John, what the heck you doin out here?"

"Checking the tarps. The one over the Sakrete partly blew off. I'm getting them good and tight or we're gonna end up with a couple hundred fifty-pound concrete stepping stones. Looks like this thing won't be letting up anytime soon."

"Yeah, the National Weather Service said rain again tomorrow."

"Right."

"You need help? I can send Bobby out."

"Naw. I've checked them all. Everything seems okay. Oh, Roger ... hey Roger." Roger turned around with his hands out in the *what now* position.

"I got food on the stove, John."

"You might want to have Bobby check your camper. When's the last time you had that fabric sealed?"

"I'll do that later. Come on in. I've fried up some taters and onions, two pounds of sausage, and I'm gonna fry some eggs."

"Great, Roger. You're the best, buddy."

Roger is a great cook. He barbecued racks of ribs last night, and they were as good as any I've ever eaten. Richard's focus is on beer. He borrowed my Ford Taurus for nightly beer runs to the Rendezvous until I found out he didn't have a driver's license; he was, in fact, DUI'd twice in Alabama. Bobby's interest is women, so he was happy as a clam to be Richard's driver, that is, until he realized how futile it was to play his game in Erwin. All the beautiful women here are taken and not about to look a guy like Bobby in the eye. So, needless to say, Bobby was getting a little restless. I wasn't worried though. It would be at least sometime in March before rafting outfits start hiring. Bobby needed a place to winter over, and he had the couch, a steady job, and three squares he could count on. Bobby wouldn't be going anywhere soon.

"John, you got a call while you were out there."

"Did you get a name?"

"Of course, little momma. It's on the pad. Brady Sleeper. Isn't that the guy, the burrito guy you were telling us about? Pass the fried potatoes, partner."

"Yeah, he and his cute little pregnant wife came by when you were in Birmingham rounding up these two jackleg carpenters." And saying this, I gave Richard and Bobby a wink to signal the tease.

"Surprised me. Snowing like the dickens and suddenly there was this knocking on the door. I expected to see the Sheriff, or something. Who else would be out in that kind of weather? Here was this young couple knocking snow off their boots. They heard about the hostel. Said they were opening a Mexican restaurant in town. Thought we might work together. He said he knew about trail hostels; was a hiker himself. In fact, and I just remembered this, Roger ... he and Lisa, his wife, were hiking, getting real hungry and craving burritos. When they camped the night before coming into Erwin, there were three hikers in hammocks. Brady joked with Lisa saying he didn't like hammocks. Thought they were dangerous. Looked too much like a bear-sized taco, he said. Danged if he didn't have a dream that night. He was sleeping in a hammock and a bear wearing a bib and a Mexican sombrero tried to eat him."

"Damn, John. Did you just make that up?"

"No ... no, they were telling me that. Crazy, huh. Anyway, they came off the trail at Chestoa, hitched into town looking for some Mexican, and that's how they discovered the restaurant opportunity. Heck of a coincidence, isn't it? Same as me. Did he say why he called?"

"Said he'd been working on the remodel twelve hours a day and hoping you'd come by and take a look. Wants to show you the place. Thought maybe you'd have some advice."

"Well, let's do it. We ought to go over there. Real nice people. Want to help them all I can. Soon as he mentioned he was opening a burrito place, I decided that's where we would take the dinner shuttle."

"I can see how you can help him, but how's he going to help you?"

"One thing he mentioned was doing some trail magic together. Up at Indian Grave Gap."

"Trail magic?" Richard said, looking at me with an arched eyebrow.

"That's what hikers call any kind of friendly gesture from the locals. There's nothing like ... it's almost impossible to describe the joy a hiker feels coming to a roadway running through a gap and finding people there cooking free hamburgers and hot dogs. It's magical. It's manna from heaven."

"So, what did he propose?" Roger said.

"That he would bring a thermal bag of burritos, and I could bring a cooler of soft drinks and maybe some Snickers. You know ... we'd meet hikers coming through Indian Grave Gap, and tell them about Erwin. About our hostel. Give um some of your brownies."

"Sounds like a plan. Pass those potatoes again, partner."

"I told him having a place like his, a couple of friendly, helpful proprietors where I could take my guests was partnership enough. And by the way ... Brady was the one who recommended his accountant when I needed to incorporate. Both Bubba and Bob Manuel insisted that I form a corporation rather than a proprietorship. His accountant drew up the incorporating papers. But, then we had to come up with a name right away. Had to call the hostel something if we were going to incorporate."

"What name did you come up with?" Bobby asked. "I've never heard you say any name but the hostel"

"Well, when Bubba asked what we were gonna call the corporation, I said The Nolichucky Hostel. Then Bob Manuel said, no, no, no ... make it Uncle Johnny's Nolichucky Hostel. Everybody broke into big grins and started chuckling, so that's what I chose. Uncle Johnny's Nolichucky Hostel."

"I'll take the rest of those potatoes," Roger said.

* * *

For the first few weeks, the camp-out in DeHaven's old house was fun for all of us. Almost everything we did had a comic edge. We joked and teased each other unmercifully. We were all so different, the diversity itself lent a charming patina to our daily activities. Roger was serious and fatherly. A one-time alcoholic, he had been cold sober for years, and had grown a little intolerant of even the presence of the Devil's brew. Our sneaking around and his arched eyebrows we all found hilarious. I, of course, was all serious business, and the guys began calling me Ahab, after the captain of the whaler in Moby Dick, and my hostel got renamed the Pequod. Richard, even at three sheets to the wind, was a great story-teller, talked constantly, and kept the project running. He was a skilled carpenter and a great teacher for Bobby. We taught Bobby to drive nails and cut, but in general, Bobby was the work-site mule. Like any construction crew, we gave the new guy a hard time. When we were ready to raise the first wall, we sent him searching through Roger's truck for the Sky Hook.

Because it became dark and cold when the sun set behind the ridge, our evenings in the house were long and active. Shortly after supper, one or another of Richard's posse would show up and carry him off to the Rendezvous. The three of us, Roger and Bobby and I, would usually settle down into long conversations, always interesting, about adventures we had enjoyed; characters we had met; trails we had hiked; rivers we had run. When these conversations turned to whitewater, Bobby was the star. He was, Roger and I silently acknowledged, an especially talented boater. On one of these occasions, Bobby asked me if he could borrow my Taurus some weekend. He wanted to run the Wilson Creek Gorge over in North Carolina. Roger, more experienced than I and less tolerant of foolishness, immediately took interest. He got up, went to the couch, bent over looking into Bobby's box, and returned with a book.

"This yours?"

"Yes?"

"*Steep Creeks and Rivers of North Carolina*?" Roger read from the cover, and then held it up for Bobby to view. Bobby nodded his head, and Roger took his seat again in the blue chair and put on his granny glasses.

"And you've read the section on Wilson Creek?" Roger asked, looking over his glasses. Bobby nodded again. "You know they don't name these rapids for nothing." Roger pushed his glasses in place and read … "Ten Foot Falls, Boatbuster, Thunderhole, Triple Drop, Bitchslap, Hidden Eddy … hidden eddy! Man, oh-man. These are all Class IV," Roger said, ducking his head and looking at Bobby over his glasses. "And you're going to run this river alone?"

"Not a problem, Roger," Bobby said with a proud grin and a shake of his long blond hair. "I've been on a bunch of rivers alone."

Roger looked down at the book and read, "At the end of a good-sized pool, the river will become choked up with boulders." Roger slumped back in the blue chair, crossed his legs, and read from the book held high in front of his face. "Starting midstream look for a slot on the right above Idaho rock that isn't really wide enough to punch thru. Hug Idaho rock, line up and bang on down." Roger rolled his head sideways and looked at Bobby.

"Just below … is the entrance to Ten Foot Falls. Now, look at that. Got a picture of it right here. Ten Foot Falls looks really … really interesting. It says, start with a four-foot-tall boof, into a tricky class-three entrance rapid. Then take a left and line up for the big plunge; a ten-foot-tall, forty-five-degree slide into a sometimes interesting hole. That's what it says here, Bobby, *a sometimes interesting hole*. I guess that means sometimes you can't paddle out and you drown."

"Oh, come on Roger," Bobby said laughing. "You're so melodramatic. You should have been an actor."

"Triple Drop is a three-tiered drop. The main thing to avoid is the sticky hole at the bottom. Sticky. I'm sure you know what that means, Bobby. If you go in wrong, you're stuck. You can't get out. Anyway, the author says the hole is backed up by a rock about eight feet downstream that keeps everything kicking back into the hole. But, man, oh-man, listen to this. If you get through Triple Drop alive, you come to Maytag. Get that analogy? ... Maytag? Now the writer says of Maytag, this is the most dangerous place on Wilson Creek." Roger sits up on the edge of the blue chair and looks over his granny glasses at Bobby.

"Roger, you're a scream, buddy. You're talking like I never been through a sticky hole. Cum'on man. You've been avoiding rivers like this, but I love um. I've been down a bunch just like ... listen, Roger. When you put a boat on the river, it's controlled chaos, controlled because you've done it lots. You're experienced. But, bottom line, you don't know how it is going to work out. And Roger, that's the fun of it, that's why, the uncertainty, that's why we do it."

Ignoring Bobby, Roger looked down at the book and continued reading. "Many otherwise manageable ledges have very ugly keeper hydraulics below them. Knowing where to go is important. First-timers should have a good guide-person." Looking up, his humorous, playful bantering fading to an expression of fatherly seriousness, Roger asked, "Have you been on this river before?"

"No, but listen, Roger. You avoid this kind of river. I look for them. I've never been caught in a hole where I couldn't paddle out. I have a gym membership. I can press two-seventy-five. I can run ten miles. Look. I'm young. You've grown old and cautious. You're looking at this from a different perspective. But, buddy...I've never been in trouble I couldn't handle. Period."

* * *

The weather was off-and-on bad. The idle time was not a good thing for Richard. Since Bobby had become less interested in driving him around, he had hooked up with a couple of boys down the street. Then he had met and become friends with the Bobs, the two bozos Roger called Bob One and Bob Two.

Richard, being a cut above the others, smarter, and having bossy tendencies, had become the leader of this camarilla, stumbling ingloriously into an unnoticed, at least by him, standoff with the regular afternoon crowd.

Richard, in spite of some faults, did have certain special qualities. He was an excellent paddler. Had met Roger years ago, back in the day when Roger could match him in downing cheap brown whiskey shot for shot. In those days, whitewater canoeing required a tandem canoe, preferably a Grumman aluminum. The tandem was the boat of choice in the early whitewater days. But, you needed a good, reliable partner.

They met on a canoe outing with the Birmingham gang and decided to do the Ocoee River together. The Ocoee had been discovered by whitewater enthusiasts early in the development of the sport. but not many paddlers from Birmingham knew the river. Certainly not the team in question. They met Friday afternoon at Roger's place and organized their gear, then went to a local pub. Around midnight, Roger invited a half-dozen friends back to his house for tequila shots and late-night omelets, and the party stretched on into the early morning hours.

Without much sleep, and feeling miserable, they suffered through the four-hour drive up through Chattanooga and on to I-75 stopping for driver exchange twice. They took the turn onto US-74, a crooked, two-lane highway that parallels the river through the mountains; a breathtaking ride for a normal person with a sharp mind and a quiet stomach. For our intrepid canoers that morning, the trip up that curving road was more than a little painful. When they reached the put-in around 9:30 that morning, the river was anything but breathtaking. They found a bucolic, lovely little stream suitable for a Cub Scout outing. Unimpressed, and puzzled by the other paddlers diligently unloading canoes and equipment, Roger expressed his exasperation and disappointment. What's the big deal? he said to a couple of guys standing nearby. This doesn't look like much of a river to me! Roger told me the two guys gawked at him for a moment and then one said to the other, these fools must not know the release is at ten. And they walked away, wanting to put a little distance between themselves and these two newbies.

The Ocoee River has its beginnings in the mountains of Northeast Georgia, and drains an area of 492 square miles. The river flows into the Cherokee National Forest where it is impounded by Tennessee Valley Authority's No. 3 dam. What Roger didn't know at the time is that the whitewater paddlers unloading their cars and vans were waiting for the water to be diverted from power generation and sluiced from the dam to provide whitewater recreation downstream. This section of the river has an average drop of fifty-four feet per mile and is considered a Class III and IV river. I would love to have been there when, about fifteen minutes later, a deluge of water measuring 117,000 cubic feet per second came surging past them. Their eyes must have popped out.

* * *

In spite of his superb carpentry skills and all the affection received from Roger and me, Richard's performance began to wane early on. He saw himself as Project Superintendent and spent less and less time pounding nails and more time with beer in hand pointing and shouting. It was getting on my nerves. Then one night, the two Bobs lugged him home from the

Rendezvous drunk as a skunk and with what they thought was a broken nose. His gang of toadies, it seems, egged him into a confrontation with a wiry guy about five inches shorter than Richard and the little guy beat the crap out of him. We cleaned him up best we could, his nose wasn't broken, and put him in bed. It was still early, so I jumped in the Corvette and drove to the Rendezvous to make sure there would be no repercussions. John, the bartender, explained what happened, how it started, and assured me it was nothing new for him or the Rendezvous, but still, he was concerned for my sake. Leaning forward with both forearms on the bar, he quietly advised me that Richard was not a good person to represent me and my new business. That the good people of Erwin could tolerate this kind of disturbance from their own, but such goings-on from an outsider was an inexcusable breach of civility.

"I'm thinking of sending him home, Roger. What do you think?"

"God, I would hate that, John. I'll talk to him again."

"Talking ... we've both talked to him. Talking doesn't appear to be helping. We're not going to keep him out of the Rendezvous, and he's giving us a bad rep."

"I think it has more to do with his posse. Maybe we could talk to them ... get them to ..."

"No, Roger. Those guys ... Richard's the best thing ever to come along for them. He's their leading light, and he loves it. Besides, they haven't the brains of a barnyard chicken among them. No, I'm for buying him a bus ticket. Just get this over with."

"Yeah ... yeah, you're right. I hate it though. Me and Richard ... we've had some good times. I want to take care of him, but there's nothing we can do. So, yeah. Let's send him home."

We carried Richard to Johnson City and put him on a bus. It didn't bother him. He seemed happy to be going home, like he'd had enough hammering in a drizzling rain; fishing nails out of a pouch full of water. Amazing how often, when driving a nail home, that last blow against the wood sends a spritz of water right in the eye.

* * *

"Roger ... it's your wife." I stood, holding the phone as Roger turned, and I could see his eyes grow wide as he read my face.

"What's wrong?" he said to me, reaching for the phone.

"She's upset. I don't know ..."

"Diane, are you okay? What? Are the kids ... calm down, come on ... calm ... Diane, take a breath, honey. Are the kids okay? ... Who? ... Dale? Wait a minute, honey. Wait a minute. Just take a second and ... Dale? Dale Adams? No ... where? Where? When ... today? No, man, no, no, no. Diane, are you sure? And she told you herself? She called you? Oh, my God. Are you with her now? Who was with him? What happened? ... Where? Listen, Diane. You need to calm down. Listen. Let's hang up. You settle down. And call me when ... yes, yes. Okay. Call me as soon as you can. Yes. I'll be coming home. I'm coming ... yes, right away."

"Christ, Roger. What happened?"

"Dale ... Dale Adams. He drowned today," Roger said as he slumped into the blue chair.

"Are you sure ... could Diane be ..."

"Dale's wife called Diane. No question."

"But how? Dale was the most cautious paddler I ever knew. He never took an unnecessary chance, and not even that if too risky. So how ...? Where did this happen?"

"Little River Canyon."

"Every time I called Diane, she said it was raining. This rainy winter has all the rivers running at high water levels. But Dale was so experienced. He's been down the Upper Two lots of times. He was up there just ... last week! Diane was telling me when we talked ... last week. If I had to guess, I'd say Dale's been on that section of the river, the Upper Two, six or seven times in the last year."

"Did Diane say what happened?"

"Well, you heard. She was pretty broken up. She said it was Roadblock rapid. Rolled the kayak, got caught in the hydraulics for a minute or so, and then washed free, face-down and unconscious. That's all she said. Missed his line, I guess, and dropped in the hole at the base of Roadblock. I've seen pictures. Never been on that river, but Roadblock's a big V-shaped drop, looks maybe five feet. Diane said there were six kayakers with him. Threw ropes. Couldn't get to him."

"Damn. Of all things. Dale Adams would be the last ... I've never been on that river either. Never wanted to be on that river. I'm not that great in a kayak, but all the guys I've ever met think safety first. They scout the rapids. I'm thinking if Dale had been down the river just the week before, he thought he had it figured."

"Impossible to say. The guys who were with him probably don't know what happened. But I'm sure they got help. Lots of kayakers on that river weekends."

"The kayaker that died up there in December. They took him out with ropes up the side of the gorge. Said they carried him to a clearing. Flew him to the hospital in a helicopter. Guess that's how they got Dale out." Roger's voice trailed off.

Neither of us spoke of it, but we knew those canyon walls were upwards of six hundred feet. Thinking about that stopped us short. Our good friend, dead. Strapped in a Stokes basket being hauled up the side of a cliff.

Bobby didn't say a word. Just sat there looking at his hands. Silently fragile. Drawn up tight. We knew he thought of himself as special. Unusually qualified. Hard to imagine what might be flashing through his head right now. Had he been on that river? Had he fought his way out of that same hole? Bobby never spoke of it, and we didn't ask.

Dale loved life and lived it hard. We spent many weekends paddling; camping, all of us together, wives, children, Charlotte and Claire. All our good friends knew Dale and his wife. We talked on into the night. Quietly at first; Roger, slumped back in the blue chair; Bobby leaning forward, asking questions. Eventually we began telling stories. We even laughed at some of the goofy things Dale would say, and the misadventures we had experienced together.

* * *

Less than a week later, it snowed again. Snowed all night long. We woke to a foot of snow. They had closed the Interstates. Traffic on I-40 was backed up thirteen miles. Up on the Cumberland Plateau, they were having wind gusts to fifty miles per hour. It was bad. I've got a hostel to build. Got to be open first of April.

Now, it's just me and Bobby. Roger left early that next morning. We talked yesterday, and he's not coming back. Said the Dale thing won't let go. He needs his wife and children. Missed his dogs, I know that. Mentioned them pretty often when he was here. I called Charlotte, of course. We talk nearly every evening anyway, but talked a couple of times a day after Dale died. Charlotte was past-president of the paddling club, and knew Dale before she met me. Turns out nobody had their eyes on Dale when he went into that hole, so nobody knows what actually happened. Charlotte kept me informed. She went to the funeral.

Now I'm in a pretty pickle.

Roger's long-bed pickup was essential to the operation, not to mention his strong back and steady presence. And, by-god, not least, his cooking. I'm not much of a cook and Bobby's worse than nothing.

"You're going out?"

"Can't sit around in here all day," Bobby said, pulling on his coat. "I'm gettin the snow off the bathhouse deck. Soon as it stops snowing, we can stand that wall."

"It'll take you all day with that round-point shovel."

"Way head of ya, Uncle Johnny. There's a big shovel under the shed. I was lookin at that Old Town canoe, and it was under there. Not a snow shovel, kinda heavy, but it'll get the job done."

"Oh, yeah man, I saw that back in the summer. That's a grain-scoop, Bobby. You're right. That's a heavy shovel. Shovel weighs more than the snow. Bust your back, man."

"I don't care. I need the exercise. Besides, I like shoveling snow. I like being out in the snow when it's coming down."

"Okay, buddy…while you're doing that, I'm gonna create a workshop. Clean out the small bedroom. Take the bed apart and store it under my bed. Move the table and that little chest out here in the living room You'll have to keep sleeping on the couch. I'm turning that room into a workshop. We need a place to work inside on bad weather days."

"We're not gonna do anything until we get power back."

"Of course not, Bobby, but we can get ready. We're losing too many hours to bad weather. We need to build bunks for the hostel and several picnic tables. Get that room cleared out, we can build them in here. I've got lumber for nine bunks and six tables. Got that out in the yard. We can do the measuring and cutting in here. We'll assemble them later. Cut the parts and stack … stack the parts and pieces wherever we can find space."

"You know how to build a bed?"

"I do now. When I was in Birmingham, I came across a magazine titled something like *101 Workshop Projects*. Had both designs … a bunkbed designed for a hunting camp, and a great design for a big, heavy, park-style picnic table. Got together with Richard. He suggested some modifications that make the job simple as pie. Build the bunks by laminating two-by-four studs. Ninety-nine cents each. Glue and screw-um for the thicker pieces. So, yes. You and me, partner. We're gonna become instant bed-building experts."

* * *

We were without power for ten days. El Niño was kicking the crap out of us. The damned thing gave us a wet, heavy snow that brought limbs and trees crashing down on powerlines from West Virginia to Georgia. I had suspected this would happen the minute I walked out to check the tarps. That much wet snow would be trouble, and it was. Shortly after breakfast, we lost power. DeHaven had warned us about frequent power outages, so I had brought along a couple of Coleman lanterns, four gallons of fuel, and a WhisperLite stove. We had the barbeque grill on the front porch, some charcoal, and nearly 200 gallons of kerosene in the big tank out back. No problems there, but work could not continue without the circular saws, drills, and screw guns. Thank god for the Warm Morning heater. It had a circulating fan that needed power, but it still produced heat, being fueled by the gravitational flow of kerosene from the tank in the back yard. The house stayed toasty warm.

The low temperature during the storm was barely thirty degrees, warming to forty the next day. By the third day, and through the following week, the highs were in the upper forties. The snow was melting, but the power was still off. As soon as they plowed River Road, Bobby and I drove into town hoping to find something open. We didn't want to run out of fuel for the WhisperLite, and the Coleman lanterns.

The IGA grocery was about two miles down the road toward town. The parking lot was half-full of cars. Puzzling to me. Bobby leaned forward and squinted and asked me what the heck was going on. The line came out the door. When we inquired, they were letting small groups go in as others walked out with bags of groceries. No lights in the store.

When it came our turn, we entered the dark store to discover a long line at just one checkout counter. The manager, Sam Tabbi was checking out customers using a hand calculator. I heard him say, "Alright, Mr. Toms, I'm just adding round numbers. Twenty-five dollars is close enough for me. Okay for you?" Then he called out in a loud voice...No credit cards, folks. Just cash. You gotta have cash. Then he added, please buy all the meat you can handle. Won't be any here tomorrow. What's left, I'm gonna feed my dogs.

We learned that he had just opened. Bobby took off in one direction to pick out the canned goods and the snacks he wanted. I headed for the meat counter making a point to remember we ought to pick up a couple bags of charcoal.

That evening, we went back. In the panic to get what we thought we needed, we forgot a few things. The manager was still punching the numbers into the little hand calculator. No bread. No milk. No batteries. No ice-melt. And the meat long gone. We snagged two more bags of charcoal.

* * *

I did my best during this difficult stretch to use down-time efficiently. Thank goodness, the phone worked. I touched base with Laurie Potteiger at the Appalachian Trail Conference and brought her up to date on our progress here. She was happy we were under way, and vowed again to help us however she could. Laurie's trail name was Mountain Laurel. She had thru-hiked the trail in 1986 and then found her life's work as an ATC staffer. Hiking through Harpers Ferry in '86, she thought it was an unfriendly trail town. Of course, it is a wonderful trail town today, and maybe Laurie had something to do with that. Since she had seen an important trail town from both sides, I took her advice and suggestions seriously.

I described the bathhouse and my intention to provide endless hot water. We must have talked for a half-hour about the value of a trail-side hostel here in Erwin, and then she gave me a little run-down of what she had learned from hikers about what they expect and look for when they come off the trail. My enthusiasm was renewed by the prospect of having a good friend at the ATC.

In the process of calling around about prospective suppliers for my outfitter store, I came across a man named Nolan Davis who was into the second year of his new business, Outdoor Sports Marketing. His was a husband and wife team, both having extensive experience in whitewater paddling and backpacking. His company represented a number of equipment manufacturers that made products I hoped to carry; MSR, Therm-a-Rest, Platypus, SmartWool socks, Osprey packs and so forth. He understood my need to start small and grow, and assured me he would have my back as we built lines of communications with his suppliers. There was a sincerity and a willingness to help that told me I had found the right guy to get my outfitter store up and running.

We were having rotten weather but it came hand-in-hand with a spurt of amazing good luck. The day after we shipped Richard back to Alabama, I placed an ad in *The Erwin Record*, our local newspaper. The lead read, Looking for an Experienced Carpenter. A thirty-something couple showed up at our door; Mike and Cindy. They had just moved to Erwin. Mike was not a professional carpenter, but he had worked as a handy-man since leaving the Army. His wife, a strong looking woman, wanted to work with him. So, I got two for the price of one; two amateurs for the price of one professional. And I had Bobby. Richard and I had worked with Bobby teaching him nailing techniques, how to cut a straight line with the circular saw, and how to measure and cut a board to the nearest sixteenth inch. Bobby was smart, and listened carefully. He didn't at all mind me looking over his shoulder, and seemed to enjoy learning the tricks of the trade. With Bobby, Mike, and Cindy, I had a team of enthusiastic amateurs willing to help me build the finest hostel on the Appalachian Trail.

* * *

"Uncle Johnny! ... you need a hand with that?"

"Deputy Handel. Good to see you. You allowed to swing a hammer when on duty?"

"Wouldn't be the first time. How can I help."

"Bobby's nail belt ... over there, grab his hammer and some nails. When we stand this wall, see if you can square up that last stud with the corner post. Punch a nail in there somewhere ... temporary. Don't drive it home. I'll do the same on this end. Bobby, when I secure my end, you shift over here by Cindy and set that two-by-four brace like I showed you, and I'll nail it."

Handel steadied himself and carefully walked up the bouncy, two-by-twelve ramp we were using to get up on the bathhouse deck. I say carefully because he was wearing those classic, lemon-yellow galoshes which are great in snow and mud, but not so good for walking up a wet plank.

What we had going is called platform-frame construction. The floor joists, attached to girders and band joists and those bolted to the six by six posts under the bathhouse, are completely covered with deck-planking to form a platform. This is the type of construction used in building houses. It creates a surface upon which exterior walls and interior partitions are constructed and erected. It is common practice to assemble wall-framing on the floor and tilt the entire wall unit into place.

We were raising the long front wall; scary for two reasons. First, the deck along this side was three, three-and-a-half feet above ground. Secondly, the wall was framed for vertical planking inside and out. It had the standard double plates, bottom and top, but just a single stud every four feet separated by four horizontal stringers. The wall is stabilized and strengthened by the vertical planks. Without the planking, the wall has no strength or integrity. Even with the four of us, the wall was trying to twist. I had my end good, and Mike was in the middle, but Bobby and Cindy didn't have the right grip. Half-way up, I called out for them to put it back down.

We had three walls standing before the snowstorm and loss of power. The front wall had been built, but not raised into place. Bobby had cleared most of the snow from the deck, and the sun had melted a good bit of the remaining snow caught between the framing of the long wall lying on the floor. That little bit of remaining snow, however, created a slippery surface, and the possibility of dumping the entire wall overboard and onto the ground was real in the minds of Bobby and Cindy. Neither I nor Mike gave that a second thought, but when we attempted to raise the wall, they were slipping all over the place struggling to control the pitch and twist. Deputy Handel's arrival was perfectly timed.

In minutes, we had the wall up, squared, plumbed, and nailed in place. And that was it. Without power, construction had come to a full stop. We invited Deputy Handel inside for a cup of coffee. Cowboy style. Coming through the front door, I could see Bobby had a quart of water boiling on the WhisperLite and he'd just poured a bunch of ground coffee straight from the bag.

"Good lord, Bobby. You tryin to kill us. Every day, you make that stuff stronger."

"Just trying to work you up to some level of manhood, Uncle John. Now, you watch that carefully. Don't let it come back to a boil."

"Seven minutes, right?"

"Yeah, but the electric clock's not workin, You got your watch on? I'll get the donuts; that is, if you left any for us."

Settling the grounds with a splash of cold water, I waited a bit and then divided the coffee among five mugs.

"Deputy Handel, this snowstorm keeping your life interesting?" I said, handing him a cup of steaming, very black coffee.

"Well, we did have one pretty scary event. Couple of girls up on the trail. Got caught in the snow. Sisters, in fact. Local section hikers walking north from Sams Gap. Their parents were gonna pick um up at Indian Grave. We were hoping they'd hole-up in the No Business shelter, so that's where we went first, couple deputies, EMS guys, and the rescue team ... the Unaka Mountain Search and Rescue Team ... heard of them? ... any of those guys been by here yet? Bunch of really nice people."

"So you found them?"

"Oh, yeah. No Business Knob. Asleep in the shelter," Handel said, taking a quick sip with a grimace. "Smart girls. Our worry was they'd be out of water. The spring, well, you know this, the spring's a good ways down the hill, and eating snow is dangerous...worsens dehydration and can produce hypothermia, but the girls had their water bottles, those camel things, in the sleeping bag with them so they wouldn't freeze. Good thing too, because it was in the twenties with a pretty stiff wind."

"No Business Knob's not the cheeriest of places, even in bright sunshine. I'm surprised they didn't push on. Lucky thing they didn't."

"You're right about that. The Knob's about 3,200. We measured way over three foot of snow up there."

"They were okay?"

"They were okay. You know how it is, parents were a wreck, but the girls were just laughing and having a good ol' time. Didn't understand why we come after them. They had winter gear. One of the girls said ... Mom! It's a winter hike. That's why we were up there! But, you and I know, deep inside, they were glad to see us. I can tell you for sure, John. When we arrived, they had that look."

* * *

The snow melted away long before our electrical service was restored. The weather warmed appreciably, and during this downtime, the sawmill delivered the pine planking. I was in the yard covering the stack with yet another blue plastic tarp when a young man came striding into the yard.

"Are you Uncle Johnny?"

"John Shores," I said, smiling at his reference. "How can I help you?"

"I've come to talk about that canoe you have stored over there," he said, pointing at DeHaven's pile of junk. "I apologize for trespassing, but I was driving around over here the other day and got curious about what you had going on. I love looking over new construction. Nobody was around, and then I noticed the canoe. Took a look at it. A really old, Old Town canoe. I like the old ones, so, Mr. Shores, I'm wondering if that thing is for sale. Looks like it's been in storage for some time."

"Well, I don't know. I'm a paddler myself, and I like the old ones too. Now, if you think you're about to snag a valuable antique, well, I've checked the serial number, and there's nothing special about that one."

"No, sir, that's not my objective, it's just ... I'm going to school up in Elizabethton, and my canoe is back in Minnesota, I'd love to spend some time relaxing ... do some flatwater. Maybe Lake Davy Crockett, and I need a canoe. Hoping yours won't ... you know, it needs a patch or two, hoping it's within my budget."

He was a nice looking kid. I was inclined to just give the thing to him, then I got an idea. "That your pickup over there?"

"Yes-sir."

"Tell you what. I had a pickup truck ... my partner's. Long story short, he had to go back home. How bout ... you need a canoe; I need a truck. Would you care to make a trade? You can have the canoe for nothing. You help me haul some stuff for a couple days."

"Wow! You mean it? For that canoe? ... I'll give you more than a couple of days. Besides, I like helping out. School's pretty intense. I'm thinking about the canoe to get away from, to take a break, you know? ...weekends. But ... working with you, that would be fun, too. Yes, sir. You've got a deal." And he offered his hand.

"Where are you ... Elizabethton? You're talking Tennessee? What school is in Elizabethton?"

"Moody Aviation."

"You're in school ... studying to be a pilot?"

"I'm majoring in missionary aviation technology."

"Missionary. You're going to be a missionary?"

"My goal is to serve the Lord as a missionary pilot. I've completed my theological studies at Moody Institute ... that was up in Chicago, now I'm getting FAA certified training as a pilot and in aviation maintenance ... all the technical things I'll need to know to fly a plane in some remote place, lots of people living in places like that never heard the Gospel, and there's medical emergencies. People can't get the help they need. I'm hoping they'll send me somewhere in South America."

"Well, that's a new one to me, but it sounds like you're gonna have an exciting life."

"Yes-sir, but I could use a little excitement right now. It's a tough course. Very intense. You know, we get certified as an airplane mechanic in just one year. It's a meat grinder. I need to get away. I'm free on the weekends."

* * *

And the very next day, the two Bobs came by looking for Richard. That infamous pair had it in their heads he was coming back. They were very disappointed to learn he was not coming back at all. They brightened considerably, however, as it slowly dawned on them that with Richard gone I might be looking to replace him. They asked almost in unison if I needed help.

* * *

After ten, long, frustrating days, I awoke to the sound of the refrigerator rumbling and the alarm clock's digits blinking. The days following the snowstorm had been generally sunny, and the gravel along River Road had dried. Rounding the house one morning, I noticed a small stream of water trickling along the side of the road.

Could this be a spring, a wet-weather spring on my property? I began tracing it upstream and discovered it came from close by the house. A spring … under my house? Standing there in wonder, I became aware that Bobby was taking a shower. I could hear the water running. When Bobby finished his shower, I informed him we had a leak under the house, that water from his shower was running down the street. Would he stand by as I crawled under the house and would he turn on the water when I shouted? This was a major leak, and I expected, with my command, to see water gushing from somewhere.

With my headlamp and a large-lensed six-volt spotlight, I crawled through the access door dreading the spiders and snakes I might come across more than the nature of the leak I would have to repair. Okay, Bobby, I shouted. Turn on the shower. I couldn't believe it. Shut it off, I hollered. When the water stopped, I shouted; turn on the kitchen sink. Okay, okay. Shut it off Bobby. Hey Bobby. Shut it off!

"You won't believe it man."

"Well, John. This is an old house. You gotta expect things like that," Bobby said, combing the water from his long, blond hair.

"Not what I mean, buddy. There is no drain."

"No drain? What do you mean … no drain."

"No drain."

"No drain?"

"Just runs out the shower onto the ground under the house. Same with the sink."

"Under the house?"

"Yep. Since 1955."

DeHaven had admitted that his house didn't have a real septic system. He explained that the wastewater line ran a short distance out the back and into a steel fifty-five-gallon drum buried in the yard. Not too buried, he said. About five or six inches under the sod. A fifty-five-gallon barrel with its bottom cut out filled with rocks, he said. He didn't happen to mention that the grey water simply dropped to the ground under the house. Dropped into a sea of sudsy mud. Under the house.

* * *

I had made several attempts to gain the trust and friendship of the neighbor whose house sat just across the property-line where we were building the privacy fence. Not once when we talked did he make eye contact. A potential friendship seemed to hang on my willingness to join his church. Every attempt I made to explain the kind of business I was building and the effort I would make toward maintaining a good neighborly relationship was countered by another description of his church and how I would benefit were I to join the congregation. Then, back on the day we began nailing up the fence-planking, we spotted him pounding a for-sale-by-owner sign in the ground out by the edge of River Road.

The property sold quickly. As soon as the county plowed River Road, a small moving-van backed into the yard, and by noon, the house was empty. A few days after that, I opened to a knock on our door to find the new neighbor and his family coming to introduce themselves. In short order, Danny Honrath, his wife, Leslie, and teenaged son, Daniel were to become our good friends. He was a retired electrician, he said, and offered to take a look at the job, should I need advice or suggestions. Young Daniel offered to mow our grass come summer. Said he'd be hunting for part-time jobs.

* * *

One of the items I wanted to check off my list was the waterproof mattresses I would need for the hostel. They needed to be waterproof, but not for the reason one might imagine. Like most hostels, we would not provide bedding ... no sheets, blankets, or pillows. The guests would be sleeping in their own sleeping bags and using their laundry bags for pillows just as they would on the trail. Often, the sleeping bags would be soaking wet. Sleeping in a wet bag was almost the norm out on the trail. The warmth of the hiker's body will actually dry or come close to drying the bag during the night. It is for this reason I would need specially constructed, waterproof mattresses. But where to get them?

I called the Nantahala Outdoor Center.

The NOC is located near Bryson City, North Carolina, out in the far western corner of that state, on the banks of the Nantahala River near where the boundaries of North Carolina, South Carolina, Georgia, and Tennessee come together.

Nantahala is Cherokee for "Land of the Noon-Day Sun," a word that perfectly describes this location. The Nantahala River runs through a landscape of long, steep ridges, and narrow valleys. The NOC, sitting on the bank of the river, is hard up against a long ridge, and to the east, across the river, another high ridge. So, just as with my property in Erwin, the sun rises late over the ridge to the east, and sets early behind the ridge to the west, giving them, like me, at best, six-hours of sunlight.

Spread over 500 acres deep in the Nantahala National Forest, the NOC offers kayak, canoe, and rafting trips on six rivers coursing through the higher parts of the Southern Appalachians. From this home-base, the NOC operates five other whitewater river outposts. In addition to all this, the NOC operates a world-renowned paddling school where athletes in kayak and canoe events train. The school is staffed by Olympic athletes including Joe Jacobi and Scott Strausbaugh, the only Americans to have won an Olympic gold medal for the United States in whitewater, which they did in Barcelona in 1992.

The Appalachian Trail passes right through the heart of the property, crossing the Nantahala River over a bridge next to the outfitter store. If you hike the trail out of Georgia, you can't miss it, and if you are the typical hiker looking to replace poor-performing or inappropriate gear, you'll stop and spend some money.

In the beginning, it was tiny. Founded in 1972 by Payson and Aurelia Kennedy and their partner, Horace Holden. The original property consisted of a few acres around the Tote 'N Tarry, a tiny roadside motel, cafe, and gas station. Payson, Aurelia, and Horace were childhood friends. They and their families were church people, belonging to the First Presbyterian in Atlanta. But they were outdoor enthusiasts too, all of them. The three families spent many summer weekends at the Tote 'N Tarry canoeing the Nantahala and hiking the Appalachian Trail.

Reaching adulthood, the three friends went their separate ways. Aurelia became an elementary school teacher, Payson got his Masters in Library Science and went to work as a librarian for the Georgia Institute of Technology. Holden was the entrepreneur. He had several business interests including Camp Chattahoochee, a popular day camp for Atlanta children.

Holden never recovered from the nagging feeling that the old Tote 'N Tarry sat on a gold mine. In the winter of 1971, he took a room at the tiny inn. Of the two pieces of luggage he carried, one was a portable typewriter. He initiated a carefully-constructed negotiation with the owner that began with the question, how was your summer? Not so good was the answer. I doubt you would ever sell this place, though, Holden cautiously replied. Oh, well, I might. Been thinking about that lately. And the old portable typewriter hammered out the contract.

Holden was just as cautious with his approach to the Kennedys. Both of them worked for schools. Both had the summer off. How would you like to run my little motel? was the question Holden proposed. Give you a chance to spend lots of time on the river, he skillfully added. Horace Holden's business strategy was to solve big problems one little step at a time.

The Kennedys jumped at the offer. Before the summer was over, Holden had put together a partnership. The Kennedys quit their day jobs in Atlanta, cashed out their retirement, sold their home, packed up their four teenaged kids, and headed into a new life on the banks of the Nantahala River.

Payson had, in the previous year, been the technical advisor and Ned Beatty's stunt double in the blockbuster movie *Deliverance*. I've never heard it said this was Holden's inspiration for buying property in the middle of nowhere to start a business that had never existed before anywhere, but the opening of that movie, coupled with the fact that whitewater slalom would become an Olympic sport, both in the year of NOC's birth, leads one to believe that Horace Holden was … well, let me put it this way. It is wrong to think of an entrepreneur as a risk taker, nor would any entrepreneur worthy of the name plunge into the wild-and-wooly on a whim or for the fun of it. An entrepreneur is one who can see an opportunity, is willing and able to seize the day, and has the guts to hang on through thick and thin.

Payson and Aurelia, who, by the way, started dating when they were fourteen, and their good friend Horace, were passionate outdoorsmen, experts at whitewater canoeing, and avid hikers. Long before they ever imagined themselves owning the Nantahala property, they had hiked the trails around that portion of the Smoky Mountains. They had hiked the Appalachian Trail and, I'm just guessing, had walked across the bridge that leads to the front door of the old Tote 'N Tarry to buy a couple of hot dogs and a half-gallon of ice cream. It's pure fantasy, I know, but I like to imagine them sitting on the porch there eating the ice cream, passing the container back and forth, looking at the river. And then looking at the bridge. And then, looking at each other. And then allowing their eyes to follow the Appalachian Trail across the bridge. Their eyes tracing the footpath all the way up to the steps to the store. And then, I like to imagine them turning toward each other and laughing, just like I did standing at the foot of the Chestoa Bridge, shaking my head in wonder that this man's property stood not sixty feet from the trailhead. Location, location, location.

* * *

Whoever the person was that answered the phone, I didn't catch her name, knew exactly what I was talking about. Over the years, they had purchased several hundred of the type mattress my hostel required. They, too, had hostels and employee bunkhouses at the NOC and at their outpost locations. Assuming the worst, I asked where they got them. You can't imagine, first the shock, and then the huge relief coming with a burst of laughter, when I discovered the only supplier of such mattresses in all of America was located in my neighboring town: Johnson City, Tennessee.

I called and placed my order immediately. Two weeks later, I was informed they were ready for pickup. Learning that Chris, the aviation missionary, buried to the neck in preparation for some kind of mechanical performance test, would not be available until the weekend, and the manufacturer being closed on the weekend, I took off in my Ford Taurus with every tie-down strap I could find.

The men at the loading dock very reluctantly helped me stack all nine mattresses on top the Taurus. None would help me with the tie-down. Looking at that pile of straps, straps in every make, kind, and color, they said, oh, no, no, no; not having any part of that. Wish I'd not helped you at all, they said. You're gonna kill somebody, man.

Never deterred by such talk, I tied the damn thing myself. I eased out the parking lot, and discovered driving wasn't as bad as one would expect. However, reaching the Interstate, I quickly realized that about thirty-five miles per hour was the limit the load would take. Creeping up over that speed sent the Taurus waving oscillation-like from side to side. I backed down to thirty miles per hour just to be on the safe side.

It was not long before I noticed, in my rearview, a Tennessee State trooper coming up behind. Just as they always do, and I'm sure it's intentional, he followed me for about ten miles before throwing on the blue lights.

"What do you think you're doing? Mr. Shores," the trooper said, looking over my driver's license and registration. "This is not just dangerous, it's illegal."

"These are mattresses for my new hostel," I said, brightly. "I'm building an Appalachian Trail hostel up by the Chestoa Bridge."

"The Chestoa Bridge?"

"Yes-sir."

"I know the place. I've hiked up to Beauty Spot many times. Fished that river, too. Great fishing hole just down from the bridge. You say you're building a hostel?"

"Yes-sir. That little white house at the foot of the bridge."

"Know the place. You're building a hostel there? ... for hikers?"

"Yes-sir. Well underway. Got the bathhouse nearly closed in," I said with a proud lift of chin. "Getting ready to remodel the house into a hostel and a store ... outfitter store. You know, hiking gear and......" Suddenly awakened to my climacteric situation, I continued quietly in humble deference. "These mattresses. For the bunkbeds in the hostel," And, with a quick, cautious glance at the trooper's name tag, I lowered my eyes to examine my hands on the steering wheel.

"Mr. Shores, you are aware they make trucks for ... listen, Mr. Shores. I'm going to let you off with a warning. Only because I'm a backpacker myself. I admire what you're doing. I don't admire how you're going about it, but you take the very next exit, and you drive the back roads the rest of the way to Chestoa. If I see you out here again, Mr. Shores ..."

"No-sir. Yes-sir. I'll take the next exit. And Officer Cooper. Next time you're up my way, please stop by. I'd love to show you the place."

* * *

With a break in the weather, JM Harris called. Said he would start the septic tank installation the following day. And he did, arriving in the cab of the machine he called My Baby, the biggest backhoe excavator I ever saw. So big, he didn't have a truck to haul it. Drove it right down River Road to my place. Burying a 1,500-gallon septic tank, digging and placing 400 feet of field lines, and running a ditch to the house for the toilet tore up nearly every square foot of yard not covered with blue-tarped building materials. JM was right. Baby chewed through rock like they were M&M's. The quantity of newly-exposed rock strewn over that expanse of raw dirt was shocking, exposing yet another daunting task I had not imagined. Somebody had to pick up those suckers and carry them to the river.

Shortly after JM finished his work, we framed the roof of the bathhouse and installed the metal roofing. That sheet metal roofing was another lucky break in my streak of good luck. Someone I had talked to in the process of finding a supplier said they had spotted metal roofing salvaged from one of Clinchfield's buildings. It was a bargain, but it consisted of several odd sizes. I moved the pile to the hostel site with Chris's help and his long-bed pickup. Bobby and I sorted and measured the lengths of each sheet, and we designed our bathhouse roof system based on those sizes.

The bathhouse ended up with the look of a tidewater saltbox-style building; a modified gable roof with the ridge member pushed toward the front, creating a short, steep roofline covering the porch and a long sloping roofline reaching toward the back. Because Unicoi County did not have strict building codes, we were at liberty to put together a very economical structure designed to accommodate the materials we had at hand. Rather than county officials demanding solutions based on the engineering of national codes and standards, the determining factor was the lengths of the sheet metal and the availability of beautiful one-by-twelve planking from an Appalachian Mountain sawmill. So, the original design evolved into a big airy structure with ceilings up to twelve feet high. In addition to its pleasing good looks, I just knew this bathhouse would sustain good air quality in spite of its four showers and four toilets.

Now that the walls were up, the roof framed, and the metal roofing installed, we began installing the vertical exterior siding planks. Some of these were sixteen-feet long. This task was a mixture of beauty and misery. White pine has a distinctive smell, and that was wonderful. It feels good to handle, cuts easily, and looks great. Personally, this phase of the construction gave me great satisfaction, but with a heavy trade-off in pain.

First, we were working on ladders. And each plank required seven nails spaced evenly and perfectly aligned from one edge of the plank to the other. Each plank was nailed to six horizontal stringers. These included the rim joists at the bottom, and the top plate of the framed wall. Forty-two nails. Forty-two nails per every linear foot of siding all the way round the building. Forty-two nails driven with a twenty-ounce, long-handled hammer. Bobby did the cutting. Cindy carried the planks and passed them up to us. Mike and I nailed. And nailed. And nailed.

With the bathhouse closed in and water tight, it was time to call Al No-Drip Higgins. During every rainy day, and there were plenty of those, we had cut and assembled the component parts that would become the hostel's bunk beds. We had knocked out the side-wall of the front bedroom, and added to the room an extra ten feet. This bedroom would become the hostel's bunkhouse. We had stripped the sheetrock from the walls, and installed stringers between the studs in preparation for nailing up the pine planking. While the stud walls were laid open like this, No-Drip would run the Romex wire and install the outlet boxes needed for the hostel. The design of the house was such that we had a perfect little nook in the hostel for a desk and a computer. No-Drip would also run the Cat-5 cable to the modem in the office.

* * *

"Uncle Johnny!"

"Al, good to see you again."

No-Drip had backed his blue cargo van into the front parking lot. Just as I came onto the porch to greet him, he bounced out with a big smile apparently very happy to have a good winter job. Al had that type of physique you often see in an older man. Like Don DeHaven, he was very fit, thin and wiry, six-foot-one or two, and moved with energy.

"I see what you mean, John. The yard back there's occupied. Either its mud and rock, or blue tarps. Parking here's just fine."

"Can I give you a hand?"

"Sure, grab that tank. I'll get the toolbox. That's all I'll need for right now. You get the copper?"

"Yep. In the bathhouse. And the PVC, too."

Al had a hose and torch attached to a twenty-pound propane tank. He had opened the rear doors to the van, and pointed toward the rig sitting next to the toolbox. The van had been outfitted with shelves along the left side. Each of a couple dozen cubby holes held fittings and electrical devices of every imaginable size and kind. A coil of rope and several extension cords hung on the right. A Milwaukee Sawzall, his miter box, and several other tools in plastic cases were scattered about the floor, along with short lengths of various kinds of pipe and other debris from his last job.

"Grab that, John. I'll get my drill-motor and toolbox. Have you got an outlet in the bathhouse?"

"Yeah. Well … no. Not an outlet. We ran a piece of Romex to a four-plex box. It's just lying on the floor in there. Long enough. You can pull it around where you need it."

"Good. Grab that twenty-five-foot extension cord, then. The yellow one."

No-Drip followed me around the left-side of the house and toward the bathhouse.

* * *

Charlotte and Claire had come for a visit the week before. They stayed at the Holiday Inn. Our camp in the DeHaven house was impossible. The living room, part storage shed and part workshop, provided a narrow pathway to the kitchen. Tools were everywhere. Bunkbed and picnic table parts were stacked all along one wall. The master bedroom was clean and orderly, but, with all the construction chaos, even that was not suitable accommodation for Claire and Charlotte's needs.

The front bedroom was well on the way to becoming a hiker's hostel. Mike and I had worked the inside, stripping the walls down to the studs, ripping off sheetrock, tearing out the old electrical wiring, pulling nails, and knocking down anything loose. It was almost fun. Bobby, Cindy, Chris the aviator, and the two Bobs carried debris to Chris's pickup truck by the armload. Streaming single file through the opening in the new wall we'd not yet framed for a door, they looked like a column of army ants.

Bobby left soon after demolition day. The Nantahala Outdoor Center called, following up three references Bobby had listed on his resume.

"He says he's a pretty good carpenter," the manager explained. "Know anything about that?"

I wanted to laugh at the irony, but I managed to stifle the obvious response, like I taught him everything he knows, or he's been a carpenter for all of two months. But I didn't. I kept my voice calm and level. Explained how I liked Bobby. Knew they would too. He was a clever, honest, faithful, hard-working young man.

"He's good enough," I said, "but he's an expert paddler, what's the deal about carpentry?"

"Oh, we're hiring him for his boater skills, that's for sure," she explained, "We're sending him to the Chattooga outpost, our most challenging assignment. But, we've got several buildings to repair before the season begins. The sooner he can get over there the better."

So Bobby packed his gear.

Spread across four southeastern states, NOC operates trips on six different rivers, and each of those rivers has a dedicated outpost. It is generally agreed among boaters that the Chattooga is NOC's premier whitewater river. It was federally protected in 1974 by the Wild & Scenic Rivers Act, forever preserving the rugged river gorge as pristine wilderness. The Chattooga delivers breathtaking scenery and awesome whitewater. In fact, the Chattooga was the location for the movie *Deliverance*. This is where Payson Kennedy served as a stunt double for Ned Beatty. The editors of Southern Living put rafting the Chattooga first on their list of things to do in the south. Section IV, the river's most thrilling section, involves navigating Seven-Foot Falls, Raven's Chute, and the famous Five Falls where five Class IV and V rapids unfold in just one-third of a river mile.

Chris volunteered to carry Bobby, his gear, and his Crossfire Dagger kayak over to the outpost near Mountain Rest, South Carolina. I can see it now. During the nearly three-hour trip, Bobby will infuse Chris with his passion for the sport. During the solo return, Chris will visualize paddling my Old Town canoe on placid Lake Davey as pure stodge. He'll turn to designing a plan for noodging me into a trade for my Perception kayak. Ain't gonna happen, partner.

* * *

Charlotte and Claire spent four glorious days in Erwin. I had reserved a room with two queen beds, knowing that Claire would love sleeping in a big, luxurious bed like her mother. Standing outside when Charlotte arrived, it seemed like a year since I had last seen her. Watched her park the car. Watched her step out and around to open the passenger door; her hair blowing in the gentle wind. Gorgeous strawberry blond hair with reddish bronze highlights. Like Nicole Kidman in *Batman Forever*.

I couldn't move. Just watched her gathering luggage and tending to Claire. And there was Abbo, Claire's constant companion; amazingly calm and attentive for a part Scotty mutt.

I planned to take them to dinner that night. I had discovered a wonderful restaurant; the oldest in Johnson City. The Peerless served an unbelievably good prime rib. Claire would be happy to hear they have the best mac and cheese I ever tasted. But, I had a more important agenda in mind. I wanted to show Charlotte the Johnson City Medical Center. She was director of a hospice in Birmingham, a position with a salary that surpassed my own when I was director of human resources at the *Birmingham News*. It would be hard to coax her away from that.

Her hospice is a division of Carraway Methodist Medical Center. As a member of the morning manager's meetings at the *News*, I was privy to some startling information about that company. Part of our marketing effort was to schedule periodic surveys of various core industries in Birmingham. We would make these studies and our consultants available to our larger clients. One of the clients was Carraway Methodist. Belden and Associates out of Dallas, Texas, handled this work for us, and they had three young, smart, marketing experts assigned to Birmingham.

Their surveys discovered that the hospital was heading into financial trouble. Built in Norwood in 1907, what was then an up-scale community, the hospital had thrived for decades. By the '80s, they were Birmingham's most innovative hospital, operating on the leading edge with new technologies. At the same time, downtown Birmingham began changing as the more affluent families flocked to the suburbs. Norwood became a declining community of older residents and unemployed youth and, worse, the location of several subsidized housing projects. Belden's consultants listed two factors responsible for the institution's financial decline—the decay of the Norwood neighborhood, and decades of decisions favoring patient care over profits. I knew what Charlotte didn't know. She would soon be looking for another job. I was determined that job would be in Erwin, Tennessee.

After taking a look at the Johnson City Medical Center, we would drive through the campus of East Tennessee State University and its James H. Quillen College of Medicine, a beautiful campus situated on rolling hills. An easy, thirty-minute drive from Erwin.

* * *

The big event was a picnic up on Beauty Spot. Beauty Spot is well named. It's a treeless knob in the Unaka Mountain Range where the Appalachian Trail passes along the Tennessee-North Carolina border providing a beautiful panoramic view best known for its sunsets. Getting out of the car at the Beauty Spot parking lot, we caught the swirling eddies of a vicious wind whipping across the bald. I looked at Charlotte, and we both knew our picnic would not take place as planned.

Wrapping my jacket around Claire's own, the three of us hustled up to the highest point for a quick look around. From the bald's grassy ridgeline, I pointed toward a stunning view of the mountain range stretching far into the blue-hazed distance. The Appalachian Trail, I explained to Claire, extends through those mountains all the way to Maine.

"But, see there," I said pointing. "Way, way in the distance where the mountains become purpley-blue? those far mountains, which are as far as we can see from here...they are still in Tennessee."

Looking right we could see a good view of Erwin. We could see nearly the whole valley of the Nolichucky. I explained to Charlotte and Claire, the locals call what we were admiring the Valley Beautiful. Then we scurried back to the car and down the crooked, narrow mountain road toward Rock Creek Park.

Rock Creek Park is beautiful and quiet with towering hemlocks. There are many amenities, the most popular with the locals being a large picnic area with widely-spaced tables, each with a barbeque pit. There is a campground with thirty-eight sites, free Wi-Fi, and electrical service. A bathhouse with showers and plenty of hot water. A play area for children. Trout fishing in the creek. Hiking trails, and a very popular mountain-bike pathway.

The original portion of the park was built in 1933 by FDR's Civilian Conservation Corp. The coolest thing about that early project was a spring-fed swimming pool that looks more like a big, concrete pond. Originally twelve feet deep with a tall diving platform, it is filled to only six feet today. It has lush, grassy banks and a sandy beach. The pool, surrounded by tall trees, collects the warming sunshine in midday, shadowed again by early afternoon. Adults seldom take the plunge. This natural-flowing swimming pool, the picnic area, and the bathhouse were all originally built by the CCC.

Plan B was a trail-side picnic by Rock Creek Falls. To get there, we followed a nicely maintained blue-blazed trail that takes you around the campground and along the Creek. It was a beautiful, warm, blue-sky day that had the three of us chattering away like so many birds. Shortly, we came to the first of four places where the trail crossed the creek. This part was unanticipated. Fortunately for me, the creek wasn't high, or we would have been forced to lunch in the less-exotic picnic area.

Rock Creek was running boldly, but Claire crossed easily, hopping through a series of flat rocks someone had intentionally and strategically placed in the creek. On the other side, Claire looked back at Abbo. He barked three times, and cocked his head. Then, seeming to understand, he scampered across the rocks as though this was a qualifying run in a dog agility contest.

After the forth crossing, the trail got steep, but Charlotte and I took Claire by the hands and up we went. The trail followed the cascading creek the entire distance, carrying us past two lower waterfalls on the way to the main attraction. Reaching the upper falls, we found ourselves in a box canyon facing a two-tiered, fifty-foot waterfall over a sheer, rocky cliff. It had rained up here recently, and we were treated to the warm aroma of earth and wet rock, a carpet of spongy hemlock needles, and a light breeze scented with pine. Claire was delighted and so was Charlotte … and I by them.

* * *

I had visited with the burrito couple, Brady and Lisa Sleeper, several times, and we had become friends. I wanted Charlotte and Claire to see their uniquely interesting house. Besides, they lived in a commune.

Up by Spivey Gap, not too far from Don DeHaven's new place, a woman by the name of June Trexler owned twenty acres spread upward in a steep mountain gorge. If you visited her and she took a liking to you, she would invite you to come live on her land. You could build a little place, or park a graffiti-festooned old school bus, or pitch a teepee; whatever.

When I first met her, I was quite surprised by Ms. Trexler's look and demeanor. I had heard she ran a commune and I expected to meet a wild-haired, hippie, mountain momma, or some kind of religious guru wrapped in a long, colorful swath of silk. Such was not the case. June Trexler was attractive and normal. This was East Tennessee, after all, and the women here seemed to be uniformly attractive...at least to my knowledge so far. Furthermore, she looked and dressed like the VP of a local bank. I later learned that she was a therapist at Frontier Health Clinic, a regional mental health facility.

Brady and Lisa were Appalachian Trail thru-hikers who had taken a couple of zeros in Erwin. Upon discovering the opportunity to open a hiker-friendly Mexican restaurant, they decided to commit themselves to that project. Somewhere along the way, they had met June, accepted the invitation to build on her place, and after reaching Katahdin, put weeks of hiker-planning into action.

It seemed, from my observation, that this was the highlight of Claire's visit to Erwin. Lisa was about eight months along in her pregnancy and Claire was fascinated with the fact that you could feel the baby moving and kicking, could actually feel and watch the impression of its tiny foot moving along under the skin. She had never seen wild deer, and here were three of them grazing in Brady's front yard. She had never visited an outhouse. Brady and Lisa had built an amazing outhouse complete with sink and running water, electric heat, and a library.

The water came from a spring 100 yards up the hill, far enough and high enough to be unaffected by the several outhouses scattered about the community. The water came down through a black plastic pipe in the bottom of the creek flowing past the Brady place. From there it was pumped by a small, submersible water pump to a thirty-gallon tank uphill on the other side of the house, and by gravity it flowed from the tank through the faucet in the kitchen sink and to the odd little sink in the outhouse.

The house was a modified A-frame, mostly glass, with a pleasing array of different kinds of windows that Brady discovered in an architectural salvage yard. They had a wood stove in the very center of the room, the black stovepipe rising straight up and through the peak of the vaulted ceiling. There was a sleeping loft, and Claire could run up the stairs and look over the railing down on the adults seated at the dining room table. On my part, I liked the floors: solid maple salvaged from a defunct bowling alley. The highly-lacquered surface still showed the bowling-alley markings.

In a month, we would both have our businesses up and running. On the way back to the Holiday Inn, Charlotte confirmed my confidence in Brady and Lisa. The Burrito Company would be a key factor in the success of the hiker hostel. Having been there ourselves, we knew from our experience that, next to a hot shower, hikers coming off the sixty-eight mile trek up from Hot Springs or coming south from Hampton are dreaming of food. The free dinner shuttle we would offer hikers to the little shop on Main Street would become valuable word-of-mouth information ricocheting up and down the trail.

* * *

I drove to the Holiday Inn every morning, and met Charlotte for breakfast. Margaret, the motel's general manager, and I had met several times in the past month as I briefed her on how we could coordinate services for hikers. Maybe half the hikers coming into Erwin would be looking for the comforts of a motel, and the new Holiday Inn, being the nearest, would likely get the lion's share of that business. I thought it would benefit the hostel if Margaret understood what hikers needed and the services I had to offer. Margaret, who had no experience with hiking or the Appalachian Trail, had no idea what to expect, and was eager to learn about these things. In the process of these discussions, we had become friends. So, Margaret would not only comp my meal, she would also join us during her free moments and seemed charmed by Charlotte and Claire.

"Charlotte, honey, I swear. Takes half-a-minute for some of your words to fully develop. I thought I had a southern accent until I heard John, but you beat all. Where'd you grow up, honey?"

"Birmingham. Same as John. But, you've got another level to go. You should hear my momma. A southern belle like she grew up with Scarlet O'Hara."

"Oh, my, I do love to hear you talk. Soft as an early morning rain."

During the final day of her visit, Charlotte and I looked at a few rental properties we'd seen advertised in *The Erwin Record*. One of those was the Rutter place, owned by Pete and Patricia Rutter who lived next door with their teenaged daughter, Danielle.

It was a nice property, high on the side of a wooded ridge. I was inclined toward buying the place, but Mr. Rutter didn't want to sell, at least not until he had a clear notion about what kind of neighbor I'd be.

"So, you rent it," he nodded, "and later on we'll talk." He was eyeing Charlotte's little dog, Abbo.

"No pets," Rutter said. "I think I listed that in the ad." Abbo mooched up to him after sniffing his pant leg. Then Abbo sat on his haunches. Cocking his head quietly, he gave Rutter a lovable doe-eyed look.

"Guess this dog will be okay," he said, smiling down at Claire.

Later that day, with hugs and kisses all around, I loaded luggage and off they went, Claire waving vigorously out the open window.

* * *

My first inkling of the problem I would have with No-Drip came that very afternoon. Hearing loud laughter echoing from the bathhouse, I found Mike and Cindy sitting on five-gallon buckets and No-Drip holding forth like a stand-up comic.

"Uncle Johnny," Mike shouted. "You should hear this. I asked No-Drip how much moonshine his uncles had made, and he said about enough to float the Queen Mary."

And they all laughed again.

"Yeah, John. They were pretty prolific. My uncles were the ones gave No Business Knob the name. Back in the '30s they built a still up by that spring. It ran bold and year-round back then. People all over these parts said, ain't nobody got no business up by that knob. That's where the name come from, No Business Knob. People were skeert of my uncles." With this, No-Drip backed up a little and looked closely at Mike and Cindy.

"People think moonshiners locate by a spring for the pure water but that's not the case. Need cold water for the flake stand. That's like a rough-built wood box where they put the coil; the copper coil's what cools the alcohol steam back to liquid, they put that in a box called a flake stand and the flake stand pipe runs directly from the spring. Need a stream of water 'bout the size of your thumb, at least. If cold water ain't running pretty strong through the flake stand and back out on the ground, the coil will get mighty hot, hot enough to bring water to a boil, so you need a constant stream of cold water."

I started to interrupt, but Al was on a roll. He talked fast and I couldn't get a word in edgewise.

"Spring water's the best cause it's colder'n creek water. Anyway, John," No-Drip looked back at me and made a little turn in front of his audience and a long ash fell from the lit Marlboro.

Before I could say anything, Al threw out his hands and said, "People back in those days were skeert of moonshiners. They were pretty rough ... my uncles." He squinted his eyes at Cindy in a menacing way.

"They were known to be uncompromising. Some bear hunters stumbled upon them one day, and my uncles and a couple of still hands surrounded them at gunpoint. Marched them down the mountain to a logging road and lined them up. Those poor guys could hear angels singin and Gabriel a-calling their names. But, one of my uncles got right in their faces one-by-one saying very quietly, you ain't seen nothin, you hear. And he moved to the next and said quietly, you ain't seen nothin. Well, don't ya know, the hunters kept it quiet. Nothing came of it. And they must have warned other hunters because far as I know no other hunter ever had any more business at No Business Knob." And he laughed at his own joke. And so did Mike and Cindy.

"Al," I said loudly, seizing the moment. "We've all got work to do." I smiled and I patted him on the back. "You guys grab your buckets and get back to picking up rock. It might rain tomorrow and I'd like to get that dirt raked out before it rains again. Get some seed planted."

"John, you ever hear that song, *Copperhead Road*? Mike and Cindy turned around, each with a bucket hanging slack.

"Right near here in Tennessee. You run out Main Street here in Erwin, north, out past Limestone Cove, jess keep a-going bout another fifteen mile till you get to US 321 there in Hampton. You take that on out toward Mountain City. Half-way along there you turn off left toward Watauga Lake, and right up there past the lake is Copperhead Road. You've heard that song, was a big hit few years back."

And then No-Drip started singing:

> Well my name's John Lee Pettimore
> Same as my daddy and his daddy before
> You hardly ever saw Granddaddy down here
> He only came to town about twice a year
> He'd buy his yeast and some copper line
> Everybody knew that he made moonshine

"Al, I'm serious here, we've got work…" Al held up his hand, smiled a big grin, did a little shave-and-a-haircut jig stomping his foot twice in my direction on the two-bits part, then picked up his right-angle drill, and went back to drilling a three-inch hole through the bottom plate where the sink drain would connect under the bathhouse to the soil line. He had already run a four-inch line to the septic tank. Mike and Cindy were filling the ditch with rocks they were picking up. JM Harris had left frying-pan-sized rocks strewn everywhere he dug.

*   *   *

A cold front, colliding with yesterday's record warm air, announced its presence by a single clap of thunder just at dawn. A transient, gusting wind buffeted the old house and rattled the windows. From my bedroom, I could hear the blue tarp we'd tacked over the unfinished door-opening pop and snap. I groaned, and crawled out of bed. Another one of those days.

By the time Mike and Cindy arrived, I had coffee going and the storm had turned to a gentle morning rain.

"Hey Uncle Johnny," Cindy called out.

"Cindy made another one," Mike said closing the door after her.

"Just like you like it; a little sugar and cinnamon on the bread," Cindy said.

Cindy was carrying a sausage and egg casserole wrapped in a bath towel. While I got out plates and forks, she unwrapped it and a delicious French-toast aroma filled the kitchen air. For several weeks now, she had provided our breakfast. Uninterested in cooking my own, I had proposed this, and offered to cover the expenses. I also covered the cost of lunch every day. It was worth it just to keep them on the property where I could manage down-time. Cindy's casserole was like any other, cooked sausage, milk, and eggs poured over ordinary sliced bread, and baked in the oven. But, she would spread softened butter over lightly toasted bread, and sprinkle that with a little sugar and cinnamon before adding the rest.

"Oh man, Cindy. That smells wonderful. Thanks so much."

"No problem, Uncle Johnny. What have we got going today?"

"Mike and I will finish screwing down the deck planking out front. Al's gonna plumb the shower drains so we can set those shower stalls in place, and I'd like you to clean out the hostel and organize this stuff." I waved my hand at the cluttered living room. "I want Al to shift to the hostel as soon as possible. Install the electrical boxes and run the wire so Mike and I can nail up the pine paneling. From now on, the three of us will focus on completing the hostel. We're starting to get some traffic, and I want to offer more than the couch and space on the floor."

Our first hiker had arrived in February. Little Hoof had survived the big snowstorm; had holed up in the Spring Mountain Shelter. But, with the warm weather and the way wet snow settles and compacts, he was able to continue by the third day. It was slow going, though, he was slipping and sliding on every north-facing ridge. It took him ten days to cover the fifty-eight miles from the shelter to here. What a happy hiker he was to find a warm, dry place and something to eat after an unexpected three-day fast.

The minute we finished breakfast, Cindy started gathering plates.

"Alright guys, hop to it. I'll take care of this. Now scoot." And she punched Mike in the arm.

Cindy was a no-nonsense type that enjoys work; enjoys getting the job done, I should say. If Mike lagged a little, Cindy would poke him, and give him a fake glare. It always worked.

She rarely smiled, but she was pleasant enough; a strong-looking, strongly built, serious woman.

I've spent so many years at the *Birmingham News* interviewing thousands of applicants, I couldn't help wondering about Mike and Cindy. What you learn in my business is that people who seem to be failing in life lack purpose. It's especially true if they think of themselves as a failure. This couple seems to have no reason for being in Erwin. Seems to have no reason for choosing to work with me. I haven't asked, because it would pain me to see their faces. But, if I were to ask: Why are you here? Do you have a purpose? I'm sure I'd get a blank stare. They don't know where they are going. Don't know why they do the things they do, and worse yet, don't know there ought to be a reason. If you are not constantly aware, aware of the coming next thing and how it will appear, you drift down the wrong track, and if you go down that road far enough you'll lose the idea of who you are, where you should be, and why. I jump on every opportunity to use myself as an example for Mike and Cindy, hoping they will learn from me. Once, Cindy asked if I was scared ... scared that all this work and money would go for nothing.

"No, not at all Cindy. When you constantly think and talk about what you want and how to get it, there's no room to be scared. It simply never occurs to me. Not even at night. If I wake up in the dead of night, I'm busy thinking about how to do what needs to be done in the morning."

"Well, I would be scared. If I had money like that, I'd want to hide it somewhere."

We were finishing up parts for the bunk beds, gluing and screwing together a pair 2x4s, creating the 4x4 legs. Cindy was performing the role of a human clamp, holding the glued pieces together while I drilled pilot holes and drove the screws.

"It takes money to make money, Cindy. It's an investment. I expect to get it back."

"How do you know you'll get it back?"

"Because when you believe something will happen, it usually does. But, in my case here, building this hostel, it's more than just wishful thinking. Let me tell you something, Cindy, this place was a future hostel, a hostel about to happen. It's been a hostel about to happen for thirty or forty years. Funny thing is, nobody ever looked at this place that way until I came along. Lucky for me. Best piece of luck I ever had. Took one look and saw an opportunity."

"But, I don't understand how that can make you feel good when you're the only one thinking that way; you just said...for forty years. Isn't that wishful thinking?"

"What I saw, and I saw this immediately, Cindy; I saw a house and some land just sixty feet from a hiking trail. Then I saw in my mind's eye a hiker's hostel. Now, and this is important Cindy, if no such thing ever existed, I might have a problem, but, I'm an experienced hiker and I've seen that combination many, many times. South of here, you have hostels at Hot Springs. Going north, you have hostels in Hampton and Damascus. Those were the reasons to believe there ought to be one here."

"Yeah ... I can see that. But still, how do you know you can make it work since nothing has ever been here before and all those hikers got along fine without it?"

"The universe is driven by laws, Cindy. If I throw this pencil into the air, the law of gravity says it will come back down. Civilization, society ... society is driven by laws just as certain as the law of gravity. One of those laws is called the law of reciprocity. That's a big word, but you follow that law every day. Let me ask you; what happens when someone does something nice for you?"

"I don't know ... what do you mean?"

"Don't you feel that you have to do something nice back? When someone does something nice for you, it's human nature ... compels you do something nice for them in return. Isn't that right?" I waited for Cindy to nod. "It's universal. People everywhere behave this way. I've been a long-distance hiker.

I've spent lots of time talking to other hikers. I know what they need. I know what they want. If my business here meets those needs and wants, solves all their problems, and if I throw in extras, like free meal shuttles, endless hot water, folding their clothes when we wash them, in other words, demonstrating my willingness to help them every way I can, then reciprocity kicks in. They'll want to do something nice back. And what would that be?" Cindy slowly shook her head, puzzled. "Talk about the hostel. Say nice things about the hostel. That's the way they can pay me back. Up and down the trail. Reciprocity. It's an iron-clad law of civil society, just like the law of gravity."

* * *

Until I put an end to it, I have to admit, I was responsible. It always started the same way. All of us working and Al "No-Drip" Higgins would be talking; not necessarily talking to us, but just talking. He'd be down on his knees pulling wire or something. I'd be up on a ladder. Mike or somebody else would be measuring or carrying. And Al would be talking. And sooner or later, one by one, we'd stop and start listening, because he was that good. Al could tell a story like nobody else. His animated face worked with the story, grimacing, or gawking, or rendering astonishment; whatever the story required. He paced about. He would pause and glare at you. He waved his hands. He would lean over and point. He would lean over and point the fat index finger of his big hand at this or that.

It wasn't intentional. Honestly, I don't think Al thought of himself as a story teller. It came from him as part of his personality. I think the term is raconteur. A raconteur tells his stories naturally. A storyteller puts on a rehearsed performance. That's not what Al did. With Al, it just happened. He liked to talk. In fact, he talked if nobody was around to listen. But if people were around, it would start off as a conversation. We'd all be talking, and Al would remember something. And that's how it would begin. He was a raconteur. We don't have a word in English for a person who tells stories so naturally. Our words are all in the negative; gasbag, BS artist, blowhard, chatterbox, magpie, talker. Talker. I guess that comes close. But still, a raconteur is a person who talks and you can't help but stop and listen; talks so naturally it makes you laugh hard or want to cry. But that was Al. Next thing you know; we'd all be listening, and the job would be forgotten.

* * *

"Heck no," Al shouted.

We were talking about whiskey. Tennessee whiskey, in fact. He was down on his knees pulling Romex up through a hole he had drilled.

"Cause anybody could do it back then. You didn't need no license or nothin. That's why Tennessee bourbon is so good. And Kentucky too. No other part of the country was so casual about distillin. In Tennessee, by god, anybody could do it, and the competition was fierce. Only the best distillers survived."

That's how the story about the Town of Rock Creek got started.

"William B. McNabb was his name. He made whiskey. That was his business. His distillery was up on Rock Creek. This was back in the 1890s, and you didn't need a license from nobody, just pay the government tax, state and federal. The government inspector would come around, they call him a gauger, the gauger come around and inspected the whiskey. Collected the tax. Put a government seal on each and every barrel. No seal, the whiskey was illegal. But, guess what? Lots of McNabb's whiskey was sold untaxed. He had a saloon up there on Rock Creek. You walk around back that saloon and there was a little door in the wall bout the size of a breadbox." No-Drip feigns surprise. "Open that little door, put fifty-cent in there." No-Drip stops, looks around from side to side like he's being stealthy. "Shut the door." He whispers. "Knock on the wall three times." No-Drip cocks his head and cups one ear like he's listening. "There'd come a single rap on the wall other side." His eyes open wide with delight. "You open the little door and take out a pint of untaxed whiskey." And here, No-Drip goes through the imaginary motions of opening the door and taking out the whiskey, then he hoots and skips a little one-legged hopping circle holding the imaginary bottle tight to his chest, stops, takes a deep breath, pulls out his pack of Marlboros, lights another cigarette, and resumes his serious look.

"Now, how that saloon come about is an interesting story. The people of Rock Creek wanted a saloon. Problem was, only a legally incorporated town could issue a license for a saloon. Otherwise, it was illegal in Tennessee to open one. The state, don't you know, was responsible for the morals of the people, and they left it to the towns to see to that. The town had to want a saloon, had to want the responsibility of looking after the morals of their citizens, and so the state said only a town could authorize one into existing.

"So, the people up and down Rock Creek got together and declared themselves a town. Now, they wasn't a town, not at all. They was scattered all up and down along the creek for a couple of miles. Just a bunch of houses and farms. But the passion for a saloon united them, and they got together and voted themselves into a town, thirty-three to nothing. Not a single dissenter. Of course, only the men got in on the voting. So, with that vote, they appealed to the State of Tennessee. See, you had to do that. You couldn't just begin calling yourselves a town. No-siree. You had to apply for township from the State of Tennessee, and they did that and they got themselves chartered as a town. The Town of Rock Creek. Weren't no town any way you look at it, but they become a town.

"Then they needed an official body what could issue licenses, in particular; they wanted to issue an official license to establish a saloon. That was the point of the whole shebang. So, they elected themselves a Board of Mayor and Aldermen. Now, John, you're from Alabama. A Board of Mayor and Aldermen is what in Tennessee would be a town council anywhere else. The legal body what runs a town. So the Board then presents McNabb a license for a saloon, and all them men got together and built it, built themselves a saloon. Weren't much to look at according to the pictures I've seen, and all the men what built it looked about as straggly as the saloon they built.

"Now, another problem was they didn't have a town hall or a courthouse. They had become a town, but there weren't no place where they could act like one, so the saloon became that. The town hall, the courthouse, the mayor's office, the post office, the school board meetin room, everything. Of course, still, it was a saloon. All the men came there. I don't think they let women in, but men would be there all the time drinking and socializing and when it come time for the Board of Mayor and Aldermen to meet, they closed the bar. Would be no drinking during the meeting. Everybody would sit down and remove their hats, that was the law, and the mayor would hold forth, and the town policeman maintained order...they had hired themselves a town policeman. Out back there was a shed of sorts they called the Calaboose. It was the jail. The bartender would sell all you wanted back in those days, keep set'um up on the bar till you fell on the floor, didn't care about that, but if you got to acting up, raisin hell, and fightin, they called the town policeman and he'd lock you up. Then the saloon would become a courthouse. The mayor, Jonathan Lafayette Winfield Carathers, would hold court, and the feller would be let out the Calaboose and hauled before the judge. He'd fine the drunk three dollars or something. Bang the gavel. Court would end. They'd open the bar, and the feller would go back to drinkin. Meantime, the mayor and the cop would split the fine fifty/fifty.

"Well, it went on like that for years. All the prominent locals went there. All the town leaders, the doctor, the publisher of the Erwin newspaper, lawyers and druggists. All of um would come by wagon and horseback from Erwin, would take that five-mile trip from Erwin up to Rock Creek to the saloon for socializin. And people come over the mountain from North Carolina where drinking weren't so legal, lookin for the socializin and drinkin, that is, like they did it in McNabb's saloon up Rock Creek. Then along came prohibition in Tennessee, and changed everything. McNabb sold the saloon, well it weren't a saloon any more when he sold it, just a raggedy ol' barn, but he sold the place and moved to Virginia where whiskey-makin was still legal. Now, you know what that building was used for?" No-Drip bent over, hands on his hips, glaring at us until we began shaking our heads.

"A Sunday School!" he shouted and roared with laughter.

* * *

"It's crunch time," I said, pausing to look at each of them. Mike, Cindy, the two Bobs, and Chris the aviator were all eating breakfast. They were seated and I stood with arms folded, presenting the situation with as much gravity as I could muster.

"I have a new rule, and I expect all of you to stick by it. Every time any of us come anywhere near No-Drip, he stops working and starts talking. I know he's a character. I know he's an interesting character. Even I get caught up in his stories. All of you stop for a minute. Look at me. We've got decent weather for a change. I told Al yesterday, we got to jump on it and get this job done. Now, here's the new rule. Don't any of you, and I include myself here, don't go near Al No-Drip Higgins. Don't go anywhere near No-Drip. I'll make sure to schedule him and us in different places. We've got a little over three weeks. Let's get this job done."

Chris had come in on Friday. We have several loads of trash to haul, some tear-out, scrap lumber and cutoffs, and a good bit of DeHaven's junk still under the back shed. Next, we enclosed the yard around the shed with a ten-foot wall and created a big, secure storage area. The front bedroom had become a bunkhouse, and we were assembling the bunkbeds. With the crew completing these tasks, the hostel was ready for opening day. No-Drip had connected the house to the septic system, and the barrel of rocks buried in the back yard had been retired after fifty or sixty years of service. The privacy fence had been completed weeks ago. The rocks had been gathered and carried away, the fill dirt raked smooth, and new grass was sprouting, turning the back yard green again. Uncle Johnny's was definitely taking shape.

* * *

No-Drip arrived early every morning and parked out front. Inevitably, someone would pull in behind him. So, every afternoon, he would come to me saying he needed this or that fitting, some solder, or whatnot, and we would have to jockey vehicles around and let him out. This happened regular as clockwork every afternoon. When he returned, he would be carrying a brown paper bag, and the object in that bag looked suspiciously like a six-pack of beer. He didn't say anything, nor did I, but whatever was in that bag kept him whistling and working for another couple of hours.

I appreciated his dedication. And I appreciated the quality of his work. No-Drip was a craftsman. His lines ran perfectly parallel. His solder work was barely visible; a thin ring of silver solder around the copper fitting with maybe a tiny solidified drip on the down side. Every joint exactly the same. It might seem pointless for a plumber to be proud of his work, considering the fact that every bit of it is hidden under the floor or behind the wall, but men like Al Higgins are proud. When my father built a house, he hired the best he could find. He was a proud man too. I have worked with framers who carried a block plane. Imagine that. If the cut for a cripple-stud over a door was a 32th too long, they would shave it to a perfect fit. Most framers wouldn't know a block plane if you hung one around their neck. Al was proud of his work. It gave me pleasure to walk through the bathhouse after he had gone for the day.

In little over a week, he was finished and gone for good. The whole crew worked at paneling the interior, building stalls, and hanging doors. We had built shelves and installed racks, shelving, and hooks for displaying gear in the outfitter store. I found a used chest-type freezer, and that was filled with ice cream, popsicles, and frozen prepared meals; all the stuff hikers would be looking for. A bankrupt restaurant provided a reach-in refrigerator for water, fruit juices, and Gatorade. Mike and Cindy had just finished the portion of the deck that would hold the Pepsi machines. Two of them were sent over and installed by the local distributor. I had purchased several cases of Snickers bars. Outside, on the front deck facing the trail where it crosses the bridge, I hung a big sign —40¢ Snickers.

In one sense, the place was a mess. We had built the center portion of the front deck, just enough that people could walk up to the front door safely. The six by six posts that would hold the roof over the deck were standing like Plain Jane totem poles. We had hung a large Grand Opening banner from them. The smaller post that would become the hand-railing outlined where the deck would eventually extend. Yellow construction tape, the caution-type, strung between these posts, fluttered in the wind.

Landscape timbers marking a pea-gravel pathway around the left side of the hostel led straight to the bathhouse steps. More caution tape, strung between temporary stakes, marked another pathway along River Road. Here, the fluttering yellow tape led to the only surviving grassy stretch in the back yard, a space about twelve feet wide running along the privacy fence. This would be a limited tenting area until new sod covered the septic tank and waste field lines.

We still had blue tarps covering the remaining construction materials. I could count on Mike and Cindy finishing the front deck, including the roofed-over portion, but I would, and this was a serious problem in my mind, I would have to extricate myself from building the hostel and begin running the hostel. We were averaging eight or nine hikers per night over the last couple of weeks and I had the excuse that we were not officially open. But when April arrived, I would have to give all my attention to the needs of my guests.

We weren't ready, but time was up.

* * *

Crap! 2:15. Six hours till morning. Opening day. Oh, ... so tired. Exhausted. Man, I need some sleep. What have I got myself into? So much work. No money. Where did it go? Missed the call on so many things. God, I must be crazy. I could be in Nicaragua. Own a dive shop. My god, the money I've spent here; I could own five of them. Be in the water every day. Live like a king. Erwin. Who would name a town Erwin? Nowhere. I'm in the middle of nowhere! Nine hikers in the hostel tonight. A grand total of $180.00. The gas bill is more than that. Endless hot water. They must stand there for an hour. Look at that bill. Bills sitting on my desk. Bills. Bills. Bills. Me, I'm subsidizing their craving for Snickers. Do they appreciate that? Hell no! Not a word. Man! Not a word. Nobody. Nobody appreciates anything. They want more. Like

I could do all this for free, or something. They cling to me. But ... I know ... I know ... yeah. It's so hard. Erwin. They've been on the trail three weeks ... four weeks? Walking long days. Seeing beautiful sights and meeting great people. Living a dream. Pancakes with Gary and Sandy Poteat. Chili cheeseburgers at the Nantahala Outdoor Center. The indescribable beauty of the Smokies. Hot Springs, with everything that town has to offer. The views from Big Bald. And now Erwin, Tennessee. You look down on the bridge over the Nolichucky. You come down the mountain. You step out onto the roadway, and there it is. Uncle Johnny's. Your body automatically winds down. I'm here, they shout ... silently thrilled, collapsing into happiness and exhaustion. Tired and relieved. Another goal along the way. My god, I made it to Erwin. I'm special. I'm one of the fifty-percent ... I get it ... the essence, the essence of the commitment ... I've been there many times. I get it.

I had awakened with a start. The train whistle is something you get used to, but if you're half-awake, it's loud. There is a crossing over Chestoa Pike just across the river; maybe 200 yards from here. The Clinchfield engineers have this whistle pattern I've come to notice. One long blast as they approach the crossing. Followed by two short blasts. Then, when they hit the crossing, another short followed quickly by an extra-long blast. Once I counted the seconds. That last blast lasted eight-seconds. That's a long, loud sound at two-o'clock in the morning.

Pacing around holding the Mountain Dew against my head, I opened the front door. Stepped out on the porch, I jumped out of my skin seeing a dark shadow; the back of a man about five feet away.

"Christ, man. You scared the crap out of me!"

"Looking at the moon." The hiker pointed at the hair-line-thin, waxing, four-day-old crescent moon in the clear sky over the Nolichucky. "My daughter, back when she was five, six years old, called it a fingernail moon. Every time I see one, I think of her." In the dark, I could hear and feel the emotion as he took a deep breath and let it out.

"You miss your family?"

"Yes I do, very much."

"How many?"

"Married twelve years. Got three daughters."

"I'm Uncle Johnny. Got a trail name yet?"

"Timex," he said, as we shook hands.

"You a thru-hiker?"

"Yes. Left Amicalola State Park February 27."

"That's okay, man. That's great. You're making good time."

I had motioned toward the open window and the hostel full of sleeping hikers, and talking quietly, we had begun moving slowly down River Road toward the bridge. I was grateful for the company. I could tell he was comfortable walking along with me, and my anxieties about tomorrow evaporated.

"How do you feel? Gonna make it?"

"I don't know. It's a lot harder than I thought. Almost quit back at Neels Gap. Came very close. I actually walked down the road and tried to flag down the first car I saw. Didn't stop, so I went up in the woods and sat down. I was really tired. Rolled over on my side, pack and all, and went to sleep. When I woke up, had a long talk with myself. Got back on the trail."

"Well, good for you, Timex. You can teach yourself skills and technique, but getting to Katahdin takes something else. Takes grit. Can't teach yourself grit."

"Well, maybe I discovered grit, but there was a trick to it."

"You discovered you had drive and tenacity … already in you. You don't pick grit off a tree. You're a tough guy, I hear it in your voice."

"Let me tell you what actually happened. Back in Amicalola, there was this guy … name was Misery. I walked over to join a fire circle, and he was talking to a bunch of young hikers. An older guy. Older than me, said he'd thru-hiked the trail three times. He talked about a number of things hikers need to know, but his main piece of advice is what saved me, and it was a trick. He said, if you want to give up, don't make that decision when you've twisted your ankle, banged your head, or if you're hurting, tired, disgusted, pissed-off, or about to go insane. When you say f-it, I'm quitting, just accept that, make that decision, and then, pitch your tent wherever you are. Rest, and get a good night's sleep. You'll sleep well, because it's over, you're going home. Then, in the morning, ask yourself why you're quitting. If you can come up with a really good reason after a restful night's sleep, then you ought to go home. If not, pack up, and get your butt back on the trail."

"That's wonderful, Timex ... I don't know Misery, but he gave you good advice. Stop, rest, and give grit a chance."

"Give grit a chance. That's a good one."

"Well, when bad things happen, there's just three responses, you give up, or get angry, or look for the possibilities."

"Grit defined. The guts to stop and look at what's possible."

"That's what winners do, Timex. You've got your goal, you've got your plan to get there, but when something happens, all that flies out the window."

"Boy, I second that. I thought I had it all figured."

"I know. We all do. I'm always surprised when things fall apart. But, the fact is, the line between here and Mount Katahdin isn't straight, even on a map. The line between you and your goal, whatever it might be, is never straight. But, that's the way we plan, like a list, I'm going to go from here to here, we say, and we're thinking like a straight line. Then you take one step and everything falls apart."

"And then you start scrambling."

"You're fully absorbed in the only way out, you're in the moment, engrossed, riveted, you lose sight of everything but the next instant. When you're completely focused on a challenge you care about, everything else disappears from your mind. The joy, even exhilaration can flow out of that concentration."

"The higher the risk, the greater the exhilaration."

"Exactly right. Timex. That's it. I've never thru-hiked, but I've section-hiked since I was a Boy Scout back in the fifties. I've canoed many challenging rivers, deep-dived some of the most demanding ship wrecks. So I know, big projects take serious planning, but it's always more difficult than you imagine. That's the definition of big. Shortly after you plunge into whatever you've chosen to do, you say ... whoa! —I didn't know it would be like this, and then..."

"You're out on the highway trying to hitch a ride home," Timex laughed, sadly shaking his head.

"No ... well, yes, we get knocked back. We pause, if we can, and survey the situation, but then, just as you said, you start scrambling. Your mind goes to work. The worse the problem, the more it sucks up everything you have."

"Like a scene from MacGyver, you ever watch that show?"

"Oh man, yeah, MacGyver, loved that show, yes, just like MacGyver. He's scrambling, as you say, concentrating, puts everything he has into creating fire, or using his Swiss Army knife some way nobody else ever thought of, would save himself by making some ingenious thing out of an ordinary object like a coat hanger or a spoon. But, whatever it was, the situation absorbed all his attention and energy. Like MacGyver, that's what I'm saying."

"I've never thought about it exactly the way you've put it, Uncle Johnny, but I'm seeing your point. A 2,000-mile hike to a certain mountain top isn't about standing on that sign, it's about what it took to get there, about the unexpected, and what you do with the unexpected. That's what you remember. That's what you tell your grandchildren someday."

"And whether you actually ever get there or not is in the hands of fate. In fact, that's why I came out on the deck tonight. I wanted to walk out here to the bridge, get away from those four walls, out here in the wide open, walk out here and remind myself that we live by minutes and hours. Tomorrow is a big day for me, but it's just another day to be lived best I can. If I give it all I've got, what happens ... what happens to whatever it is I'm trying to build here, well ... that's in the hands of fate."

"You're certainly right about fate, Uncle Johnny. Something terrible happened to me one time. I'm not particularly religious. Some think life is in the hands of God, but I see it as the law of averages, or the coincidental nature of events. I would imagine that an x-number of thru-hikers break a leg or something. So, dream all you want. Plan down to the most minor detail. You break a leg and you don't make it to Katahdin. Whether that person is me or somebody else is decided by circumstances. I don't mean what I suffered was like drawing the short straw. Your chance to have your picture taken with your arms raised in victory behind that sign on Mount Katahdin is not totally random. More like playing rummy. Statistical significance. The chance that you'll draw an Ace rather than a Ten is one thing, how you play um is another. One night I went home as usual, happy as usual, thinking nothing particular as usual, and halfway up the steps to my apartment, I suddenly collapsed. I could barely move. Couldn't move my legs at all. I managed to drag myself up to the door, get it open, and crawl to the phone, call my sister. She came over. Called the EMTs. Got me to the hospital. It was a bug. A virus. Where I got it, how I got it, nobody knows. Just fate, you know. But, it was a virus that paralyzes. It's called Guillain-Barre syndrome. My immune system attacked itself by mistake...attacked my own nervous system. Inflamed nerves caused muscle weakness leading to paralysis."

"My god, man. That sounds horrible. You were paralyzed?"

"Just my legs and trunk muscles. I could still breathe. People have died. It can happen to anyone. Rare though. But what I'm saying is, fate drew my number."

"Obviously you recovered. How long did it take?"

"Months in bed, almost eight months. My sister came and took care of me. Friends helped too."

"You weren't married then?"

"No, recently divorced from my first wife."

"How about your job? Eight months is a long time."

"I was really lucky there. Work for Amtrak. Soon as I was ready, got my old job back."

Timex and I had moved along slowly, had stopped for a time and talked while leaning against the iron railing looking down into the black, tumbling river below. With very little ambient light, the dark sky above filled with stars, more light fell upon us from the hint of Milky Way than from the sliver of moon hovering over the ridge. Now, just past the middle of the bridge, we stopped and sat on the concrete abutment.

"You were ... doing what? ... your job at Amtrak?"

"I'm a chef," and Timex laughed quietly. "Sort of. I'm the executive chef on the Auto Train. Heard of that?"

"Yes. But, don't know anything about it. Runs to Florida? Ships you and your car to Florida, I believe."

"Right. Direct from DC. Non-stop from Northern Virginia to near Orlando, Florida; Sanford, actually."

"You run the dining car?"

"Right. In fact, three of them."

"Three dining cars?"

"Three cars, three seatings each, three times a day. For instance, for dinner, we offer seatings at five, seven, and nine o'clock."

"You must have a lot of people to feed."

"Just under five hundred, plus a twenty-six-member on-board crew. We pull a bi-level sleeper-car just for them. All of the cars are bi-level, so we have a lot of room and pack um in. Passenger railroading on a grand scale. Typically, we have two F40PH locomotives pulling seventeen bi-level passenger cars, twenty-nine double-decker auto-carrier cars, the crew sleeper, two lounge cars, and the three diners...over four-thousand feet of train. Run by a four-man operating crew: two engineers, conductor, assistant conductor. We're not actually non-stop...we stop for a few minutes in Florence, South Carolina and change operating crews."

"And automobiles. How many of those?"

"Exactly 225 every trip coming and going."

"So, I guess people who want their own car with them in Florida save money on the trip, or there wouldn't be a market."

"You save money if you ride coach. The sleepers are pretty expensive. I think it's I-95 that sells us. Have you ever driven I-95 to Florida? I tell you what, it's brutal. You call 511, the traffic advisory thing, anytime during daylight hours when you're driving down 95, and you'll hear about a dozen delays, construction sites, and accidents. Accidents galore. Interstate 95 from the Georgia state line down to where you exit onto I-4 toward Sanford has the highest fatality rate of any road anywhere in the United States. Just on that stretch alone, there are almost two thousand accidents every year. Six hundred or so injured, twenty-five, thirty dead—just on that two-hour stretch."

"Thanks, but no thanks. I'll take the scenic route through the Chattahoochee National Forest, steer to port, give Atlanta a wide berth, and pick up I-75 South."

We heard hiking boots crunching loose gravel, and then saw light dancing on the roadway. Turning, we both shaded our eyes in unison when the eye of light steadied on us.

"Hellooo, hiker," I sang out.

No response, but the light stayed on us as the hiker continued walking.

"Must have been a tough go coming down the hill with no moon," I tried again. The hiker kept coming. As he drew close, and I could tell it was a he, I could see him struggling to remove his pack and, drawing abreast, he plopped it on the ground as though making a statement.

"Was tough, but I'm tough. I like hiking at night. Used to it. Came off at the campground up there and took the road."

"Where you headed?"

"Uncle Johnny's. Is he open yet?"

"Not officially, but open, yes. How can I help you? I'm Uncle Johnny."

"Oh ... Uncle Johnny, huh. Got any room?" he smerked

"No, sir. Very sorry about that. The hostel is full. Got space for a tent, though."

"I hear you have hot showers."

"We do. Endless hot water. But, the store's closed. You got a towel?"

"Yes."

"Soap and shampoo?"

"You don't provide soap and ...?"

"We do, but it has a tendency to disappear in the dead of night. Poltergeists. Soap ghouls. We supply the underworld with bath soap and shampoo in these parts, so I can't guarantee..."

"I got soap."

"Then you're in business. Follow me. I'll take you to the shower. Keep it quiet though. We'll be walking right past the hostel. Timex, you ready to turn in?"

"Not yet. I'm taking a zero tomorrow, I'm going to hang here for a little bit and concentrate on the lessons of my struggle." And he laughed quietly. "Thanks for the advice. I enjoyed talking with you, Uncle Johnny."

"Zero? You're sticking around tomorrow?"

"I'm exhausted, Uncle Johnny. Taking a zero."

"You're in a tent, right? How'd you like a free berth in the hostel tomorrow?"

"And the catch is...?"

"You're a chef? I need a grill man. I'm grilling burgers and dogs all day tomorrow; starting about eleven. Need portion control. Need just-in-time delivery. Sleep in. Get your rest.

Help me tomorrow and I'll give you a free berth in the hostel. Fill up your fuel bottle. Shine your shoes."

"If that means I get to eat all day, you got a deal, Uncle Johnny."

"Thanks. See you in the morning. You ready, young hiker?" Turning to the young man, I waved for him to follow me.

"Free food tomorrow?"

"Yep. Opening day. Our grand opening...Uncle Johnny's Nolichucky Hostel."

* * *

Benton MacKaye's idea that the Appalachian Crestline could become a living community was realized, but in a way he never imagined. It is, as many have observed, a long skinny village, a linear settlement of temporary residents measuring up to all the criteria any definition of a village might have; leaders and celebrities; insiders and outsiders; its own rules and customs; caring for the sick and injured; the homeless and the occasional village idiot. And it is huge; skinny, but huge. The whole Appalachian Trail is a gargantuan social community threading through fourteen states, its residents sustained by a network of trail crews, hostel owners, resupply merchants, and shuttle drivers. And just as would be the case with any other community you wish to examine —built, maintained, owned, used, and protected by the people who live there.

Hiking the AT is by no stretch of the imagination a wilderness experience. It is a people experience. That portion of the Appalachians stretching from Maine to Georgia, abutting the majority of the nation's population, is accessible to millions for a half-day's ride. If wilderness has a role, that role is containment. It keeps its thousands of daily travelers fearfully focused on the trail. The Middle English word, *wildeornes*, meaning wild beast, echoed by its cousin *wilddeoren*, meaning wild savage, was coined as a cautionary word, a warning, describing a place to fear, a place you don't want to go. A hiker's first order of business is to stay out of it. His greatest fear, if not of wild beast or the wild savage, is to be lost in it.

Wilderness and nature are two different things. Nature dominates. The trail, the shelters, and everything man-made is secondary. The trail crews and the ATC made sure of that. Everything, including the humans moving north and south, must harmonize with the natural setting; a vision of *The People* visiting a place that celebrates the individuality of man and a closeness to nature. Walking the trail, the hiker is forced by the wilderness to focus narrowly on the natural surroundings, the pathway before him, and on his purpose.

Every village is a location with a purpose. The Appalachian Trail Village is no different. People come for a reason. Not so special, that. After all, human beings are animals that move with reason. What's special is the simplicity of the typical AT hiker's purpose. They come to the trail either full of something they want to purge, or empty and seeking to fill up. That's it. All of this I understand as a human resource professional. Human resources, the personnel business, is a people-changing business. You understand purpose. You understand failure and its causes. You understand success. You understand change. Every people-professional comes to know that change is so difficult and finding change so rare, that discovering a fool-proof method to bring it on is something people will talk about. With that message spreading further and wider, the Appalachian Trail will never disappear.

Today, April 1, 1998, another hostel has been added to that network of sustaining forces that make the AT doable and worthwhile, and its community sane and safe. I was not the first, and I will not be the last. Hikers have been streaming down that hill straight to Uncle Johnny's for several weeks now. Thank you, Roger.

I had called Roger, knowing he had produced posters and flyers for various canoeing expeditions. He knew the computer software and produced great camera-ready copy.

I made a special trip to Hot Springs, the nearest full-service stop hiking north toward Erwin. Cindy came along as a runner. While I met and talked with the more important trail heroes like Elmer Hall, she walked around town looking for bulletin boards for hanging our flyers. So we could expedite this process in the future, she made a list of bulletin boards she found. A prime location was Elmer's hostel, the most famous in all of Hot Springs.

Elmer's hostel is a historic, old, Victorian two-story house on the corner of Walnut and Broad Street. Elmer named his place Sunnybank. It has seven bedrooms, six porches, a music room, a common room, two dining rooms, and a kitchen with a well-loved cast-iron stove. There is a garden in the back, and a fire pit that sits below swaying pecan trees. The Appalachian Trail runs along the sidewalk right in front of Sunnybank. Elmer's hostel is a magical, restful place according to all I've heard. Elmer had been very helpful, answering all my questions and offering suggestions during the planning stage of my own project. Elmer is quite the character, and hikers love him. Having his endorsement was huge.

There were other hostels north of here; Kincora on Dennis Cove Road and Braemar Castle in Hampton. We put up posters everywhere we were allowed and tacked up flyers on as many bulletin boards as we could find. It was tremendously helpful to be listed in Wingfoot's thru-hiker's guide. As soon as I got my copy, I called to thank him, expressing my appreciation for his trust.

These simple marketing efforts worked. Every hiker heading north must come down the mountain and cross the Chestoa Bridge over the Nolichucky. These north-bound hikers coming down the hill have full view of the Open House and 40¢ Snickers banners. Another tacked up between the unfinished posts read *Free Town Shuttles*. It seemed to me that every hiker coming down the hill stopped, if for no other reason than to buy a cold Gatorade and one to go.

* * *

Our grand opening was rowdy and nearly unmanageable. I had picked up eighty hotdogs and buns. Twenty pounds of hamburger and the equivalent in buns. Ten big cans of hotdog chili. Onions, mustard and ketchup. Timex fired up the gas grill around eleven. The night-hiker volunteered his service as grill mate, and never stopped eating the whole time. One of our very large picnic tables was nearly covered with food preparation. Bags of buns. Paper plates. Rolls of paper towels. Hikers dug into their food bags and produced a full spread of Ring Dings, Ding Dongs, Cosmic Brownies, Twinkies, and Raspberry Zingers. Chips and salsa appeared as if from nowhere. I counted five bags of potato chips I had not purchased. Hikers I had never laid eyes on were chopping onions. Lots of laughter and pushing around. I couldn't watch. I had to walk away. I half expected a full-blown food riot any moment.

Unlocking the store, I was followed by five hikers needing fuel. Reading my I-will-return-soon sign, they had patiently waited. Before it was over, I had filled twenty fuel bottles. It was not long before I began to see the full dimension of my problem. I'm the shuttle driver. I'm the clerk in the outfitter store. I'm the registration desk. I clean the showers and toilets, sweep out the hostel, wipe down the mattresses with sanitizer, carry the trash to the dumpsters in town. And you would not believe the amount of trash we collect in a single day. Hikers, following the leave-no-trace rule carry in the empty packaging, cans, and wrappers; waste from the food and fuel they have consumed on the trail. Dozens of resupply boxes are opened every day, each producing an empty cardboard box filled with empty wrappers. Nearly every hiker during resupply brings back six-packs of beer and soft drinks, bags of chips and donuts, ice cream containers, melons, and fruit too green to eat. The waste from thirty or forty hikers in one day, collected in heavy, black-plastic bags, would fill the trunk and back seat of the Taurus. So, in addition to the multiple shuttle runs, at least one run each day goes to the Erwin trash-collection point.

After I filled that twentieth fuel bottle, a hiker came in for three Snickers. Just then, an unaccustomed sound penetrated the shop.

"A trumpet? Am I hearing a trumpet?" I asked the hiker.

"Guitar, trumpet duet. The other guy has a Martin BackPacker guitar."

"I just hear the trumpet."

"Well, there's a guitar player out there too."

"Are they hikers?"

"Yeah...camping out by the fence. Walked with them for three days. They played every night. Pretty good."

"Imagine you're a coon hunter in the middle of nowhere, and you hear *that* at two in the morning."

"Your dogs'd start howling at the trumpet; forget about the coon."

"The upside is the fact that it could be an excellent bear repellant."

"Hiker repellant, too. Older couple joined us one evening; complained so much the players quit. Next morning, the couple packed and left by dawn."

"I don't know why. I play trumpet and I can tell you, that guy's pretty good."

"Bunch of people out there listening to them. They built a fire circle."

"A fire circle? Where! ... in the yard?"

"Yeah, you didn't know?"

"No. I did not know. Where in the yard?"

"That level spot. You know, bout halfway between the hostel and the fence."

"On this side of the yellow caution tape?"

"Yeah ... oh ... the tape. The yellow tape? They took that down."

"They took the ..."

"You didn't know?"

"No, I did not ..."

"Yeah. Took it down."

"Oh, lord. My grass. They're trampling the grass. The new grass."

To get instant green coverage, I had seeded the yard with thirty pounds of annual ryegrass. Thanks to a night of misting rain, the seed took hold and grew quickly. Ryegrass produces a dense, shallow root system, and I hoped enough of it had developed to hold up to the foot-traffic it would get tonight. Tomorrow, I will replace the yellow caution tape and add a few signs pleading for cooperation. The yard will be renovated in September using a heavy over-seeding of perennial rye and fescue, the grass seed mixture, chosen by the All England Lawn Tennis and Croquet Club, the venue for the Wimbledon Championships. The event is the only Grand Slam tennis match held on grass. A mixture of 70% perennial rye and 30% creeping red fescue produces a sod tough enough to hold up during the tournament. Seemed like a safe bet it would hold up to hundreds of boot-shod Frisbee players.

* * *

The next several weeks were as stressful as any in my lifetime. Our living area, the front deck, was incomplete and being constructed beneath the feet of my guests. There was the pressing need for a large passenger van but absolutely no time to go looking for one. I felt that every moment verged on chaos. Most of my problem were the result of inefficient systems.

Take, for example, the simple process of filling an empty fuel bottle. Nearly every hiker carried some kind of stove for boiling water and cooking meals. These stoves burned either alcohol or Coleman fuel. Typically, a hiker carried just enough fuel to get to the next re-supply. So, nearly every hiker that stopped by or spent the night needed fuel. And they were coming and going constantly. Every time I turned around, I had to unlock the store and fill a small bottle with fuel at 19¢ an ounce. Of course, fuel resupply was a very important service, but each incidental filling seemed hardly worth the trouble.

If I had to single out the most devastating problem I faced during this early startup phase, it would be the complications and distractions caused by having not yet found a decent passenger van I could afford. Shuttles were my major problem. I absolutely, positively had to provide shuttles, shuttles into town, shuttles to breakfast, lunch, and dinner, shuttles for slackpackers, shuttles for section hikers, shuttles for resupply, shuttles to the post office, shuttles to USA Raft, shuttles to the bus station, shuttles to the airport......!

And I had no money to hire a driver. I needed a shuttle driver. As the only shuttle driver, I had no recourse but to hang the Be Back Soon sign on the front door and leave the premises. Needless to say, every time I returned some kind of problem had surfaced, and I would barely get whatever it was settled before I had to leave again.

In the meantime, my old Ford Taurus was the shuttle van. It held five hikers, and if a girl agreed to sit on somebody's lap, six. If nine hikers signed up for the breakfast shuttle, it took two trips. Carry five hikers to the Huddle House and return. Pick up the remaining four and skitter back over to the Huddle House hoping that at least four hikers from the first trip were fast eaters. Run them back to the hostel. Pick up the two guys wanting a ride to the post office, drop them off, skip over to the Huddle House and pick up the last of the breakfast crew.

Back to the hostel, and drop them off. Back to the post office. Back to the hostel. And during returns to the hostel, fill fuel bottles. Take the money and make change for five Snickers bars and a Gatorade. Return three phone calls. Run to the bathhouse and plunge an overflowing toilet. Plead for a hiker to come down from the roof of the hostel. Yes, I know the view is pretty neat up there, but the roof is a hundred years old; please consider that. No ma'am, you can't lie topless down by the river. Yes, it's completely private, and I personally don't give a dang, but it's not my property. It's posted, didn't you see the sign? And that would be my morning. Followed by a repeat at lunchtime. And at dinner. Over and over. What the hell had I gotten myself into?

Within just a few days, I understood what had happened. I got so involved in the building process, I failed to realize, fully realize the necessity of acquiring the largest passenger van I could get my hands on. Then, when the hostel opened for good, I had no time. And it takes time. Of course, I began my search. I put the word out every chance I got.

The opening, the startup phase, seemed to drag on unendingly. The hikers were generally happy. For most, we were a blessing. Coming down the hill, getting the full view of Uncle Johnny's was like meeting Jesus on the trail. Instant relief. Instant adoration and joy. Praise him. Alleluia; a hot shower. Hooray. Oh, look! Snickers…40¢.

But it seemed the pride and honor of receiving this kind of enthusiastic approval was wiped out by the stabbing pain of some jerk's snooty criticism. Most of the locals were either neutral or very supportive, but, there were those condescending few who, by mere facial expression or body language, could dash every ounce of joy I felt.

Once, I had jammed seven boisterous hikers into the Taurus. Amidst laughter and playful mockery, they tumbled out in front of the IGA grocery, and when they had cleared the walkway, I saw Josh Greer from USA Raft shaking his head, chuckling in cavalier dismissal. I was embarrassed.

"Hey, Josh," I said, faking a happy, feeble grin.

"Un-cle John-eee," he said; stretching my business name into a sneer. "You gotta tie a couple lawn chairs on top that thing."

"Yeah, I know." I smiled, shaking my head. "I'm looking for a passenger van. Let me know if you come across one for sale."

"What makes you think you need a van? By June, your Taurus will be plenty big enough to handle the hikers dribblin down the trail this summer."

"That's not true, Josh. The ATC is expecting ... estimates more than fifteen-hundred hikers will attempt a thru-hike this year. Half of them will reach us at ..."

"What you got out there ... nine beds? You overbuilt that bathhouse, son. Gawdamighty! You built the Taj Mahal of bathhouses! No-Drip Higgins was braggin and I just had to see for myself. What a hoot. What possessed you build that monster, John?"

"It sells the hostel, Josh. We had thirty hikers last night. They came for a hot shower."

"It ain't always gonna be like that, John," he said slowly, shaking his head with an expression of faked forbearance. "You'll be gone in a year," he said, "you and that ... that friend of yours, that burrito guy."

"Brady ... Brady and Lisa Sleeper. Doing a heck-of-a job, Josh."

"Yeah, selling burritos the size of a football. You guys, neither of you ..." and here, Josh put both hands over his eyes, tipped his head back, and laughed, "... got any sense of proportion."

"Come on, Josh. Give it a rest."

Dropping his hands and looking at me gleefully, he laughed again. "No ... you guys ... you got no sense of proportion. Both of you be gone by ..." And he laughed again.

"Nice seeing you, Josh. Got to get inside ... check on my guests."

* * *

The news came up the trail that Earl Shaffer was hiking the AT for the third time, had undertaken his third attempt to hike the entire thing end-to-end in one season, this time to celebrate the 50th-anniversary of his historic trek in 1948.

First I heard, got a call from Laurie Potteiger, with the ATC. Then Roger called. Said he'd read about it on one of the websites he follows. I immediately called Elmer Hall to let him know Shaffer was coming his way, and we discussed how he might encourage Earl to stop at the Nolichucky. I asked Elmer to tell Earl I would comp his stay at my place; pay for everything. Tell him to expect a little trail magic in Erwin.

Earl was almost eighty-years old. The trail was over 100 miles longer than it was in 1948. And, more troubling, the trail had been re-routed away from roads and more towards the mountain peaks. Hiking the trail had become much more difficult since his second thru-hike in 1965 when Shaffer was thirty-three years younger.

I was told 327 thru-hikers had registered with the ATC last year. The number of thru-hikers had grown each year since Shaffer became the first, and Wingfoot's recent *Thru-Hiker's Handbook* states that more than 2,000 individuals have hiked the trail end to end in one season. One thing would surely be different for Shaffer this time. He would have plenty of company. If he got into trouble, if his heart failed him, or if he fell and broke his hip, he would likely get help right away.

Wingfoot had said when Shaffer completed the first thru-hike, it was like Lindbergh's solo flight across the Atlantic; something nobody believed was possible. This amazing man has set two AT records so far. If he completes his trip this year, he'll have achieved a third. First person ever to hike the

Appalachian Trail end-to-end in one season. First to hike it both ways; south to north in 1948; north to south in 1965. And, if Shaffer makes his fiftieth anniversary hike, if he does make it to Mount Katahdin before the park closes for the winter, he'll have the record as the oldest thru-hiker; seventy-nine years plus five or six months.

In one sense, Shaffer blazed a trail for generations of hikers, launching an era of long-distance hiking, proving it's possible to survive and thrive for months or three-quarters of a year in the American wilderness.

Roger had read that Shaffer was hiking just as light, or nearly as lean as he had in 1948. He was carrying forty-pounds in an Army-issue backpack. No cell phone. No tent. A single change of clothes. Cold food; he didn't even own a stove. For sleeping, he carried an Army surplus blanket and two blue Walmart tarps. Both of these were light tarps he had cut down to size, one for the ground and one to cover himself if it rained. He has Wingfoot's trail guide this time, Roger said. A small can of baby powder, a knife, and a foam sleeping pad salvaged from an old chair. He preferred to sleep in the open. If it rained, or if it looked like rain, he would gauge his pace to reach a shelter but, often enough, he would climb into his bedroll in spite of the rain and cover himself with the tarp. He carried two quarts of water and tried to drink a gallon every day, all of it from mountain springs. And that small can of baby powder? He shakes that into his boots every morning in place of socks. Socks are the cause of blisters, he says.

* * *

The first indication that Shaffer would arrive that day came from a three-hiker vanguard striding jubilantly down the hill. They climbed up the ramp to the hostel deck full of grins.

"He's coming," they said. "Earl Shaffer. Just behind us."

"Did you know he was coming?" another asked.

"Yes, got the word couple days ago."

"Well, he's coming. We trailed him all day yesterday. Had lunch together today. We took off first. Thought you might need a heads up."

"Thanks, but we're ready."

About an hour later, two more hikers arrived. Man and wife. They had hiked with him for a day, they said. Then Shaffer pushed ahead.

"He's very strong," the man said. "Really nice, too," the wife added. "But we got the message he wanted to be alone, so we hung back all day today, then skipped lunch so we could get ahead. Thought you might want to know," she said.

"He's coming," the husband repeated, rubbing the back of his neck, smiling, proud as punch.

"Yes, we're ready. Thanks."

* * *

I spotted him, just after four o'clock, coming down the hill wearing his trademark pith helmet, a blue flannel shirt buttoned at the wrists, and blue work pants. Still packing that Army-issue rucksack. Four young hikers were walking with him. Two of them girls. The girls were right up with him, and Earl was pointing at the Nolichucky with his homemade walking stick. He was telling them something, and they were walking close listening. The two young men followed about six yards back. They all came quickly. Didn't slow at the intersection or look at the bridge. They walked together, not breaking formation, straight toward me as I stood on the deck watching. As they approached, the young hikers fell back letting Shaffer take the lead.

"Earl," I called out as he got near.

"Might this be Uncle Johnny?" he answered. And began struggling with the straps of his pack. Swinging the pack down, he climbed the steps.

"Drop that pack over there, Earl. Have a seat and rest those legs. Can I get you something to drink?"

"No, I got water. But, I'll take two of those 40¢ Snickers," he said placing his pack on the bench of the nearest picnic table. As I went to fetch the Snickers bars, Shaffer untied a quart-sized Army canteen from his pack; the kind of canteen issued to U.S. Military troops; made of odor-free, dark green polyethylene. Shaffer had it tied to his pack with a shoelace.

"How ya doin so far?"

"Very good, Uncle Johnny. Not quite as quick as I used to be, but making twelve, fifteen miles most days."

"Wonderful! I was thinking about ..."

"Got this nagging pain in my chest. Doctor said ... haven't been to a doctor since my Army days. Not once. My brothers made me go. Insisted. Insisted on lots of things. Saw the doctor to ease their anxieties. Full physical. Passed it, too. The doctor said I might have a partially collapsed lung. But I hike every day ... all my life ... five miles or so every day. I'm a little short of breath but ... well, fifteen miles a day ... so there."

All of this came out between chomping on a Snickers and drinking slugs of water. He was smaller than I expected, about five-foot eight. One-hundred fifty pounds or so. He was vigorous and attentive, remarkably so for a man near eighty.

"Have you got room for me in the hostel?"

"Certainly. Yes, sir. I heard you were coming. Reserved you a bottom bunk, best one in the hostel. I'm sure you'll be comfortable. Everybody's waiting for you to ..."

"Look, Uncle Johnny, I'm going to stretch out for a little bit." Shaffer said, tying the canteen back to his pack and gathering things. "We'll talk later," he said, stuffing the Snickers wrappers in his pants pocket.

It was dark when Shaffer entered the store looking for a towel. Shaffer doesn't shower. When I offered him the towel and explained we had endless hot water, he said he feared athlete's foot, which he said had ended many a hiker's dream. He explained that in the Army, jungle rot had been a serious problem. He believed it came from the showers. So he never showers in public places. Does a quick wash-up any time he comes across a creek providing a little privacy.

"Here's how I do it," he explained; "I stand in the shower stall wearing boots laced up tight. I get the shower running a little dribble of water, then I wash up just as I would creek-side."

I led him around the hostel and pointed out the bathhouse. I stood watching, and was surprised that when he went in, everybody else came out. No one, it seemed, was comfortable in such a private place in the presence of someone as hallowed as Earl Shaffer.

People left him alone. All of them were jittery, excited by the fact they had happened by pure chance to stop here with the great Earl Shaffer. One young man came up to me and blurted out ... here we are in the same place with the Great One! I can't believe my luck. Just the best, Uncle Johnny. Thank you.

But, in spite of their reverence and adulation, or, maybe because of it, they left him alone. All went about the business of cleaning up. Getting out cooking gear. Preparing supper. I had ordered pizza delivered, and when it arrived, Shaffer and the couple that had walked with him and several other hikers sat together on the deck. A car-load of local section hikers went on a beer run. Others gathered driftwood from the river and started a fire.

Danny, my neighbor, learning that something big was happening, came over. After meeting Shaffer, he went back home and got his son Daniel. They brought extra chairs. People were quietly gathering around the fire, some lying in the grass, some sitting on backpacks. And it got quiet when Shaffer and I arrived carrying chairs from the store. No one said a word. Joining the others at the fire ring, I immediately shared their communal admiration; an overwhelming feeling of reverence, both grand and wonderful.

The arc of faces beaming out at Earl Shaffer, faces lit by the fire, lit by awe, lit by the sense of good fortune, the miraculous good fortune of being here in this moment, mellowed the lines and leathery neck of the man himself as he told his story, and his words rippled through them.

"The first thing I want to say," Shaffer began. "All of this." And he waved one arm and then the other, indicating the hostel and the mountain and the trail along the crest of the mountain he was facing. "All of this is different for you than it was for me. You are far more comfortable. You can afford to be fearless. You are inundated with the tips and steps and techniques for the long hike. There are books and articles and websites. I had none of that. I suspect that you are not so astonished by the experience as was I ... every turn, surprised by another thing, another frustration, another tense moment. If you are not so struck by the mystery, I probably contributed to that. I wrote one of the first books on thru-hiking, but there are dozens upon dozens now. There is very little mystery left, I suppose. Where I had to relentlessly trust myself and my judgment, each of your resupply boxes brings another section of your thru-hiker's guide. Don't get me wrong. I'm not saying things ought to be different. No, not at all. And I'm not saying your victory will be any less than mine. I'm just saying ... I'm struck by how different this is, my walk this time. How different it is from before."

And with that, Shaffer poked at the fire with his walking stick, and grew quiet.

The ring of faces glowing in the fire remained transfixed as one young man hesitantly spoke,

"Mr. Shaffer, I ..."

"Call me Earl. You, ..." and here he flapped his hand good-naturedly to indicate all of them, "just ... call me Earl."

"Earl, I'm just wondering, was it the war? People say ... well, you say in your book that you were ... you were in the Pacific during the war, and ..."

"That's right. When world war two broke out, I joined. I volunteered for the Army."

"So, it was really bad? I mean, like ... you witnessed horrible things?"

"I spent my time in the Pacific theater...it was bad. Yes. It was bad. I don't like to talk about it. But, yes ... I was in combat areas of the Pacific; a couple of years without furlough or even a short rest leave. When I came out, I didn't know what to do. I was ... I was in a state I didn't like, confused, maybe depressed. Growing up, I had hiked a lot. Spent time in the woods. My best friend back then ... we had vowed we'd hike the entire trail; the AT from Georgia to Maine. Then the war came along."

"I heard that your friend died in your arms," another hiker said.

"No. That one's not true. Not at all. My buddy was a Marine. In 1941, when it looked like we might get drafted, we volunteered. We knew the draft was coming and didn't want to wait. I joined the Army and Walt ... his name ... my friend's name was Walter Winemiller, Walter joined the Marines. He died in the Battle of Iwo Jima. The landing at Iwo Jima. I was in the Pacific for over three years, the Army Signal Corps, based in Hawaii, but for most of the time I was on those combat islands. The Marines would take them; we, the Army, we would move in and clean up, round up the enemy troops hiding in the brush, the snipers, you know. My job was to install radar stations, build towers, sometimes we built airstrips. When the war was over I couldn't settle down or do anything. I told myself I've got to do something so why not do something that's never been done? That was my motivation. The closer I got to Katahdin, the more I wanted to keep on hiking. I wanted the trail to go on and on. I hated it was the end. But, I did reach Katahdin, and the long cruise was over. And it ... did ... it straightened me out, more or less."

"So, you and your buddy. You hiked a lot when you were kids?"

"Walt ... he was my best friend since when we were five years old. We grew up together. He was the finest outdoorsman I ever knew; even to this day. I got my love of the wilderness from him, and ... so, when I got out of the Army, I thought perhaps this trip would be the answer. I would walk the AT, the whole thing just like we planned ... I would do that in Walter's name. I dedicated my hike to him. I was trying to wipe out the bad parts; that wartime service in the tropics, and substitute good memories of Walter."

"So, that's why you ended up hiking the AT. Are you still hiking with that memory?"

Except for the pop and crackle of the fire, there was silence. Shaffer paused for a moment and seemed momentarily taken by the cradle of shining faces, each with a hint of smile, looking back at him.

"Well, just like you, I have reasons for being out here. If you enjoy being out here, if it's your thing, as they say these days, there are probably two basic reasons why you enjoy it, why you're having fun. If you boil it down to the essence ... two basic reasons. First, you simply enjoy the experience. I mean ... by experience, I mean, using your knowledge, the skills, using your knowledge of the equipment, the guide books, the maps, how you plan each day, preparing your meals, all the stuff you know ... all those skills. You are good at that. You know you are good at it, so you get joy from that. Secondly, it's the activity. These are two different things. First the knowledge and the use of the skills you have; honing them; getting better each day. Then, the activity itself. The walking. That you enjoy the physical effort of moving along the trail, being out there, and, for whatever reason put you in that moment, getting on, doing it, striving, driven by the mental activity of making sense of your purpose, whatever that is. Those two things define who you are … hiking the trail."

A young woman stuck up her hand and excitedly interrupted.

"Mr. Shaffer … Earl, I mean. I know exactly what you're saying. The activity itself. I'm very happy … of course, there are bad times … hard times … but mostly, I'm very happy out here. Back home when I'm doing nothing, or simply going through the motions at work, it's nothing like when I'm out here stretched to the limit, stretched to the very limit, but knowing I'm in control, accomplishing something I know is difficult … but … difficult, but worthwhile."

"Voluntarily," Shaffer added. "When you are home doing nothing or at work going through the motions, as you say, it's not voluntary. You are doing what your life requires. All the planning and preparations and then the actual activity of hiking the AT … you volunteer for that. The commitment is to yourself. Keep that in mind. Explains why you're happy doing it. The wilderness focuses your energy. When you get to Pennsylvania, you're gonna hit rocks like you won't believe. They can cut right through shoe leather. You're going to be miserable, but guess what? You will be completely absorbed in the activity of climbing and avoiding injury. You will feel strong and alert. If you are in love with your skills, your hiking and equipment, your knowledge, you're gonna feel in control, strong, and alert. Behind that … sheer happiness."

"Earl, I just noticed your boots. No heels. Did you lose your heels somewhere?"

"Took um off. You don't see athletes running in shoes with heels, do you?" And he held his boot up so everybody could see. "Hiking is as athletic as anything, isn't it?" Then he stretched both boots out together. "Indian-style," he said. "A lot better for your knees and ankles than turning them out like a duck."

"Mr. Shaf ... uh, I've heard you don't cook on the trail. You eat everything cold. What kind of food supplies do you carry?"

"Mostly peanut butter." Shaffer said, to his fans' laughter. "Peanut butter and brown sugar, jelly's too heavy. Crackers. For protein, hardboiled eggs and Knox unflavored gelatin. I buy eggs if I know I'll have a chance to boil um. I carry a pot for that. Oatmeal most mornings, but I don't cook. I soak oatmeal overnight in water. If I have raisins, I add that ... and brown sugar. I always have brown sugar." And the hikers laughed again.

"What is your favorite thing, Earl?"

"I just like to walk in the woods and sleep on mountaintops."

There were cheers and a couple of whoo-hoos, and laughter.

"No, let me correct that. I'm a writer. I think of myself as a writer. That's my favorite thing, especially poetry. I've written over fourteen-hundred poems ... mostly about the AT and my experience in the Pacific."

"Is that what you do when you are not on the trail?"

"Oh, no. I spend most of my time keeping my old VW bus running. Out in the barn, I've got three more junkers just like mine and thirteen VW engines," he laughed, and the hikers laughed with him.

"Poet and grease-monkey," one hiker hollered.

Another said, "Barn? ... you have a farm? You live on a farm?"

"Yes, I have a farm. Small one. It's in Pennsylvania, not too far from York where I grew up. North of Gettysburg ... you know where that is? Just a few miles from the Appalachian Trail. I have cats and a goat for company."

"I heard you never married," one of the girls added, with an expression of sympathy.

"No. That's one thing's never happened for me. I spared some woman a lot of misery. I like solitude, love solitude, don't like people putting expectations on me, waiting for me, you know, counting on me. The cat's got expectations, but she can't say anything about it. If I feel any nagging responsibility, it's to the trail. I've spent lots of time during my life working with clubs maintaining the trail, built six shelters during that time, worked on important relocations, that sort of thing, guess that's been my hobby, so to speak, my hobby. Not always fun, frustrating sometimes. Too many cooks in the kitchen."

"What do you do for mon … what kind of work do … you know …uh, … employment."

Shaffer crossed his arms and leaned back, looking skyward. He frowned and pursed his lips. After a moment, his eyes darting here and there, he said, "As little as possible," and the hikers burst out laughing again. Laughing with them, he continued, "I do some carpentry. I'm a good carpenter," he said. "I buy and sell antiques now and then, refinish some of them, work with auctioneers, this and that. I don't need much, no electric bill, cook on a wood stove, heat with wood, kerosene lamps, sell honey, got some beehives too," he said.

The hikers were chuckling and looking at each other, and all of them glowed with admiration and awe.

* * *

The conversation that night ran late. Shaffer didn't show up again until about ten in the morning. He is known for his long naps and sound sleeping. It is not uncommon for him to nap for two or three hours at the end of the day, boots on, wake up, eat and go off in search of water, chat for a while if there are others camping near him, and then retire for another ten hours of sleep.

Shortly after he appeared in the store, he asked if I could take him to a grocery store.

At White's IGA, Shaffer purchased a loaf of cheap white bread, a half-dozen eggs, a two-pound box of dark brown sugar, a big jar of peanut butter, and some Fig Newtons.

When we got back, Shaffer and I boiled the eggs in the kitchen and continued a wonderful conversation that had started on the way back home from the store. Shaffer surprised me when he took the loaf of bread and compressed its length to about four inches. I asked why he was doing that—it did not reduce the weight—he said it traveled better that way in his pack. He asked for a dinner knife, opened the jar of peanut butter, and demonstrated how he would peel off a smashed-thin slice. Smearing peanut butter on it, he folded the slice in half and downed it in two bites.

About the time the eggs were out cooling, Bull Frog, a hiker who had asked about work-for-stay, stuck his head in the door and called out to me announcing the arrival of the first reporter. I had asked him to be on the lookout for reporters from two local newspapers who were coming to interview Shaffer.

"I was hoping to go at least halfway before letting the word out that I was trying to do it," Shaffer said. "In Hot Springs they had a Trail Days celebration. They did a big to-do about me, had me put my footprints in cement. It's nice, and the people are nice, but it takes a lot of time."

Out on the deck, I met Brian Woodson and Charles Edwards for the first time. Woodson was the principal reporter for the local newspaper, *The Erwin Record*. Edwards was the photographer. When I called Woodson to explain his opportunity to write about the most famous Appalachian Trail hiker ever, that he would be here in Erwin in just a few days, Woodson had been very excited, already knowing, as a local Scout leader, who Shaffer was. However, Woodson called yesterday morning and said he would only have a few minutes for Shaffer; he had been assigned another important story. The five-minute interview lasted a couple of hours. That lets you know how engaging Shaffer can be, especially to an active Scout leader with prior knowledge of the rigors of the trail.

Later on, after the interviews, after Shaffer had shaken hands with the hikers taking a zero, the other hikers having left earlier, I accompanied Shaffer northward across the bridge, into the woods, and up to Beauty Spot. That's a very tough climb, and several times Shaffer stopped to catch his breath. He would lean over, his cheek against the walking stick, and breathe hard. Each time, he recovered quickly and moved on briskly.

Topping the ridge and coming out into the grassy bald, we stood for a while taking in the view, the magnificent view of the Valley Beautiful that gives this place its name.

Shaffer spoke first. "John, I want to thank you for your hospitality. Thanks for the groceries. I want to pay, but I respect your desire to support me this way."

"Well, Earl, the honor is all mine. I'm so thankful you stopped. I've been told that you almost never stay over in trail towns."

"I do stay in trail hostels from time to time, never in a motel. Never in a bed-and-breakfast. I rarely eat in restaurants. In fact, I don't often come off the trail at all. I resupply as quickly as possible and get back on the trail. Hitch a ride to the nearest store for food, then back to the trail."

"Is there a reason?"

"Connection. Staying connected. I don't want to lose the spirit of the trail. I think hikers make a big mistake when they disconnect. You hear of them leaving the trail to attend weddings and school events. If parents or friends live near the trail, hikers seize the opportunity to leave and spend a few days in civilization. That's a bad idea. It breaks the spell."

"But you do stay in hostels."

"Oh, heck yeah. That'd be different. Like a shelter or a trail-side campground, hostel's full of hikers talking trail. You don't lose the spirit. In fact, if your head's right, can strengthen it. Strengthen your resolve."

"I know exactly what you mean about the spell. After eight or ten days on the trail, you come to a crossing road and hitch a ride. It's the weirdest feeling, speeding along fifty miles per hour after days traveling at three. Feels foreign and out of place."

"That's why I never take a zero. Think about this. Almost every thru-hiker says that, leaving Springer Mountain, it takes at least two days to catch the mood. To get the swing. Develop trail legs, they say. Why would you want to lose that and have to start all over? The swing, the mood, trail legs, that's the spirit of the trail. Gasping and panting, you breathe it in. It becomes part of you. Once I get that, I don't want to lose the connection."

"I think you're right, Earl. I hope you didn't lose too much of that spirit by staying with me."

"No. I got a great night's sleep. Your place was very comfortable ... accommodating. It was good. Very good. I loved the sound of the river, the Nolichucky rushing by. The train whistle. Liked that too. The rumbling train put me right back to sleep every time."

"Do you think I'll make it, Earl?"

"John, you hang in there. Do this right. You know, I've crossed over the Nolichucky twice without staying in Erwin. The trail needs your hostel. Thru-hikers, especially, need your hostel."

"So, you think I've got a chance?"

"Of course."

"There are those who don't, you know."

"Who cares what they think. Thinking something doesn't make it so. You just pay attention to those who actually know."

"I'm trying, Earl. God knows I'm ..."

"John, do you know how many people walked the entire Appalachian Trail by the time I hiked it southbound in sixty-five?"

Without waiting for an answer, Earl said, "Thirty-seven.

"And, do you know how many had achieved that goal just one decade later? By the end of the seventies? ... over seven-hundred, seventy-five.

"The eighties? ..." Shaffer asked, looking astonished by his own words. "Fourteen-hundred! John, the ATC projects that since it opened in thirty-seven, well over three thousand hikers will have hiked the entire trail by the end of this year. If the gods are willing, I'll be one of them."

"Yes, I know those statistics."

"Well, John. That answers your question."

"The rising tide ... you mean when ...?"

"There's more to it than that."

Shaffer stopped, planted his walking stick, and bent over, resting his cheek against it. He looked at me for a long moment. "If you finish building the hostel like you've described to me, you'll have a great place. Not only that, it's being run by the right guy. You're the key to it all, John."

Saying this, he straightened and stood standing square, looking me in the eye.

"No two ways about it, Uncle Johnny. You're gonna make it."

[To be continued]

Epilogue

650 hikers stayed at the hostel that first year.

John and Charlotte continue to operate the Nolichucky Hostel to this day. Thousands of weary hikers have enjoyed the restorative power of showering in endless hot water.

Mike and Cindy completed the front deck, and the pergola covering the main portion of the deck, and transformed the brother-in-law's room into Cabin A, the hostel's first private room. With John Shores as a solid reference, Mike and Cindy expanded into general carpentry and home repair.

Over the next several years, six more cabins were added to the hostel complex. During the summer of 2016, volunteer hikers built a 16' x 50' hammock pavilion to accommodate the surging preference hikers have for sleeping in a hammock vs. the more traditional tent.

In 2000, Charlotte resigned as Carraway Methodist Medical Center's Director of Hospice and moved to Erwin. In addition to her role in the hostel, she was employed full time by Frontier Health in Erwin.

On August 6, 2001, Charlotte and John were married on a snow-white beach in Negril, Jamaica by a 4' 9" Baptist Minister. All members of the wedding party were barefoot. Charlotte retired in 2014 and now devotes all her time and energy to the family, her pets, and the business.

Claire graduated from the University of Alabama at Birmingham in 2013, and although she has a Bachelor's Degree in Social Work, she has chosen to work full-time for the Hostel.

Anjanette Harris became a secretary for the Unicoi County Middle School, a job that allowed time for husband and family. Her natural enthusiasm and engaging personality continues to attract new friends wherever she goes.

Mr. DeHaven suffered a stroke in 2012, shortly after his cherished wife Betty had passed away. He now lives with his son

Donald and daughter-in-law Ruthie a few blocks from the hostel.

Brady and Lisa Sleeper sold the Burrito Company and their home in the commune near Spivey Gap in 2001 and opened the Boone Saloon near Appalachian State University in Boone, North Carolina. Later, they relocated to Asheville, North Carolina, where, with partners, Brady opened The Universal Joint and the Walk, two highly successful restaurants. Brady and Lisa have two lovely children, Forest, eighteen, and Bella, sixteen.

Bobby Bentley, the kayaking wizard that was the quintessential California surfer-boy type, worked at NOC on the Chattooga River for several summers, then headed for the West Coast. He settled in Santa Cruz and traded his canoes and kayaks for surfboards, boogie boards, and skateboards. His excellent balance, agility, and water skills allowed him to quickly become an accomplished surfer. He remains a free-spirited bachelor.

Ben Edwards, John's driver in 1997, advanced from guiding on the Nolichucky to guiding on the Gauley in West Virginia, a 25-mile run with 49 major rapids—mostly class IV and V. After eleven years, Ben got his dream job; guiding 13-day, 225-mile oar trips through the Grand Canyon.

The banker, Garland "Bubba" Evely, and John have remained good friends. Bubba heads the Erwin branch of the Bank of Tennessee. He is still happily married to Leanne. His son Benjamin is the principal of the Love Chapel Elementary School and his younger son, Thomas, is a second-year resident in orthopedic surgery.

Josh Greer, the river guide who questioned John's judgment and doubted he would survive the winter, no longer works for USA Raft. He now sells used cars in Elizabethton, Tennessee.

USA Raft was sold in 2012. John and Charlotte have an excellent relationship, both personally and professionally, with the new owners and all their employees. USA Raft has become the premiere rafting company on the Nolichucky, employing over fifty-five fine river enthusiasts.

Roger Perrin has been married to Diane for 43 years. He remains an excellent chef and one of his great joys is cooking up fun food for his three grandchildren.

Richard "Sir Richard" Duncan, the master carpenter that kick-started the building of the hostel, married his long-time canoeing partner, Millie, in 2000. They moved to Jolly Bay, Florida, a tiny fishing village near Freeport. He remains a world-class builder with a passion for high ABV beers.

JM Harris and his Baby are still in business and have spent the last eighteen years digging holes and planting septic tanks all over Unicoi County.

Elmer Hall, now nearly 80 years old, has operated the Sunnybank Inn for the better part of four decades. Elmer's hospitality is legendary and his mouthwatering vegetarian meals are the talk of the trail. His hostel continues to set the standard.

Bob Manuel passed away on January 24, 2011. He practiced law for 34 years. Being an avid traveler himself, he started Volunteer Travel in 1993. His children, following in his footsteps, continue to operate his law practice in the same location in downtown Erwin.

Al "No-Drip" Higgins, now in his 80s, did some repairs at the hostel just last month. He's still driving his old blue cargo van, helping friends in need, and is as entertaining as ever.

Bob Slagle, the second of the Two Bobs, not the skinny one who lived in the tenant house out at the Bruce nursery, the other one; the one that lived with his mother, Miss Mellie. That Bobby, the heavier one, became Uncle Johnny's first shuttle driver. He did a swell job. John had no complaints until he discovered that Miss Mellie had her son shuttling the Nolichucky guests to her home in downtown Erwin.

The *Birmingham News* ceased publishing daily on September 30, 2012. The *News* closed its Washington, DC bureau citing budget restrictions. The paper vacated its six-story, 1917

Jacobean-style building and its $25 million, 110,000 square-foot production complex, and moved its 55 employees into a renovated warehouse. Victor Hanson III retired at the age of 52.

Clarke Stallworth passed away on June 27, 2008. He had retired from the *News* in 1991 and was teaching writing seminars all over the country. He has three popular books still in print: *A Day in the Life of Alabama* and *One Day in Alabama vols 1 and 2*. He remained a close friend to the very end and encouraged the writing of this book.

Vincent "Mickey" Townsend, John's mentor at the *News*, has recovered fully from his heart attack in 1997. He remains a very eligible bachelor and still lives in what locals call the Tiny Kingdom of Mountain Brook, Alabama.

Zack "Chief" Cross passed away February 26, 2009. He was 85 years old. Chief provided over 35 years of full-time professional service to the Greater Alabama council of Boy Scouts. A current book, *Chief: A Biography of Zack Cross* is available through major book stores. It presents the philosophy of leadership, how to train servant leaders, and how to effectively manage any organization.

Bobby and his Crossfire Dagger arrived at the Nantahala Outdoor Center just as it entered a period of tremendous growth. Payson Kennedy and his team were in the process of building NOC into the largest outdoor education and recreational center in the world, becoming during this time the premiere boater training center, attracting and producing national and Olympic paddling champions. Staff and former staff include twenty Olympians, two Gold Medalists, and numerous national champions and elite athletes. Nearly half-a-million guests spend some portion of their vacation days at one of NOC's seven river outposts, a $15 million per year operation with a fleet of 1,000 rafts, 120 busses, and countless canoes, funyaks, and kayaks. "One of the best outfitters on Earth," according to National Geographic Adventure Magazine.

After more than twenty-five years hiking and living on the Appalachian Trail, Dan "Wingfoot" Bruce moved to Atlanta.

He lives in a small suburban community away from the hustle and bustle of big city life. Dan Bruce has built a new career writing and publishing non-fiction Christian books focused on sacred chronology and interpretative prophecy. He has published nine books on these themes. You can check out his current work at the Prophecy Society website. His most recent book, however, is a memoir about his first end-to-end hike up the Appalachian Trail in 1985. The book is titled: *Walking with Wingfoot on the Appalachian Trail.*

Nimblewill Nomad, one of the truly outstanding citizens of the AT community, arrived at the Nolichucky Hostel in May of that first year; hiking what he called the Odyssey of 1998—a four-thousand-mile trek beginning in the Florida Keys that included all of the Appalachian Trial and extended to the far northern edge of Quebec. "A desperate search for peace" was what drove him to such lengths. When he arrived, he was 114 days into this odyssey. His trail journal for that day reads:

> I pitch in the cool, lush grass behind Uncle Johnny's hostel along with many thru-hiker friends: U-Turn, Tween, Sam, T-Bone Walker, Long Distance Man, Fletch, Joliet Joe, Innkeeper, Dave, and Joyful Girl. Johnny had the grill going for burgers. Beer is permitted on the premises in cups—great bunch, great evening!

Now, buried in this fascinating slew of facts is an important detail. By May 14, the date of Nimblewill Nomad's arrival, the second Thursday in May, the grass was cool and lush. Lush, he said. Uncle Johnny's turf management efforts had produced this splendid affirmation in just six-weeks in spite of the unauthorized fire circles and the heavy-booted Frisbee players.

Earl Shaffer completed his 50th Anniversary hike, reaching Katahdin in 173 days. He averaged about 13.5 miles per day. "I'm mighty, mighty glad it's over," he said. "If I had another week I would fall on my face."

Eighteen days later, Shaffer turned eighty. Shaffer's walk was covered on national television, local radio talk-shows, and in many newspapers. Taking time for these interviews, he said, slowed him down. Toward the end, he fretted over these delays and worried he wouldn't make Baxter State Park before it closed for winter.

Earl V. Shaffer succumbed to cancer on May 5, 2002. He was 83 years old. David Donaldson, trail name *The Spirit of '48*, Shaffer's hiking partner during the final half of his 50th anniversary walk, was at his bedside. David later wrote and published *A Grip on the Mane of Life; An Authorized Biography of Earl V. Shaffer.*

On the night of June 17, 2011, Earl, along with Myron Avery, Gene Espy, Ed Garvey, Benton MacKaye and Arthur Perkins, was the first inductee of the Appalachian Trail Hall of Fame. Of the six, only Gene Espy of Macon, GA, the second person to thru-hike the A.T., was still living and present to accept the award in person.

The AT Hall of fame is housed at the AT Museum at Pine Grove Furnace State Park, not far from Earl's farm in Pennsylvania. The suggestion to locate the museum here was first made to the AT Museum Society by Earl's youngest brother, John Shaffer.

One of the exhibits at the museum is the reconstructed Peters Mountain Shelter, built by Earl. It was one of six shelters that Earl himself constructed during the 1950s and 60s.

An extensive collection of Earl Shaffer's photographs and papers is permanently available for viewing by visitors at the Smithsonian National Museum of American History Archives in Washington, D.C.

John Shores
2016

John Shores opened the Nolichucky hostel in 1998. As an Eagle Scout and a Brotherhood in the Order of the Arrow, John had an intimate knowledge and understanding of the Southern Appalachians and the famous trail that runs from Georgia to Maine. But it wasn't just scouting that had prepared him for his new life in Erwin Tennessee. By age 51, John had lived a very full life. He learned carpentry skills working with his father's construction crews. From an early age, he studied music. Small, but strong and athletic, he surprised his coach by choosing trumpet over football, and won a chair in the Alabama All-State Band. Joining the Army after High School, John was assigned to the 282nd Army Band stationed at Fort Jackson, South Carolina. After discharge from the Army, he attended the University of Alabama at Birmingham while working for the telephone company. He became South-Central Bell's youngest marketing sales manager. Recruited by one of his largest accounts, the *Birmingham News*, he became their Human Resources Director, managing the careers and creating opportunities for over one thousand employees. Along with three partners, he owned a dive shop, and was a certified diving instructor for both PADI and Scuba Schools International. John dove dozens of ship wrecks, and many of the popular dive sites in Australia and the Caribbean, including Cuba. In addition to all of this, John was an avid outdoorsman, hiking the AT as often as he could, fishing good rivers and lakes, whitewater canoeing, kayaking, and rafting rivers in California, Oregon, West Virginia, Alabama, Tennessee, North Carolina, South Carolina, and Georgia. Today,

John and his wife Charlotte still own the Nolichucky Hostel. During the year in which this book was written, they enjoyed the busiest period in their 18-year history. On one particular day, the nine-bed hostel was full; no vacancies in the eight cabins which accommodate 22 guests, and the camping area was filled to capacity with over 20 tents and hammocks. And even stressed to this maximum, the big bathhouse lived up to its reputation for endless hot water.

Stephen Tyler
Author

In June of 2015, I was looking for a new, interesting place to write. I had just published a book from which I had cut 600 pages. I had the notion of salvaging all that hard work by expanding the book into a series. With summer coming on, it occurred to me to look for a campground. I had all the equipment for park-style camping. I imagined myself waking at dawn, sitting at the picnic table under the rain canopy peacefully organizing several books. Even at 76 years of age, I still wasn't ready to begin living like a sane, rational human being. I googled camping places in Western North Caroline and East Tennessee, the most beautiful section of the Appalachians. I found Uncle Johnny's famous Nolichucky Hostel. One look at the amenities offered, and I was sold. I had vivid memories of driving the old road through Erwin, Tennessee and the Valley Beautiful on trips from Asheville, North Carolina to my family home in Southwest Virginia. My phone call was answered by Uncle Johnny himself. Do you take long-term stays? Certainly, how long do you plan to be with us, Mr. Tyler? From mid-June into fall. You're going to be hiking all that time? No, sir, I'll be writing. You're a writer? Yes, sir. Published? Yes, sir. Mr. Tyler, we'd be happy to have you. By the way, what's the name of your book?

Two weeks later and settling into my camp, Uncle Johnny came by and announced, I've read your book, I've been looking for a writer like you. But, I've got a project going, I said. I know, he said, but let me tell you a story. Three days and twenty stories later, I was hooked. Thus began this book.